Critical Muslim 27

Beauty

Editor: Ziauddin Sardar

Deputy Editors: Hassan Mahamdallie, Samia Rahman, Shanon Shah

Senior Editors: Syed Nomanul Haq, Aamer Hussein, Ehsan Masood, Ebrahim Moosa

Publisher: Michael Dwyer

Managing Editor (Hurst Publishers): Daisy Leitch

Cover Design: Fatima Jamadar

Associate Editors: Tahir Abbas, Alev Adil, Nazry Bahrawi, Merryl Wyn Davies, Abdelwahab El-Affendi, Marilyn Hacker, Nader Hashemi, Jeremy Henzell-Thomas, Vinay Lal, Iftikhar Malik, Boyd Tonkin

International Advisory Board: Karen Armstrong, William Dalrymple, Anwar Ibrahim, Robert Irwin, Bruce Lawrence, Ashis Nandy, Ruth Padel, Bhikhu Parekh, Barnaby Rogerson, Malise Ruthven

Critical Muslim is published quarterly by C. Hurst & Co. (Publishers) Ltd. on behalf of and in conjunction with Critical Muslim Ltd. and the Muslim Institute, London.

All editorial correspondence to Muslim Institute, CAN Mezzanine, 49-51 East Road, London N1 6AH, United Kingdom. E-mail: editorial@criticalmuslim.com

Critical Muslim acknowledges the support of the Aziz Foundation, London.

C. Hurst & Co (Publishers) Ltd.,41 Great Russell Street, London
WC1B 3PL

ISBN: 978-1-78738-020-2 ISSN: 2048-8475

To subscribe or place an order by credit/debit card or cheque (pounds
sterling only) please contact Kathleen May at the Hurst address above or
e-mail kathleen@hurstpub.co.uk

Tel: 020 7255 2201

A one-year subscription, inclusive of postage (four issues), costs £50
(UK), £65 (Europe) and £75 (rest of the world), this includes full access
to the *Critical Muslim* series and archive online. Digital only subscription is
£3.30 per month.

Page 157 'The "gypsy" Naima Akef'
Page 159 'Tahiya Carioca at the height of her fame'

Critical Muslim

Subscribe to Critical Muslim

Now in its seventh year in print, Hurst is pleased to announce that *Critical Muslim* is also available online. Users can access the site for just £3.30 per month – or for those with a print subscription it is included as part of the package. In return, you'll get access to everything in the series (including our entire archive), and a clean, accessible reading experience for desktop computers and handheld devices — entirely free of advertising.

Full subscription

The print edition of *Critical Muslim* is published quarterly in January, April, July and October. As a subscriber to the print edition, you'll receive new issues directly to your door, as well as full access to our digital archive.

United Kingdom £50/year
Europe £65/year
Rest of the World £75/year

Digital Only

Immediate online access to *Critical Muslim*

Browse the full *Critical Muslim* archive

Cancel any time

£3.30 per month

www.criticalmuslim.io

CM27

July–September 2018

CONTENTS

BEAUTY

SHANON SHAH	INTRODUCTION: MAKING BEAUTIFUL MUSLIMS	3
SAMIA RAHMAN	SELFIES AND OTHER GAZES	21
DORIS BEHRENS-ABOUSEIF	BEAUTY IN ISLAM	33
NADIA MOHD RASIDI	BEAUTY PAGEANTS	43
MAHMOUD MOSTAFA	EXPERIENCING THE MOST BEAUTIFUL NAMES	54
HASINA ZAMAN	A BEAUTIFUL DEATH	72
JONAS OTTERBECK	BEAUTIFUL (POP) SOUNDS	84
IRUM SHEHREEN ALI	WELLNESS	97
HENRY BREFO	TAMING THE BARBARIANS	109
YOVANKA PAQUETE PERDIGAO	SKIN SHADES	118
NIMA NASSERI	NOSE JOBS, IRANIAN STYLE	127

ARTS AND LETTERS

ALEV ADIL	NIGHT JOURNEY AT THE END OF THE WORLD	141
YASMIN DESOUKI	EGYPTOMANIA	151
RICCI SHRYOCK	WOMEN WRESTLERS	169
MUSTAFA ABU SNEINEH	FIVE POEMS	174
BRANDINO MACHIAVELLI	POEMS	177

REVIEWS

SAHIL K WARSI	UNWANTED BONES	185
GILES GODDARD	THE PRICE OF A RAINFOREST	192
MISHA MONAGHAN	DRESSED TO BE BLESSED	200

ET CETERA

AVAES MOHAMMAD	LAST WORD:	
	ON MALE BEAUTY	207
THE LIST	TEN MIGHTY MAKEOVERS	214
CITATIONS		222
CONTRIBUTORS		233

Errata: In the last issue, *Critical Muslim 26: Gastronomy*, the article 'Malay Bonne Bouche', written by Aimee Lewis, was wrongly attributed to Mastura Alatas. Our sincere apologies to Aimee Lewis.

BEAUTY

INTRODUCTION: MAKING BEAUTIFUL MUSLIMS
by Shanon Shah
SELFIES AND OTHER GAZES *by Samia Rahman*
BEAUTY IN ISLAM *by Doris Behrens-Abouseif*
BEAUTY PAGEANTS *by Nadia Rasidi*
EXPERIENCING THE MOST BEAUTIFUL NAMES
by Mahmoud Mostafa
A BEAUTIFUL DEATH *by Hasina Zaman*
BEAUTIFUL (POP) SOUNDS *by Jonas Otterbeck*
WELLNESS *by Irum Shehreen Ali*
TAMING THE BARBARIANS *by Henry Brefo*
SKIN SHADES *by Yovanka Paquete Perdigao*
NOSE JOBS, IRANIAN STYLE *by Nima Nasseri*

INTRODUCTION:
MAKING MUSLIMS BEAUTIFUL

Shanon Shah

There I was, a drab male lump in a queue of chic young hijabis on a sunny, crisp Saturday. We were waiting to get into the afternoon's events at the London Modest Fashion Week (LMFW) in Bloomsbury. The line was moving glacially, and it was clear the event was going to start late. People started approaching the rugby player-built security guards around – who looked like they were channelling Tommy Lee Jones and Will Smith from *Men in Black* – to check if the time on their tickets, 2pm, was right. Taking advantage of the bottleneck, a young woman – with an American accent with South Asian notes – started distributing a dissertation questionnaire to people in the queue. She focused only on the young women – I felt equal parts relieved and left out. I couldn't help but see what the young women in front of me wrote in the 'age' column – 21. I made a mental note not to strike up a conversation in case they dealt the unintended indignity of addressing me as 'Uncle'.

Why was I so self-conscious? Was it because I was surrounded by perfectly preened, young, mostly Muslim women, taking selfies and chattering away? 'I'm not some creepy, non-colour coordinated lech,' I wanted to protest aloud, 'I'm here for research.' Just as I was thinking this, two attractive English lads walked past the queue and stared, in what I thought was puzzlement, at the sea of hijabis before them. The coin dropped for one of them: 'Oh, it's fashion week, innit?' 'Course it is,' the other replied, in a tone that was both enlightened and relieved. How wonderful, I thought, that this is how they made sense of the crowd of Muslim women before their eyes – how wonderfully London.

How liberating, I went on thinking, that these young British men would associate the hijab not with some stereotypically insular or ominous-sounding Muslamic event. Surely it was only in London that they would associate the mostly brown-skinned hijabis before their eyes with style and beauty. But then I wondered if this was a double-edged sword. Were they instead perceiving these hijabis as hot because this event adopted the format and atmosphere of a pre-existing, so-called Western template – runway fashion? Was this what it took for Muslims in Britain to be seen as more than pesky, radicalised religious minorities – to dilute the markers of our faith and gently stir them into the majority's comfort zone? I realised that it was a bit rich of me to be thinking this – I am not visibly Muslim by any means and never have been. I have no beard, no *jubba* (ankle-length robe), and an accent that is difficult to pin down.

These thoughts about the politics of fashion, appearance, and identity were swirling madly in my head as we were eventually ushered into the building. Then we had to get into another queue that snaked around the basement and backstage area. The chatter got louder and more excited. I lost track of the number of 'hi darlings' and air kisses that were exchanged before my eyes at various spots in the queue. For the longest time, I was stuck in front of the 1001 Abayas stall. In an adjacent stall, there was a stylish, bearded young black man striking poses and getting photographed. When we finally took our seats beside the runway, the crowd's anticipation was ripe. Soft electronic dance music played in the background – the mood was tasteful and understated. I wondered, not for the last time, if this was so that no one would confuse this for an immodest fashion show.

Phones were then whipped out *en masse*, mine included – although I was probably in a tiny minority of people using Keep Notes rather than Twitter, Instagram or Snapchat. There was a mix of scruffy middle-aged men with cameras on tripods in one corner, obviously 'official' photographers of some description, and what I assumed were fashion bloggers or vloggers and their phone-camera-wielding fashionista followers on social media stationed in other parts of the hall.

At 3.30pm, finally, the spotlights came on. A woman announcer greeted the audience with the extended *salam* – *assalamu alaikum warahmatullahi wabarakatuh* (the peace, mercy and blessings of Allah be with you). No shade intended, but I don't think she was a Millennial, although she was certainly a snazzy hijabi. She welcomed everyone to stay and enjoy not just the runway – there were shops selling all sorts of products, from food to fragrances. For the first time, also, the event was hosting a runway for men. I did a double take when she then announced that Lindsay Lohan – yes, the Lindsay of *Mean Girls* and *Freaky Friday* fame, rumoured to have converted to Islam – was there, too.

And with that, the first catwalk show began. The clothes being modelled were loose-fitting and long yet attractively shaped, sedate yet showy in the choice of shiny material and floral textures, and innovative in the permutations of wrapping patterns for the headscarves. There were several ensembles which didn't even incorporate headscarves – the models had their hair flowing freely. But even with these designs, the sleeves and the skirts or trousers were lengthy and no cleavage was visible. This is when I recognised that modest fashion can be deeply subversive and political – especially in an age when, for example, French schoolgirls are banned from attending classes because their skirts are 'too long', or when French women are forced to remove their burkinis at the beach at gunpoint. At the same time, 'modest fashion' shows such as these fly in the face of the draconian rulings and attitudes on women's dress in many Muslim countries. In my native Malaysia, for example, online trolls – invariably Muslim men – get away with impunity for insulting and threatening even headscarf-clad women whose dressing is deemed to be not compliant enough with 'true' Islamic standards. Advocates of Muslim fashion thus always have to confront multiple opposition and criticisms. There is Western fashion imperialism on one hand, which continues to be unable to recognise Muslim clothing cultures as 'fashionable', and, on the other hand, the anti-Western, coercive dogma of traditionalist Islamic authorities. The fact is that for many Muslim women, items of clothing such as the hijab can have multiple meanings, including as markers of religious piety, political protest, personal style, and inherited culture.

There are choices to be made, however, in how these possible meanings are presented at events such as the LMFW. In this case, once the runway began, the music changed subtly, into what I can only describe as chillout Arabian Nights techno-chic. This recurring aesthetic that blended the latest in the electropop revival and a more placid and, dare I say it, 'Oriental', vibe reminded me of what Jonas Otterbeck observes, in this issue, about the emergence of Islamic pop music. Writing specifically about the oeuvre of Awakening Records, which includes household names such as Maher Zain and formerly Sami Yusuf, Otterbeck notes that the company's production values are 'clean yet rather contemporary'. He explains:

> Think Lionel Richie meets Taylor Swift. Distorted sounds or dark atmospheres are not part of the soundscape.... Musical instruments, with the exception of drums, were not used at first.... This was essential at the time as Islamic legal ethics rarely found stringed and wind instruments acceptable. Since Sami Yusuf's debut, digital sound pads have been used extensively. These pads may consist of, for example, sampled voices producing a required type of sound texture, in this case the imitation of a choir or even different instruments. Pads are also used to provide vocal basslines and swooping synthesizer-like chords, creating much larger sonic landscapes than previous recordings of the genre. Almost all mainstream pop productions of today make extensive use of pads. However, around 2003-05, opinions started to change among Islamic intellectuals and artists and in the coming years several artists that used to produce vocals-only recordings started to add instruments, including such seminal artists as Yusuf Islam, Dawud Wharnsby and Awakening's own Sami Yusuf.

Although Otterbeck is referring specifically to Islamic pop, where creating a modern yet religiously approved 'beautiful sound' is the foremost goal, much of what he says is applicable to the modest fashion sphere, as exemplified by the LMFW. In both settings, beautiful sounds are a way of redrawing aesthetic boundaries without either completely jettisoning religious tradition, whatever that means, or alienating the supposedly liberal, Western 'other'. Because, of course, fashion and music are inseparable – a glance at the most iconic videos from the likes of Lady Gaga and the late George Michael illustrates this point amply enough. The use of music in the Islamic pop and modest fashion industries can therefore be seen as the attempt to have one's trendy Muslim cake and eat it, too.

Yet it would not be right to be entirely cynical about this aural enterprise. In this issue of *Critical Muslim*, Doris Behrens-Abouseif complements Otterbeck's analysis by pointing out that the idea of music as an expression of divine beauty has been ever-present throughout Islamic history. Focusing on Arabic-Islamic literature, Behrens-Abouseif argues that in this corpus, 'music was the art to which [was] attributed the most profound impact on the soul'. This argument might come as a surprise to those of us who have internalised the idea that music of any kind is strictly forbidden in Islam. Behrens-Abouseif acknowledges this side of the argument but explains that Islamic opinions about music were not entirely unanimous or uniform. Jurists and scholars were divided about the stirring power of music, some believing that it could 'lead to the profound religious experience of ecstasy', while others held that it would result in 'the kind of intoxication associated with immorality'. According to Behrens-Abouseif:

> Although the jurists Abu Hanifa (d. 767) and Shafiʻi (d. 820) condemned music, in particular when performed by slave girls, al-Ghazali contradicted them with the argument that there is no statement in the Qur'an or in the Prophet's traditions to justify such hostility. One of al-Ghazali's arguments in favour of music was that it is perceived by one of our five senses which, together with the mind, were created to be used. He mentions the musical performances of the Patriarch David and the singing of birds which flatters the ear and refers to a hadith saying that all prophets sent by God had a beautiful voice; a preacher should have, therefore, a pleasant harmonic speech to move his listeners. He divided the influence of music into two categories – spiritual and physical. Al-Ghazali's opinion was endorsed by other theologians, especially among the Sufis who, referring to the biblical Davidic tradition and to hadith, believed music to be an attribute of Paradise.

In Muslim cultures, therefore, the concept of beauty incorporated but did not prioritise the visual – beauty was also aural, tactile and olfactory. But in the past, as in the present, the main issue – as formulated by Al-Ghazali and his supporters – was whether music provided a means of getting closer to God or an excuse to indulge in unlawful behaviour. Trying to discern the boundary between the two has never been easy, because of the sensuous and seductive nature in which beauty is described within Islam's central texts. Behrens-Abouseif goes so far as to maintain that 'in no other religion does the concept of beauty play such a crucial role as in Islam.' The proof, she argues, is to be found within the Qur'an itself:

> One of the most powerful testimonies of the significance of sensuous beauty in religion is the fact that, unlike in Christianity, the Qur'an and other Muslim religious texts describe Paradise in physical sensual terms, referring to precious materials – natural and processed – such as gems and jewellery, garments, architecture, and ornaments (55:54, 76), and to beautiful young women, or *khayyirāt* and *ḥisān* (55:70).

These arguments are persuasive enough – for me, at least – to recognise and celebrate that the concept of beauty, including the exhortation to appreciate it and strive for it holistically, lies at the heart of Islam. But do they justify the need for profit-seeking phenomena such as the modest fashion industry, or Islamic pop? In this quest to pursue supposedly Islamic ideals of beauty, who is the ultimate arbiter, or beholder, of what counts as beautiful? A *sharia*-ready response would be, 'Why, Allah, our Maker, of course.' But this, to me, would be casuistry at best and would smack of hypocrisy at worst. To behold some objects as beautiful and others as not is an act of power that too many human beings conveniently exploit in the name of divine instruction or otherwise.

The modest fashion runway is not immune from such acts of power, either. Sure, the LMFW models were admirably diverse on one level – from blonde and blue-eyed to brown-skinned and black; hijabi and non-hijabi. They were all also young, able-bodied, and slim. At the risk of sounding po-faced, I wondered why, in a show that was supposed to represent a holistic alternative to the allegedly exploitative practices of mainstream fashion, I could not see a single person who was plus-sized, older, or visibly disabled. This is not whataboutery – it's about acknowledging the deleterious effects of the fashion industry on huge numbers of women, men, and people who do not fit neatly into either end of the binary. Neither is this a call to arms to destroy the fashion industry as an icon of patriarchy, capitalism, and racism. Rather, it's about understanding the power of conceptions and definitions of beauty in people's everyday lives, especially women. As Nadia Mohd Rasidi recounts in her poignant essay in this issue, the idea of beauty – even when grounded in Islamic terms – can be experienced as a kind of tyranny for some people.

Nadia recalls sitting in her Islamic Studies lessons as a child in Malaysia, struggling with the idea that, for Muslims, 'God is beautiful and loves beauty.' What follows is a raw, candid confession of a Muslim woman coming to terms with the role of 'beauty' in shaping her sense of self:

> In a vague sense I understood that God's beauty was something beyond my comprehension but His love for beauty, to me, had to be grounded in the tangible world that I lived in. And if God loves beauty, and if, as I then believed, I was not beautiful, what did that mean for me? It wasn't that I thought God didn't love me because I wasn't conventionally beautiful. It's that it was

beginning to dawn on me that the beauty I was being told God valued still very much conformed to the parameters of human desire, and so no matter how sweet my words and good my deeds, as a fat person, my body would always betray me to other people through the ugliness of its excess.

This personal confession of Nadia's turns into unflinching, multi-layered analysis as she dissects the politics of beauty pageants. She asserts that beauty pageants, as with the fashion industry, are a product of the patriarchal, male gaze. They are designed not only to define the idea of beauty for women, but for spectators to take pleasure in watching women struggle and squirm to fit into these male-centric criteria. Beauty pageants, according to her, are all about celebrating thinness, non-disability and, most insidiously, whiteness.

In this sense, the LMFW could claim to be a force for change of sorts. Blackness, brownness and yellowness were proudly on display, on the runway and in the audience. And, to be fair, there were plus-sized women – or 'large and in charge', as reclaimed by *RuPaul's Drag Race* fan-favourite Latrice Royale – dotted about in the audience, if not on the runway. For women like Nadia, however, the battle always has to be fought on more than one front. For, in Malaysia, the appeal of events like beauty pageants is matched by the patriarchal enforcement of so-called Islamic morals and values, often disproportionately and heavy-handedly against women and religious and sexual minorities. According to a *fatwa*, or religious opinion – which, in Malaysia, has the force of state legislation – Muslim women are forbidden from entering beauty contests. The dilemma, as Nadia articulates, is this: 'On one hand, the restriction is absurd and discriminatory; on the other, arguing for inclusion in an archaic form of aesthetic assessment undeniably rankles. It raises the question, what do we understand as distinctly Muslim beauty that stands in opposition to non-Muslim beauty?'

Additionally, should Muslim women be thankful for being saved by Muslim men from the ignominy of succumbing to the supposedly immoral Western standards of beauty? Or should they fight the ridiculousness of the anti-pageant *fatwa* to claim the freedom to compete in a patriarchal assessment of their boobs, bums, and brains (in that order)? While modest fashion advocates might protest that what they are doing is far removed from the idea of the beauty pageant – with its unashamed ranking of participants, including what they look like in swimsuits – the parallels are undeniable. The similarities come into sharper focus when we look at developments in Indonesia, home of Miss Muslimah, an Islamic beauty pageant launched in 2011. In this Jakarta-based competition, open to contestants from around the world, 20 hijab-wearing finalists have to demonstrate not only their style and physical beauty, but also their religious piety, humanitarian intelligence, and strength of character. Tasks include memorising the Qur'an, visiting impoverished slums and care homes for the elderly, and hobnobbing with corporate sponsors, all while praying five times a day – 'and wearing heels'. Among the prizes offered are pilgrimage trips to Mecca and education scholarships.

Nadia's bemusement at the very existence of such an 'Islamic' beauty pageant reaches its climax at the observation offered by a photojournalist, Monique Jacques, who says:

> I thought the contradiction of a Muslim beauty pageant was so interesting and unique. In my work I'm always looking for ways to communicate the experience of young Muslim women to Western audiences. Much of the competition is similar to a pageant in America or anywhere in the West, just with headscarves.

And there's the rub. (Or one of several rubs, actually.) As worthy as their goals sound to their originators and supporters, do efforts like Miss Muslimah and LMFW merely amount to 'add headscarf to Western hegemony and stir'? Or, in the case of Islamic pop, 'add beard and stir'? Do they actually represent a thoughtful rethinking of Islamic ideals and a challenge to discriminatory attitudes and practices within and beyond Muslim contexts? Or, as Nadia puts it, 'Is the end goal then, once again, to flatten difference? There is comfort in the familiar, certainly, but such comfort only serves to assuage white and Western fears about the untamed other.'

The blanket is not all wet, though. Contradiction alert: I actually enjoyed quite a lot of LMFW. Yes, as I looked at the models parading in front of me, I did wonder about what the experience of looking entailed. What are you looking at, or for? Would it be how you imagine *you* should look, or actually look? Or would it be how you would adapt elements of the perfect look being displayed in front of you for your own unruly and stubbornly non-fashion-ready body? Or would you judge the models and the garments on their bodies with a harshness you would never resort to with someone you really cared for? Even as I was thinking these thoughts, I observed the audience around me. A group of girls beside me who were obviously friends – two non-hijabis (one Asian and one white) and a Somali hijabi – looked earnest and thoughtful, but not unkind. Two blond white men sitting across from me – representatives from a fashion line, I wondered? – had priceless reactions. They were demonstrably enthusiastic and invested in everything that passed before their eyes. Again, their expressions were devoid of the sneering judgement one would associate with the Meryl Streep character in *The Devil Wears Prada*.

These reactions, and my own, made me reflect upon what some writers refer to as 'the gaze'. The gaze, for those of us with the ability to hold it, establishes particular boundaries, hierarchies, intentions and understandings between us and the object, or objects, of our attention. In other words, the gaze objectifies. But are all gazes alike? Do all forms of objectification carry the same consequences for the one doing the gazing and the one being gazed at? Conventional feminist wisdom has it that the patriarchal, heterosexist gaze exploits and diminishes women (and men who do not conform to stereotypical masculine ideals). Complementing this idea is the decolonial or anti-colonial idea that the Eurocentric, white gaze has historically dehumanised or subjugated – and continues, in new guises, to dehumanise and subjugate – non-white, non-European peoples.

The value in these interrelated perspectives is that they make us reckon with relationships of power between the beholder's eyes and the objects they deem to be beautiful. They expose the ideologies that underline a multitude of beliefs and practices on intimate and industrial scales, including skin lightening, cosmetic surgery, and inner wellbeing. But these analyses also run the risk of being too static and reinforcing the marginalisation of those who are already marginalised by the white, heterosexist, patriarchal, male gaze. The thing is, is gazing not a two-way relationship? Do those being gazed at not consciously invite gazes, and do they not gaze back at the people gazing at them? And, in an age of selfies and wefies, do they not take pleasure at gazing *at themselves* in the way that they want others to gaze at them, and to gaze at other people gazing at themselves? Is there not a more complicated view we could develop about the nature of the gaze?

For Samia Rahman, the idea that selfie culture could contain liberating elements remains questionable. It provides but faux liberation from the Eurocentric, patriarchal gaze. In her essay on Selfies and Other Gazes, she argues:

> Filters, photo-editing, Snapchat and all manner of duplicity are employed to make a person prettier and thinner than they could possibly aspire to be In Real Life (IRL). IRL a person is flawed. A beach-ready body and perfect skin comprise an image perpetuated by elite supermodels who deny they ever diet or have a skincare routine.... You gotta fake it to make it. It's all about attitude and editing. Now that our lives are lived through the medium of virtual reality, it is an encumbrance, no an obligation, to smooth those wrinkles, trout that pout and present a super-enhanced version of your best possible self. Brushed and sculpted, using all the latest guides and trends and YouTube tutorials, you can now dare to gaze out from the black mirror and be blisteringly judged and brazenly objectified.

There are even apps now — several of them — for 'perfecting selfies'. The verdict, according to Rahman, is that there is no way to subvert the gaze. The solution is simply to stop gazing and to start seeing or apprehending each other, and ourselves, as fellow members of humanity. And so, Rahman repents ever calling anyone pretty, or handsome, because such compliments do not only exclude those who are not privileged or lucky enough to receive them, they also diminish the very people they intend to praise. 'Pretty', 'handsome', 'gorgeous', and 'hot' say nothing about each person's struggles, aspirations, gifts, and concerns.

While Rahman's sentiment is salutary, it might be a little bit difficult to put into practice. The line between physical beauty and inner fulfilment is often fuzzy. There's a reason, after all, for the enduring popularity of sentiments such as 'if you look good, you feel good'. Alongside this is the reality that attaining beauty and projecting happiness have probably always involved some level of artificial enhancement and deception, notwithstanding the rise of the selfie. An intriguing case study of how the boundaries are blurred can be found in none other than one of the former axes of evil, according to former US President George W Bush — Iran.

In this issue, Nima Nasseri reports an intriguing trend within the Islamic Republic about cosmetic surgery. No, it's not that this is booming business in Iran — it has been for a while, especially amongst women. What is noteworthy is how popular going under the knife has become amongst Iranian men now, too, who account for a third of all clients of cosmetic surgeries in the country – double the global average. By far, the most popular procedure for Iranian men and women now is the nose job. Quoting a study by Johns Hopkins University, Nasseri reveals that 'the rate of nose jobs per capita in Iran is seven times that in the US'. And no, this phenomenon is not restricted to the wealthier or upper classes. The cosmetic augmentation of the Iranian conk is also popular amongst 'office workers, university students, shop keepers, and even teenagers who choose to spend their savings or risk going into debt for such procedures'. Neither is the phenomenon restricted to lax Muslims or secular Iranians – in Nasseri's observation, the obsession is shared equally amongst the pious and impious.

Such statistics fly in the face of Iran's reputation for upholding and imposing hard-line interpretations of Islam. Nasseri argues that they actually indicate unexpected and non-organised forms of resistance against the state's official anti-Western policies, which often border on caricature. Such widespread yet seemingly apolitical actions can sometimes push the state into conflict or compromise. For example, state-sponsored websites which once condemned cosmetic surgery are now publishing guidelines on how to perform *wuzu*, or ritual ablutions, for people who are recovering from such procedures.

The majority of people Nasseri spoke with highlighted not only the surgery's tangible benefits – one cosmetics businessman underwent a nose job to attract a larger clientele – but also the wonders that it did for their self-esteem. Of course, this boost in confidence could also come from the relief of being rewarded for conforming to rising social pressures regarding physical beauty. The sting in the tail is that Iranian nose jobs also reveal a certain level of self-directed racism. According to one surgeon Nasseri interviewed, what people are really looking for is to remove the characteristic 'Persian bump' so that they can look more European. Paradoxically, because of the ubiquity of plastic surgery, the removal of this inherited 'hooked nose' now adds to a sense of Iranian pride.

Iranians, however, have not monopolised the obsession for achieving physical perfection by removing all traces of native heredity in favour of a Eurocentric ideal. As Yovanka Paquete Perdigao discloses in this issue, skin lightening products are big business in Africa and Asia. This is despite the fact that many of them have been shown, time and again, to cause all manner of harmful side effects. The percentage of women who regularly use these products in the African continent alone is staggering – '77 per cent of Nigerian women; 60 per cent of Zambian women between the ages of 30 and 39; 59 per cent of Togolese people; 50 to 60 per cent of adult Ghanaian women; 52 per cent of women in Bamako, Mali; and 35 per cent of people in Pretoria, South Africa'.

What is the reason for the popularity of these dubious products? For Perdigao, the blame lies squarely with colourism, or shadeism, which is a direct consequence of European colonialism. Early in her essay, she establishes why the politics of skin lightening are emphatically not similar to the politics of tanning for white people – the choices we make to beautify our bodies do not exist in a political vacuum. As Perdigao argues, tanning and skin lightening are not parallel phenomena because 'no people of colour had colonised and brutally ruled Caucasian people and installed a meritocracy based on skin colour. It is precisely within European colonialism that the obsession with skin lightening began.'

Before Muslims can cheer at this anti-Orientalist takedown, however, there are some uncomfortable home truths to reckon with. As Perdigao stresses, the rise of Muslim civilisations was not exactly immune from skin-colour racism either. The examples that demonstrate this are many. The Arabic word *abd*, for example, means 'slave' but is often used by Arab Muslims to describe African or dark-skinned people. And within Muslim-majority African cultures, light-skinned people enjoy higher status, for example, in Somalia. In some other predominantly Muslim African countries, skin colour remains a function of slavery and inequality, for example in Mauritania and Libya. Outside of Africa, Perdigao serendipitously gives the example of Iran, where Afro-Iranians – mostly descendants of Africans captured by Arab slave traders – remain invisible, despite their numerous contributions to Iranian culture.

The colourist bias has also permeated the modest fashion industry. The lack of representation of black women in the 2017 Dubai Modest Fashion Week sparked an uproar amongst black Muslim beauty and fashion bloggers and vloggers. Their protest against what they rightly saw as intra-Muslim anti-black racism culminated in the hashtag #BlackMuslimahExcellence, which went viral instantly. In hindsight, I wonder if this partly explains the visibility of black men and women at the LMFW I attended.

Despite these critical caveats, as I've already confessed, I wasn't exactly hunched in a corner, silently spitting tacks. As self-conscious and insecure as I was, I was intrigued about what was going on around me, in a good way. After the end of the first runway, I wandered around the venue and found myself in a hall where loads of different products were being sold. There were, of course, headscarves and other garments, sold by lines such as Mimpikita, Till We Cover, Cover Me Collection, Hafza Studio, and Deena's Style. There was Jubbas, showcasing its line of men's *jubbas* (or *thawbs*), religious books, and fragrances. When I was browsing at this particular stall, the guys who were minding it were spritzing perfume samples on a couple of hip black youths. There was also Sweetlicious – selling sweets, of course – and Two London, which was selling foundation and fake eyelashes.

I found the last stall, the National Zakat Foundation, a logical fit, yet somehow slightly jarring as well. There was something about seeing this promotion of obligatory almsgiving, an essential tenet of Islam, at a fashion show. It was logical because, of course, the event was consciously conceptualised as a celebration of a holistic, integrated, and stylish expression of Islam. And so, why not pay the obligatory poor-due after you've bought your five designer headscarves and two sets of halal nail polish?

Many commentators – of various beliefs – are increasingly critical about the societal pressures on us all to adhere to superficial standards of beauty. However, concentrating on 'inner beauty' and 'wellbeing' isn't the solution either. As Irum Shehreen Ali argues in her essay on 'Wellness', this reflective turn towards 'inner beauty' has its own exploitative, inane dimensions. The legitimate goal of pursuing 'self-actualisation' has now given birth to, as she puts it, the 'wellness industrial complex'. And it's gendered, too, because guess who the prime targets of the wellness industry are? Women, of course.

As Ali explains, it's easy to understand the appeal of the emphasis on wellness and inner beauty. In a world that hasn't quite recovered from the 2008 financial crash, and where massive problems such as violent conflict and environmental degradation seem to be intractable, people do need to believe that they can find resilience, strength, and happiness within themselves. And some advice is just sensible – eat healthily, exercise more, cultivate supportive relationships, and get enough rest. The problem is when wellness becomes an industry in which people's understandable scepticism about quick fixes regarding external beauty becomes exploited by a load of quackery about inner wellbeing. For example, according to Ali:

> In an atmosphere of anxiety regarding food, clean eating philosophies offer reassurance that if you follow the rules of this holistic way of life, you too will be healthy and whole. As a result, thousands are obsessing over chemical toxins, using coconut oil for every ailment, going gluten free despite not having coeliac disease, adopting ever more rigid and inflexible patterns of eating. Many doctors and scientists have shown elimination diets to be based on bad science. Writer Bee Wilson notes that faced with conflicting nutritional information and an overwhelming array of unhealthy food, clean eating is 'best seen as a dysfunctional response to a still more dysfunctional food supply: a dream of purity in a toxic world'.

It is not just 'clean eating' in which such potential for harm exists – Ali includes the obsession with yoga and mindfulness in the West as areas in which capitalist profit-making and fake expertise flourish synergistically. Ultimately, the main problem with the industrialisation of wellbeing philosophies is but a subtler and more insidious version of the main problem with societal obsession with physical beauty. It turns the people who do not meet these impossible standards into failures without challenging the very structures that are designed to guarantee failure for the many, not the few. As Ali argues:

> Promoting this retreat into the self as a path to inner beauty does nothing to change the very socio-economic structures of our late capitalist societies that leads to the disaffection, loneliness and sense of loss that we are seeking to heal. It is essentially a philosophy of selfishness, dressed up as spiritual awakening. It also locates the entire onus of inner wellbeing and happiness on the individual and ignores the problem of oppressive cultural norms.

It would be unfair to give the impression that the audience and organisers of LMFW did not possess this potential for self-reflection and self-criticism. After the lunch break, as I left the National Zakat Foundation counter and returned to the main hall, I managed to catch a panel discussion on the evolution of the Muslim male's lifestyle. Some of the discussion was light, fun and informative. For example, there was the chronology of how Muslim entrepreneurs in East London are benefiting from the rise of the hipster beard. Because, of course, many brown and black Muslim men in Britain were growing beards long before they morphed from being security threats into the latest fashion trend. But because of this new fad, Muslim beard-grooming outlets are now doing booming business – they're run by people who know what they're doing and who use halal, ergo 'natural', beard-care products.

The real revelation on the panel, however, came from an Asian Muslim halal entrepreneur whose appearance – bearded, muscly, tattooed, accompanied by a baseball cap, denim jacket, and skinny jeans – I can only describe as post-Salafi swank. At some point during the discussion, he said, matter-of-factly, 'Well the whole Muslim fashion industry is about privilege, isn't it?' It's about the Muslims who are becoming more middle class also becoming more visible because of their rising disposable incomes, whilst the majority of Britain's Muslims still live in poverty.

This proposition finds its corollary in Henry Brefo's contribution to this issue, on the increasing appropriation or incorporation of Muslim symbols by clothing manufacturers and other designers. The introduction of hijab-friendly athletic gear by Nike, for example, could be seen as an act of inclusion, but it could also be a cynical marketing decision to attract a growing demographic of Muslim consumers. Brefo asserts that the absorption of Muslim symbols into Western culture has a long history – but it has never resulted in a greater acceptance of Islam within the West. This discrepancy – between finding certain elements of Muslim cultures appealing whilst retaining Islamophobic attitudes – is not resolved in the versions of multiculturalism endorsed by the state and marketed by big corporations. As Brefo argues:

> Multiculturalism is acceptable so far as it conforms to the norm, even within the realm of fantasy. The celebration of Diwali, the Hindu festival of lights, must always involve a troupe of Indian women dressed in traditional garb, gyrating to public delight. This suggests that the city must once again be graced with native sexuality for the benefit of subsequent generations, who no longer have the Empire at their disposal. Africa Day can be summed up by a cacophony of colours and sounds, all too insufferable to your average UKIP voter hankering after a post-Brexit, white utopia.

If Brefo is right, then the LMFW can only find success if it can consistently find its target between the shifting goalposts of 'fundamental British values' whilst playing up Muslim exotica for its own sake. Lipstick laden Muslim women in hijab seem to fit the bill – for now. Time will tell.

Meanwhile, this year's LMFW premiered a male runway, too, which I awaited excitedly. I didn't really know what to expect, but never have I seen so many *thawbs* on a runway in my life. Every single fashion line that was showcased – including Sulyman by SO.ME, Al-Imaan by Jubbas, Ilyas X Morrison, and Sunna Style – consisted overwhelmingly of variations upon a loose kaftan. I was bracing myself to get bored, but there were surprising delights to be found here, too. Particularly memorable was when one of the young black models broke out some hip-hop dance moves on the runway, to raucous applause. Even more surprising was how, at some point, I started leaning forward in interest, despite myself, thinking, 'Well, I'd wear that. Or maybe that one, in a different colour. Or that one, in Ramadan.' And for all the critical analysis I developed on the day, I have to confess that I've actually bookmarked the Jubbas website. No, this is not product placement – I haven't bought anything. But I do have my eye on the Al Noor Wine Thobe which is retailing for what I consider to be an affordable £24.99. The only thing is I don't know if it will go with my skin tone.

Just when I thought I'd seen everything, I looked around before I left and noticed that there were no women wearing *niqab* (the face-veil). Well, why would they be here anyway, I wondered. Surely the whole point of wearing a *niqab* is to reject the fashion industry as haram. But this is why Muslims don't call God the Manifest (az-Zahir) and the Hidden (al-Batin) for nothing – as I walked up the stairs towards the exit, who should I have glimpsed entering but a woman in a *niqab*, also wearing what I would swear were fake eyelashes. Now I really had seen everything.

While I can't offer a working definition of 'beauty', I wonder if, as a Muslim, there are ways to capture its transcendent potential beyond the usual sensorial allegories of sight, sound, touch, taste and smell. The contribution by Hasina Zaman comes achingly close to offering this larger view of beauty. Zaman, a Muslim woman director of a funeral company that caters to a multifaith clientele, makes a rare yet utterly compelling case for appreciating beauty as a matter of life and death. Specifically, she asks us to think about the ways in which we can prepare ourselves, and our loved ones, for a beautiful end to our earthly lives. This is not recycled mumbo jumbo from the wellness industry, but an observation based on personal experience and challenging everyday work. Zaman begins by revealing the anguish she felt in the aftermath of the suicide of a member of her family – and the ugliness of how their surrounding community reacted to this tragedy. From this example, Zaman suggests that the callousness with which some people approach death, including Muslims, is also connected to ignorance about a host of other issues, including mental illness. To make things worse, supposedly excessive expressions of grief amongst the bereaved are often seen as possible signs of mental illness, instead of a fluctuating journey of emotional and spiritual recovery. Perhaps the most poignant observation that Zaman makes is of workshops on death, dying and bereavement which she often delivers for caregivers:

> On one such course, the carers I was teaching, all of whom were Muslim, were charged with exploring the notion of a 'Good Death'. Many were perplexed by the idea and, when called upon to close their eyes and imagine death, eighty per cent said they had imagined themselves drowning in the sea – lonely, scared, and terrified. Each carer, it seemed, had slanted towards envisioning a devastating and painful death. Only after many questions, which asked them to imagine themselves bedbound and to describe their ideal surroundings, were the majority able to describe a Good Death. Many said they envisioned an end in which they were not in hospital or in a care home, but in their own bedroom, on a sunny day with windows framed by open curtains, and the Qur'an playing in the background.

This is why, for Zaman, the capacity to conceive of a 'beautiful death is a rare and courageous gift', but one which we can only give ourselves and to others if we have appropriate examples to follow. She contends that these examples can be found at the heart of Islamic teachings – but it is rare that these are conveyed in ways that many of us might find comforting or helpful.

One powerful resource at the core of Islam that can help us reconceptualise beauty is the Asmaul Husna, or the Most Beautiful Names of Allah. In his contribution, Mahmoud Mostafa, a Mevlevi Sufi, contends that this epistemological shift can only be made possible through spiritual experience. We can't think ourselves into a new understanding of beauty – we have to experience it and live it. For Mostafa, one of the most profound impacts of contemplating the Divine Names is the revelation that while they might possess attributes which we could stereotypically regard as 'masculine' or 'feminine', they transcend these unhelpful binaries and can help us break out of them, if we would only pay attention. Mostafa narrates what happened when he meditated upon four of the 99 names – Al Halim (the Most Forbearing); Al Quddus (the Most Holy and Pure); An-Nur (the Light); As-Salam (the One Who is Peace) – at a retreat in San Francisco. Ultimately, according to Mostafa, the practice of engaging with Allah's Beautiful Names is an aid to helping us embody the one-ness of creation, or *tawhid*:

> A truly Islamic and *tawhid*-ic perspective would encourage men and women to step outside prescribed gender roles and support the realisation of the inner creative potential in each of us by virtue of our humanness. This creative potential is the Most Beautiful Names awaiting expression through each of us.

In other words, transformation is possible when we contemplate the existence of a Beholder of beauty beyond ourselves. But Mostafa's conception of a Beholder that is at once transcendent and immanent is not the equivalent of the reductive, readymade, legalistic conception of Allah that permeates so much of contemporary Islamic discourse. What Mostafa's piece suggests is that the Beholder is Beautiful, too, only in ways that we cannot hope to comprehend completely yet could gain so much by trying to, regardless. This is perhaps the beauty of the contributions to this issue of *Critical Muslim*. They all probe the notion of beauty – some more forcibly than others – but in doing so, they question how it is constructed in the first place. In other words, if beauty is indeed in the eye of the beholder, this volume turns its gaze resolutely on the beholder, and what kind of power the beholder wields upon the beheld, and vice versa. Our contributors suggest that the solution to the puzzle of beauty – 'What is it?'; 'Who gets to define it?'; 'Where do we find it?'; 'Who benefits and who suffers?' – is to put the onus of responsibility on the beholder. Because why burden the objects of beauty with ever-growing pressure to comply with fickle standards that are designed for most of them not to measure up to anyway? As Mostafa suggests, perhaps it is the self-appointed beholders of beauty who should be convinced to change their attitudes towards it, mirroring the generous and non-judgemental attributes of the Divine.

SELFIES AND OTHER GAZES

Samia Rahman

> i want to apologise to all the women
> i have called pretty
> before i have called them intelligent or brave
> i am sorry i made it sound as though
> something as simple as what you're born with
> is the most you have to be proud of when your
> spirit has crushed mountains
> from now on i will say things like
> you are resilient or you are extraordinary
> not because i don't think you're pretty
> but because you are so much more than that
> — Rupi Kaur

Did you notice, Rupi, my gaze? Lingering a second longer than it should. Perhaps you guessed my thoughts as I looked into those eyes? Wondering at the passage of time since we last met? There was a time I told her she was pretty and lavishly bestowed the most saccharine of compliments. A fleeting memory in soft focus carried within the deepest recesses of an active imagination. Could she have once adorned billboards? Tell me that didn't cross your mind too. Fulfilling the fantasies of every male gaze. Lowered or un-lowered — it's all the same. To aspire to be beautiful, adored, coveted, envied. And now? A life etched onto the skin's surface; a story emanating from every pore with the transience of youth swept aside. Women are pretty and men are brave. Society stakes its claim on feminine aesthetics and privileges the right to scrutinise. I know now. Our visual encounters so resolutely gendered as we search female faces and bodies for the covered-up truth. The mask is more than just foundations and concealers and contouring and strobing, hijabs, niqabs and *dupattas*. Men need only be bare, authentic. What is that I hear them say? A woman employs trickery to enhance? The gaze will see through her 'mask', her layers. Every attempt to present the best possible version of her 'self'.

And what of this 'self' that reveals itself, clear to the gaze that holds it in its view, objectifying and quantifying? Clumsy words defy my attempt to capture what the mind's eye beholds. Only empty adjectives are prized: 'pretty'. Who objectifies whom? Why and how? The answer is indisputable – from James Bond films to reality television, the symbolism that envelopes our lives through screens and visual imagery is created for the male gaze. The hierarchy of consumption places *his* priorities at the centre, behind the lens, directing the action, manipulating the message. Devouring every sexual detail of the female form for simplistic pleasure; objectification diminishes each and every intricate woman, it strips away her tumultuous depth and simmering humanity to a husk, a mere commodity. Insidiously, the gaze is gradually turned inward. Young girls accommodate society's insistence that their value must be measured according to their physical attributes. Self-objectification pervades, as an individual privileges physical attractiveness over all the multitude of complex, contradictory, dizzying and wondrous non-observable body attributes that make up their fulsome being.

A person becomes reduced to an aesthetic in today's social media age as the inverted gaze becomes a medium ripe for self-objectification. The compulsion to author our own story and reveal our best self to the world is inherent in our millennial selfie culture. Selfies beam down from Instagram and Facebook and Twitter. Defiant and confident, they declare they are reversing the process of objectification. What a persuasive conceit, for what else is a selfie other than full disclosure, while a female protagonist is left without anchor, inevitably shamed by the expectations of convention into which she contorts and contracts but can never comfortably fit. The emancipatory ideal falls short and we are left with a complicated gendering in pursuit of internal truth. Yet, what is this truth that we speak of? As we turn the gaze onto ourselves are we finally taking ownership of our projected selves? Is the selfie really a democratising tool that enables everyday individuals to sculpt and fashion their image exactly as they would like?

It would seem not. Ownership of the self is cast aside. The body aesthetic is held up against pre-determined standards of attractiveness and objectified by the power of its gaze. The selfie is an attempt by the narratable self to meet the gaze with its own version of its story, yet the exact dynamics of such an interaction will never be controlled. Photographs create an endless tension between image and reality when subjected to a gaze of varying context. For Susan Sontag, photography inevitably objectifies and commodifies its subject, numbing us to a person's essential humanity and taking a predatory interpretive role. In our contemporary times the phenomenon of the selfie is one that seemingly erases the distance between subject and photographer. Distance is severed and, as such, so is connection, because by turning people into objects, the gaze claims to know the person in the selfie in a way that they could never fully know themselves.

Self-objectification via the selfie is the ultimate confession in its depiction of multiple spectacles of the self. It is to bare your soul via an internal gaze with intense emotional and physical vulnerability. I knew that I found it disconcerting when my eyes locked with those of every selfie subject but I could never be sure why. Those eyes were at times intransigent, at times warm, often bottomless pools that reflect everything, yet nothing. It is what Giovanni Borradori describes as the meaning of the story in its afterlife. On an unseasonably warm March evening I sat in a gleaming room at Goldsmiths College in New Cross and listened as Professor Borradori discussed the selfie in terms of 'a representation of the spectacle of self-representation'. Devoid of autonomy, the subject is merely duped into thinking that he or she is curating the story of his or her life. Instead, by projecting the ideal self 'through the lens of imagined others', every individual is at the mercy of objectification that is narrowly defined according to established conventions of beauty. Endlessly over-exposing, over-sharing, inviting empathy and pleading acceptance, the selfie is validated only by the approval of others. Borradori describes the end result as the emergence of 'the docile political subject produced and maintained by the reversible camera'. The significance of the selfie is a celebration of what comes after – how much validation the image of your best possible self, a self that you cultivated and carefully chose to project, elicits. Yet the impact is commodified, transient and fleeting, with far from captivated or emotionally invested audiences flitting 'from selfie to selfie, glimpsed, revisited and quickly forgotten'.

Photography is a form of death, not only because it captures a moment, an object, a person, or a context that no longer exists but out of the disruption emerges something new. An afterlife. Borradori's afterlife. The gaze has faltered and we are met with the eyes of a person who invites us to let him or her contribute to our story before we have even had a chance to internalise our own perception of self in that moment. What is key is that this form of self-objectification is not done on one's own terms but seeks approval from the viewer in a desperate soliciting of likes, retweets, comments and follows. A selfie on social media seeks affirmation for the image that is being projected, the image that has been constructed purely for the objectification of others. It is the only way it will remain alive in the consciousness of those who view it. Our idealised self, representing how we wish to be perceived, can be validated solely by the external gaze, via a reaction from others. Instead of energising a diversity of self-representation, the internal gaze is a slave to the norms of neoliberal discourse. Western fashion and fads vomit out a social media sea of clones gazing out at us with their generic straightened hair, head coquettishly tilted to one side, and the obligatory duck-face expression. The commodification of the selfie is a uniquely twenty-first century manifestation of the objectification of self. We tell ourselves that photography is the prism through which we make sense of reality but instead, what has occurred is the converse. Our lives are dictated by the Instagrammability of every activity. Ego travel has supplanted traditional holiday destinations with photo-friendly opportunities for toad-licking and perilous yoga poses on cliff edges the priority for millennial 'explorers'.

Turning the gaze inward is a state of mind, we are constantly told. The 2018 film *I Feel Pretty*, starring the supposedly less-than-averagely-attractive Amy Schumer, sets out to persuade the female viewer that the only way to transcend her below-par looks, as dictated by the beauty standards of today's brutal and highly visual social media culture, is to re-set her internal gaze. After a bump on the head, Schumer's character sees herself as a drop-dead-gorgeous supermodel, and boy does she channel it! Her new-found self-image and off-the-chart body-positivity lead to all manner of favourable outcomes in both her corporate career and previously non-existent love life. This woman is turning heads, revelling in her elevated position in the objectification hierarchy and generally making men and women re-think their attitudes to beauty through her untameable inner confidence. But let's get real. The multinational cosmetics company that she works for is only tokenistically influenced to sugar-coat its industry-wide conventional definition of beauty with a sprinkling of empowerment dust. The 'revolution' is as superficial as the notion that a white, blonde, hetero-normative, cisgender, able-bodied, first-world-inhabiting woman is regarded as falling short of Hollywood's gold standard of what constitutes a beautiful woman. As far as I can tell, she absolutely *is* the template for Hollywood's objectification of women to please the male gaze. Resistance doesn't come from dismantling the patriarchal structures that set unreal and discriminatory beauty-standards. Oh no. That would be far too anarchic. Instead, responsibility is laid firmly at the door of the less-than-averagely-attractive woman who just needs to get a grip, grow a thicker skin and emanate grace and confidence in order to shatter that glass ceiling.

The self-objectifying gaze is a story of either conformity or failure. The confession becomes even further removed from all semblance of reality than the absence of finality. Filters, photo-editing, Snapchat and all manner of duplicity are employed to make a person prettier and thinner than they could possibly aspire to be In Real Life (IRL). IRL a person is flawed. A beach-ready body and perfect skin comprise an image perpetuated by elite supermodels who deny they ever diet or have a skincare routine. Yet, just like Schumer's character, we are taught that perfection ought to be the preoccupation of every female who wants to look cool or hot or just not invisible. You gotta fake it to make it. It's all about attitude and editing. Now that our lives are lived through the medium of virtual reality, it is an encumbrance, no an obligation, to smooth those wrinkles, trout that pout and present a super-enhanced version of your best possible self. Brushed and sculpted, using all the latest guides and trends and YouTube tutorials, you can now dare to gaze out from the black mirror and be blisteringly judged and brazenly objectified. You can even opt out of real life altogether and use technology to project an unreal, exemplary image of yourself. An article published in *Hello* magazine in 2015 listed the top five best apps for 'perfecting selfies'. It involves taking that raw selfie and employing the power of technology for 'whitening teeth and brightening skin or [creating] a healthy glow' or opting for total transformation and undergoing 'a full make-over including shaping your eyebrows, banishing dark circles and even contouring your face' without having to apply even a scrap of make-up. The standards of beauty located in the minds of men and women via the patriarchal matrix in which we exist are unrelenting. Do you dare to be authentic? Your fantasy projection may score you an objectified ten in the eyes of our society's gaze, but when your Tinder date relegates you to a 6.5 IRL then you know you've fallen victim to the impossible pressures an uneven playing field obsessed with digital exhibitionism and narcissism imposes.

Some sites of subversion do exist. Singer Alicia Keys declared herself make-up free in 2016, performing and carrying out public appearances with only her natural beauty exuding. The irony was not lost on me – strikingly beautiful woman, who looks immaculate without make-up, decides to ditch make-up to protest against the way 'women are brainwashed into feeling like we have to be skinny, or sexy, or desirable or perfect.' She went on to explain, 'One of the many things I was tired of was the constant judgement of women.' There is no doubt Keys has made a bold and important stand for which she deserves full respect but the news was met with a media frenzy that diluted any feminist quality to her stance. All talk was of her glowing skin and Cleopatra eyes as her make-up free comeliness continued to be objectified and analysed by society's misogynistic gaze. *Cosmopolitan* magazine was one of a number of lifestyle publications falling over themselves to slam on the brakes on those women who dared contemplate facing the world without succumbing to a regimen of aesthetically enhancing rituals. It was with great relish that they uncovered the singer's elaborate beauty prep to attain that 'natural' look. She not only ices and oils her face but, according to her 'make-up' artist Dotti, in an interview for *W Magazine* quoted by *Cosmo*: 'On some days, I'll look at her skin and say, "You need cucumber today," so I'll grate a full cucumber, then place the pulp no higher than her brow bone and no lower than her under-eye bone, not going near sensitive parts of the eye. If we've got time, I'll put the pulp all over her face until it draws the heat out of the skin and brings the blood to the top.' We all know the technique of placing a slice of a cucumber over your eyes for a quick refresh, but the implication here is that Keys, like an Olympic medal-winning athlete who enhanced his or her performance with a sly swig of cough medicine, has been caught out. Like the hipster called out for spending hours in front of the mirror perfecting the 'just got out of bed' look, the objectifying gaze never ceases to judge even the woman who decries the tools of the patriarchy. She may resist the pressure to aspire for perfection, but IRL even she is stuck on the pendulum of disappointed perfection.

The male gaze objectifies women to within an inch of their essence. But what of men? A friend recalls a period in his teens where he describes being heavily objectified by a group of girls at his school. It may sound like every young boy's dream come true but, all jokes aside, the experience was traumatising for a shy and bookish adolescent unprepared for the barrage of unsolicited sexual attention and rendered painfully self-conscious by constant remarks about his 'pretty-boy' looks. Alas, this was before Rupi came on the scene so there was not even the opportunity to retaliate with a choice quote. Kit Harington, star of the cult TV series *Game of Thrones*, which, let's be under no illusions, is a minefield when it comes to gratuitous misogyny, echoed my friend's discomfort. In an interview with *The Sunday Times* in 2016, he railed against what he termed sexism but later clarified to mean the objectification of men and said that there was a 'double-standard' in the lack of acknowledgement that men were victims too: 'I like to think of myself as more than a head of hair or a set of looks. It's demeaning. Yes, in some way you could argue I've been employed for a look I have. But there's a sexism that happens towards men. There's definitely a sexism in our industry that happens towards women, and there is towards men as well... At some points during photoshoots when I'm asked to strip down, I felt that.'

It would be a misnomer to argue that the female gaze does not exist and has no propensity to objectify men. The Diet Coke advert, which first hit the airwaves in 1994, featured a group of female office workers ogling at a handsome construction worker while he took his daily 'Diet Coke Break', which quickly became their daily 'Diet Coke Break'. The advert caused such a ruckus that it was reprised in 1997, this time with the gaggle of women turning their attention to a sexy window cleaner. There is much that is problematic about this scene, not least the issue of class, yet at the time it was argued that this example of reverse objectification was actually testament to a new-found sexual confidence as women unashamedly celebrated their right to project desire. Personally, I have a problem with anyone objectifying anyone but let's not kid ourselves that the female gaze is anywhere near as pervasive, entrenched or damaging to society and the psyche of its subject as centuries of objectification perpetrated by the male gaze has proven to be. This is the point that Harington needs to note and my friend must concede. As I mentioned, Harington back-tracked on his use of the term 'sexism' because, until structural misogyny is no longer a thing, to cry crocodile tears over reverse objectification is akin to calling an ambulance for a paper cut. It stings, it can be painful and an inconvenience and make you a little wary of paper-related tasks. But it's not going to ruin your life.

The nuance of objectification is not only gendered. It's certainly the case that we can't go wrong with a bit of misogyny-busting but it would be too convenient to forget that not only is the internalised gaze patriarchal, but the status quo is often perpetuated by women, who are more often the first to rush to judgement. Justin Bieber, adored by his legions of die-hard fans, known quirkily as 'Beliebers', is constantly having to request that they tone down their vicious hate for his latest rumoured love interest or whoever he has recently been pictured in a romantic clinch with. Male objectification may be less insidious than the rampant objectification of females that makes up our reality, but what is indeed damaging is the model of idealised romantic love that is fostered by obsessive adoration of the boy-band variety. Women have been known to fiercely renege on solidarity to become the worst critics of members of their own gender. How many times have prospective mother-in-laws deemed their son's choice of bride a disappointment in the beauty stakes? Objectification would be severely weakened if it was not upheld by female protagonists.

The Western-centric gaze, albeit predominantly male, has been pivotal in constructing an image of the ideal man and woman and imposing it on the rest of the world. Absorbing the limitations of the Western model of perfection, we now have a global culture that stubbornly refuses plurality. This is despite other societies historically managing, successfully, to incorporate diversity in their perception of perfection. It is the objectification of people as sexual beings that is teetering out of control and the sexualisation of children is a particularly worrying by-product of social media that permeates every aspect of our existence. The unresolved problem remains an inability to dethrone the concept of the ideal woman and man. Remember: men are brave; women are pretty. The West is drowning in a quagmire of individualism and the binary perceptions it projects deny the more pluralistic responses to gender that do exist elsewhere. Muslim tradition has long celebrated self-definition and it is tiresome to presuppose Islam carries the burden of misogyny alone. Rather, what the West has imbued is a denial of beauty standards that informs our opinion of ourselves. The result? When faced with a stereotype or idealised beauty or behaviour, we all declare that we don't adhere to that model, we are unique, we are worth it, we are individual, while in reality the beauty industry has rendered us all mass-marketed clones. Individualism in relation to the collective lies at the heart of all understanding of ourselves. It is here that we are afforded the ability to speak in terms of me, of I, oblivious that we are projecting an outdated homogenous trope via our blinkered gaze that negates the flexibility to be different.

Around the world, people are strangled by the gaze. Conformist societies render group thinking the norm. Non-conformism travels from the fringes only to become commodified and neutralised, breeding further social conformism and the surreal inevitability that to be unconventional you only need to place your online Amazon order and purchase your required 'look', as if it were a fancy-dress costume. The idealised aesthetic is that of the sexualised female of child-bearing age while older women are perceived to be a burden without value. Grandma sits politely in the corner to be ignored unless she can perform some useful function, such as provide free childcare. Has the empowered status of the wise and respected older matriarch been vanquished to the footnotes of history? With experience should come agency and a position of influence, whether in the home or the community or elsewhere. Western societies have an obsession with youth that objectifies women with vulgar reductivity and the rest of the world has embraced this dire state of affairs wholeheartedly.

Furthermore, as the West gazes out at the world, the difference in perception goes beyond even male-female binaries and appears diminished. It is this embrace of the binary that denies more pluralistic responses, engulfing them entirely. Modern popular culture offers no respite, whether in the form of a plot device in Amy Schumer's appalling attempt to give voice to all those women out there who 'aren't pretty', or the beauty and lifestyle magazines replete with images of flawless perfection airbrushed to unreality. Lupita Nyong'o famously talked about the way in which she yearned to have lighter skin as a child after realising that she had no role models or exemplars of beauty that looked even remotely like her. Burberry model Neelam Gill similarly recently lamented the painful pressure to be pale in a desire to adapt to society's gaze. To be invisible, average, or even remotely outside the conventions of mainstream, Eurocentric, Western beauty can stifle self-esteem, self-worth, self-value. Globalisation has only added to this conflict between the inner and outer self as individuals struggle to find their place in the world of increasingly homogenous beauty standards. To be relentlessly objectified in a manner that is excluding and alienating can only accentuate anxiety, despair and feelings of insecurity as individuals struggle under the gaze of others. On the other hand, if society's gaze decides you are beautiful then the assumption is implicit that, as a consequence, you can do no wrong.

Like Rupi, I wish to apologise to all those women I have called pretty. I yearn to retract every uncomfortable stare and judgemental comment I've borne witness to. Unspoken words articulated through cursory glances and disapproving looks make my cheeks burn with shame. The gaze has turned in on the marginalised, the minorities and the disenfranchised. Operating within the hierarchy of power, it subjugates through the structures of injustice that limit us all. Women, in particular, are subject to demands that they are pliant to the whim of their objectification regardless of the form of representation that is directed their way. For Muslim women, it is through the prism of the Western obsession with the veil that they are imagined. The gaze objectifies and dismisses Muslim women and girls as pitiful, disempowered creatures, it seeks to save them from themselves and liberate them from their garb. Fetishised and deconstructed in the minds of those who pass judgement from a watchful distance, the Muslim female is one of the most closely observed and scrutinised groups in the Western imagination. Neither is she free from policing gazes in Muslim societies. Locating the site for ideological and political battlegrounds on Muslim women's bodies is hardly unheard of in many Muslim countries as well as beyond. Freeing oneself from the gaze of voyeurs is not tangential to a piece of cloth, whether one chooses to cover or uncover. Neither is it dependant on a person lowering their gaze. Instead, Muslims are urged not to be so utterly consumed by the gaze. Believers are counselled to recover the moral principle and use it as a buffer against the all-pervasive Western-origin, neoliberal definition of gaze that objectifies, commodifies and sexualises.

The objectifying gaze is anathema in Islamic tradition. What is celebrated instead, is an equalising gaze that considers first the obligations of men, before mentioning the same obligations of women as a guide for perceiving those among whom they exist.

The Qur'an states:

> Tell the believing men that they should lower their gaze and guard their private parts... (24:31)
> Tell the believing women that they should lower their gaze and guard their private parts...(24:32)

By talking about both men and women, one is not privileged over the other or carries the burden of responsibility when confronted with the objectifying potency of watching and assessing. Men and women are both granted the ability to gaze upon others but are compelled to look upon their fellow (wo)men conscionably, in a manner that is not reductive. True, to be preoccupied with averting one's eyes when interacting with a member of the opposite sex only ferments objectification. But this is not the point. The point is, rather, that veiling is not relevant to the Qur'anic message, although it is the right of any woman to veil under her own volition if this is what she wishes to do. The anathema of the gaze is conveyed, not the lowering of the gaze. Islamic teaching advises not to look at people as objects but as a sum of all their humanity. *Purdah*, or the segregation of the sexes, is an impractical and detrimental state of affairs, yet is routinely interpreted as the optimal path in any attempt to thwart objectification. Barriers, whether they manifest in the form of veiling, averting of the eyes or the actual physical separation of the sexes, are a misapprehension. It is the actual gaze itself that we must delete from our psyche in order to create a healthy and respectful dynamic of interaction and appreciation between human beings. The Muslim woman, weighed down by the burden of the gaze, struggles to be an exemplary female in reaction to the gaze she is subjected to. Wearied and re-imagined, she is unable to escape objectification even in Muslim societies, which are often so very removed from Islamic ideals. The misconstruction of our own interpretation of the Islamic gaze is rife, regardless of cultural or religious tradition. Muslim communities and nations have only served to imbibe the worst aspects of the Western concept of the neoliberal gaze and embody its meaning without question. Without critically re-thinking the Qur'anic interpretation of the gaze, we will never get past the distractions of veiling and segregation.

I am sorry if I called you pretty, or handsome. I am sorry if I cast my eyes over your features without acknowledging the strength of your inner dignity and wisdom. Treating people as equal beings and honouring far more than the superficial mask they present to the world should be the purest definition of our understanding of beauty that exists. Let us not reduce the complexity and vibrancy of our finite selves to objectification based on transient and fleeting external attributes. As we gaze upon others, let the experience be expansive as we quench the thirst of our eyes. The gaze is powerful. The gaze is anathema. Let us make the gaze benign. All societies have an aversion to the gaze, but as we soak in the entirety of every person we observe, we are reminded that not all gazes are the same. Each of us is our own landscape.

BEAUTY IN ISLAM

Doris Behrens-Abouseif

In no other religion does the concept of beauty play such a crucial role as in Islam. The concept of aesthetic beauty or the beauty of the form begins with the Revelation itself and the belief that the Qur'an is the word of God Himself, transmitted to the world by His unlettered Messenger, Muhammad. The unique beauty of the language and literary style of its text are believed to be the compelling evidence of its divine essence. The language of the Qur'an is described as a miracle *(i'jāz)* which no human being is capable of achieving or imitating. Because the language is quintessential to the revelation, the translation of the Qur'an is not acknowledged as equivalent to the Arabic text. Early texts report of conversion through aesthetic experience, of converts being mesmerised by sound and expression of the recited Qur'an, revealing the divinity of its source. The persuasive power of beauty is a leitmotif in the Islamic aesthetic discourse.

The words *husn* and *jamāl* and other derivatives of the same roots mean beauty. Several other terms are used in the Qur'an to refer to beauty and perfection in connection with God's creation of the world such as *zukhruf, tayyib, bahīj, zīna* and their derivatives. The derivatives of *husn* are used in the Qur'an in the sense of goodness, virtue as well as excellence and perfection, as in *ahsana kulla shay'in khalaqahu* (32:7), *fa-ahsana suwarakum* (40:64; 64:3). The stem *husn* appears as an attribute of the names of God, *al-asmā' al-husnā* (59:24), commonly understood as the 'beautiful' names although it should be perhaps interpreted in the sense of 'good' and 'best'. In classical Arabic, *husn* means 'beauty' and is synonymous with *jamāl*. *Husn* and *jamāl* with their derivatives encompass aesthetic as well as moral beauty – in other words, the beautiful and the good.

The Qur'an dedicates an important place to the pleasing beauty of God's creation. God made the world beautiful in the sense of appealing to the senses, by perfecting all things and giving them ornamental attributes. The term *zayyana*, meaning 'to ornament', is used in this context: God has adorned the sky with stars. Ornamentation is an essential aspect of beauty (15:16; 18:7; 27:88; 32:7; 35:27-28; 37:6-7; 41:11-12; 50:6; 67:3-5). One of the most powerful testimonies of the significance of sensuous beauty in religion is the fact that, unlike in Christianity, the Qur'an and other Muslim religious texts describe Paradise in physical sensual terms, referring to precious materials – natural and processed – such as gems and jewellery, garments, architecture, and ornaments (55:54, 76), and to beautiful young women, or *khayyirāt* and *ḥisān* (55:70).

God not only created nature to please, but he also gave the human being an excellent shape: *aḥsan taqwīm* (95:4). Human beings are allowed to adorn themselves with beautiful garments and jewellery for which God provided the material on earth (7:26; 16:14; 35:12). The only truly narrative text in the Qur'an, 12:30, 32, which tells the story of Potiphar's wife's encounter with the Prophet Joseph, powerfully expresses the fascination with human beauty. When Potiphar's wife introduces Joseph to her female friends, they get so mesmerised by his physical beauty that they cut themselves with the fruit knives they are holding.

A rare phenomenon in the history of religions is the abundance of descriptions of the Prophet Muhammad's physical features and of how he dressed and perfumed himself. Following this tradition, the Arabic medieval chronicles often describe the physical features of monarchs. Verbal portraiture substituted for effigies.

Several hadiths (recorded traditions of the prophet Muhammad) praise human beauty as a virtue, describing the handsome believer as the utmost perfection, or saying that handsome people are auspicious: *uṭlubu al-khayra ʿinda ḥisān al-wujūh*. The philosopher and jurist Al-Ghazali (d. 1111) describes physical beauty as blessing and power (*niʿma, qudra*). The notion of beauty being auspicious is also found in the visual arts. Erotic literature and the celebration of female beauty had an acknowledged status even among members of the religious establishment.

The famous and often-quoted hadith about God being beautiful and loving everything beautiful might not necessarily be authentic, but it always had a great impact, particularly on Sufism.

From the perspective of Sunni orthodox thought, al-Ghazali's discourse on beauty (using both terms *jamāl* and *ḥusn*) is paramount. Beauty is good because it is a source of pleasure and pleasure is pursued for its own sake. God's perfect creation is comparable to a work of art made by an artist or designer (*muṣawwir*). Just as a work of art, be it calligraphy or wall painting, inspires the beholder to reflect upon the artist's talent, the beauty of the world inspires the human being to think of the Designer who created it. In long passages, al-Ghazali invites the believer to contemplate the wonders of the universe in search of God, 'pleasure being a form of cognition'. God created beauty for the human beings to enjoy so that they get a taste of the eternal bliss of the Hereafter. Beauty can be visual, as well as perceptible by smell, touch and also cognition. Al-Ghazali also referred to a form of beauty beyond the material one sensed through sight, hearing, touch, and taste, which is the intelligible beauty of knowledge and virtue perceived rather by 'inner sight'. The more exalted the subject of perception, the higher the pleasure so that the knowledge of God is the perfect perception of beauty and the utmost form of pleasure that surpasses all sensuous and intellectual satisfactions.

While Arabic-Islamic culture did not articulate an all-encompassing theory of art, it produced dispersed yet elaborate concepts of artistic experiences regarding specific subjects, such as literature and music, that together form a substantial corpus on aesthetics. Although al-Ghazali compared God's creation with a work of art, human artistic achievement was not associated with divine sources as in Greek culture. The notion of genius that would associate the human being with divine attributes is absent in the Islamic framework. Artistic works, *ṣinā'āt*, belong to the realm of knowledge that needs to be acquired through endeavour.

Because of the significance of poetry as the paramount form of art in pre-modern Islamic society, the elaborate concepts of Arab poetical aesthetics are relevant to the understanding of other artistic aspects of culture as well. Despite the Prophet's alleged hostility to poets and the rejection of music by some puritanical theologians, these arts were always highly celebrated and cultivated theoretically and practically. Retaining its faithfulness to the ideals of pre-Islamic poetical tradition and its hedonistic associations, and its emphasis on formal aesthetic and stylistic criteria, classical poetry maintained a worldly outlook and was left to thrive in the secular domain.

Classical Arabic literary criticism adopted the Aristotelian distinction between form and content. The good poet was the one who masters his art, no matter the morality of his subject matter, with literary skills having priority over sincerity. According to the Persian mathematician al-Isbahani (d. 967), in his *Book of Songs*, 'not all songs have a meaning and not all that is meaningful pleases the viewer and entertains the listener'. Meanings are everywhere, according to the Arabic prose writer al-Jahiz (d. 868) – the issue is to give them an attractive formulation. Later, historian and sociologist Ibn Khaldun (d. 1406) judged most religious poetry as inferior because of the ubiquity of its content. Meaning, which is not the poet's main concern, is like water, it assumes the shape and colour of the form that contains it. The poet's role is to shape the container. An extreme statement endorsing the aesthetic function of the poetry is a saying that poetry is associated with sin and if involved with morality it degenerates. Unlike the Greeks, who considered poetry as a gift rather than a science, the Arabs emphasised the technical aspect of poetry and other arts, which require study and skill rather than divine revelation. The poet was often compared with a jeweller operating with precious metals.

In his elaborate theories of literary criticism, the Tunisian poet Hazim al-Qartajanni (d. 1284) defined poetry as aiming to touch and move the soul rather than address the mind rationally as the natural sciences do. He emphasised the aesthetic experience where images, imagination and fantasy are involved in enhancing, exaggerating, and transfiguring reality to accomplish the required psychological effect. In the same vein, the eleventh century Persian polymath Ibn Sina qualified Arabic poetry as mainly aesthetic and subjective, made to address emotions, delight and impress without being bound by moral or ethical criteria. With these attributes it differed from Greek narrative and epic poetry, which was purposeful and engaged and aimed at influencing human conduct.

The culture of *adab* at the court of Baghdad created the concept of the *zarif*, meaning the refined person. *Al-Muwashsha* (meaning the Embroidered Gown) is a manual of the ninth century authored by a man called al-Washsha (meaning the Embroiderer), describing in detail the rules and etiquette and social aesthetics that includes a section on the hygiene of the body as well as a section on the *zarif*'s female counterpart, the *zarifa*. The *zarif* has a pleasing appearance with a slender figure, dresses with taste without ostentation, cultivates a refined lifestyle, and carefully selects the objects he surrounds himself with. He displays fine manners at table and in conversations. The epitome of the *zarif* was the musician Ziryab (d. 857), educated in Baghdad where he served at the court of Harun al-Rashid, before he became famous at the court of the caliph 'Abd al-Rahman II (r. 822-852) in Cordoba, where he introduced his own fashions in music, dress, cosmetics and cuisine.

From the litterateur's perspective, al-Jahiz emphasised the individual psychological factor in the aesthetic experience, giving it priority over fixed criteria of beauty. His approach followed the principle inherited from Manichaeism, that all things combine simultaneously positive and negative features, whose ultimate value and impact on the mind are determined by the quality and proportion of their mixture. Bad and good are not absolute values, but a matter of circumstances and subjective experience. Al-Jahiz viewed the human being as a microcosm which combines all elements and attributes that exist in nature, with all their disparity and contradictions. Addressing the subject of abstract beauty as being based on a mental process, al-Jahiz's view was that it was not a commonly accessible matter, but rather required intellectual skill to be perceived.

These concepts articulated by literati and philosophers were not detached from the reality on the ground, but rather mirrored the taste of the broad worldly environment of an urban society. The immense success of the *Maqamat* of the poet al-Hariri (d. 1122) as a literary narrative in rhymed prose, written in a highly recherché style, is one example. The hero of this narrative is a rather immoral person who makes his living with dubious methods, yet always succeeds in getting away unpunished thanks to his eloquent poetic pleadings, which elicited people's sympathy and forgiveness.

However, some thinkers, rather than literary critics, adopted Platonic concepts of beauty, such as al-Razi (d. 925 or 935), Miskawayh (d. 1030) and Ibn Hazm (d.1064), condemning love poetry and romances as frivolous and immoral. The aesthetic mainstream approach of classical poetry did not preclude the development of an engaged poetry with political, moral or religious associations as, for example, the poems interspersed in the chronicles or the poetry of *jihad* in times of warfare. Religious poetry was recited in mosques on festive occasions, notably the genre dedicated to the praise of the Prophet. The poem of 'the Mantle' or the *Burda* by the Sufi poet al-Busiri (d. 1294), is a most prominent example of such poetry, which acquired a liturgical and sacred status over the entire

Muslim world. The poet composed it in praise of the Prophet following his recovery from paralysis after the Prophet appeared to him in a dream, wrapping him in a mantle. The poem had an unparalleled echo already in the poet's lifetime. Inscriptions with its verses were widely engraved in sanctuaries and homes and used as talismans to avert illness or celebrate recovery. However, Sufi poetry symbolically adopted the conventional forms of wine and erotic poetry to address God.

Whereas poetry was conceived to incite imagination and arouse emotion, music was the art to which Arabic literature attributed the most profound impact on the soul. Its stirring power was believed to lead to the profound religious experience of ecstasy or to the kind of intoxication associated immorality. Although the jurists Abu Hanifa (d. 767) and Shafiʻi (d. 820) condemned music, in particular when performed by slave girls, al-Ghazali contradicted them with the argument that there is no statement in the Qur'an or in the Prophet's traditions to justify such hostility. One of al-Ghazali's arguments in favour of music was that it is perceived by one of our five senses which, together with the mind, were created to be used. He mentions the musical performances of the Patriarch David and the singing of birds which flatters the ear and refers to a hadith saying that all prophets sent by God had a beautiful voice; a preacher should have, therefore, a pleasant harmonic speech to move his listeners. He divided the influence of music into two categories – spiritual and physical.

Al-Ghazali's opinion was endorsed by other theologians, especially among the Sufis who, referring to the biblical Davidic tradition and to hadith, believed music to be an attribute of Paradise. In Sufi rituals, the *samāʻ* or musical performances, including singing and dancing, have been universally practised – although the debate over their permissibility has never stopped. Al-Ghazali viewed the *samāʻ* as an encounter with God that leads the mystic to ecstasy, uncovering hidden emotions and purifying the heart. Other advocates of music and poetry argued that music, like poetry or even language, cannot *per se* be wrong; their moral value depends rather on their context and use. Al-Ghazali, however, condemned the use of certain musical instruments that were employed in frivolous contexts. He approved of love songs because they arouse desire, strengthen feelings and excite pleasure, all of which are permissible on the condition that the relationship between the lovers is lawful – according to al-Ghazali, the

Prophet himself authorised music, singing and dance as a natural expression of pleasure. Music performances should be allowed on festive occasions and celebrations, for pleasure is laudable. Al-Ghazali criticised opponents of music as being incapable of perceiving the beauty of God's creation.

Mas'udi (d. 956), who compiled the classic and gigantic *Book of Songs*, considered the study of music to be the noblest bequest of Greek culture because music ignites and transports the soul – it is the highest of all pleasures. Music was not only art but also science, pleasure, and therapy – a prescription for physicians to administer to the mind or body of the diseased. As many other authors, he believed that there was a correspondence between the human body and the universe and that the humours of the body were tuned to the vibration of music.

The Ikhwān al-Ṣafā (Brethren of Purity – a tenth century secret society of philosophers), adopted the Pythagorean principle of mathematical proportions as defining the beauty of all things and as the basis of universal harmony. Earthly art is a reflection of the heavenly, superior world. The principle of earthly beauty reflecting the heavenly was adopted in Sufism, especially in its poetry, in which the love of God is often expressed using the terminology of erotic love and the ecstasy of the divine union depicted as drunkenness. Earthly music is an echo of cosmic music, produced by the movement of the celestial bodies reflecting the harmony of the universe. It can produce a perfect emotion which can exalt the soul and repel ugliness. It generates pleasure to the soul like wine does to the body. Ikhwān al-Ṣafā distinguished two aspects to the art of music – the art itself and its psychological effect.

Ibn Khaldun regarded music as the most sophisticated form of art because it could only subsist in a highly civilised and urbanised society as an expression of leisure and luxury, devoid of any function other than that of pastime and enjoyment. It therefore perishes when its cultural environment declines. In the visual arts and material culture of the mediaeval Muslim world, the depiction of music occupies a prominent place as a sign of auspiciousness. It is often associated with representations of courtly scenes, showing musicians and musical performances along other pastimes. The juxtaposition of good wishes as inscriptions to these scenes reiterates this message.

Arabic literature on kingship includes numerous references to the sages of Greece, India, and Persia, who described music both as a serious subject and a useful pleasure that educated and cultivated the mind, improved the character, and revived the spirit. It is therapy for melancholy and is therefore essential to the well-being of kings. The belief in the therapeutic effects of music, or the influence of musical modes on the mind, was based on the Greek doctrine according to which the elements and humours are in relation to particular notes and rhythms, reflecting cosmic order. The Arab polymath Al-Kindi (d. 873) was one of the great protagonists of this doctrine; he analysed the soothing combination of music, colours and perfumes. Musical scenes are one of the major motifs in the pre-modern decorative arts. As symbols of pleasure and princely life, they fulfilled an auspicious function.

Unlike poetry and music, the visual arts have not been the subject of theoretical debate in Arabic literature. In recent years, historians of Islamic art have dedicated their attention to the Arab mathematician and physicist Ibn al-Haytham's (d. 1039) discourse on beauty. Ibn al-Haytham achieved a breakthrough in the field of optics by studying the mental aspects of visual perception. Sight can only perceive the physical properties of an object, or the raw material, which it channels to the mind without analysing them. It is the mind that interprets the visual impulses that reach the eye by physical means. The perception of an object's beauty is achieved through the mental faculty of discrimination by establishing analogies, categories and associations with stored memories.

Ibn al-Haytham's psychological analysis of visual aesthetics and the mental process of visual perception converge with the theories of his contemporary, Ibn Sina (d. 1037), who emphasised the psychological factor, endorsed in most Arabic statements on beauty. Ibn Sina conceived pleasure as dependent on two factors – beauty and the perception of it. The latter is a form of knowledge and thus variable and relative. The intensity of pleasure is proportional to the degree of perfection and at the same time to the extent of its perception.

The emphasis on the pleasure factor in beauty may perhaps explain the prominence and characteristic significance of ornament in Islamic art. Decorated surfaces have been one of the earliest expressions of Islamic art. The Dome of the Rock in Jerusalem, built in 691, was decorated with glass mosaics not only on its inner walls following Byzantine tradition, but on the outside as well. The entire inner walls of the Umayyad mosque of Damascus, completed in 721, were the largest surface ever to be decorated with glass mosaics. Surface decoration also characterised Abbasid architecture and the far-reaching spread of glazed pottery from ninth century Iraq was an unprecedented phenomenon in the world at that time. The qualification of Islamic art by some Western scholars as *horror vacui* (literally 'fear of empty space', or filling the entire surface of a space or artwork with detail), although highly debatable, is a reaction to the significance of surface decoration in Islamic art and the development of infinite geometrical designs and their arabesque interpretation. Extreme orthodox opinion rejected the ornamentation of the mosque, the melodious recitation of the Qur'an and the golden illuminations of its manuscripts. However, the evidence of practice reveals a clear vote in favour of aesthetic and artistic expression as a form of religious veneration. Magnificently illuminated Qur'an manuscripts are among the greatest achievements of Islamic art as is the ornamentation of mosques. The melodious recitation of the Holy Book was cultivated according to musical rules and performance styles.

A remarkable feature of Islamic art and material culture was the investment of great skills and intense labour to adorn objects made of common or base materials, turning them into works of art for princely patrons, such as stucco on brick in architecture or copper alloys for vessels.

The dogma that the Qur'an is the word of God transmitted to humanity in the form of a book has played a decisive role in the visual arts; calligraphy was a highly regarded artistic discipline. Calligraphy was not confined to books or religious texts, being rather a major ornamental motif universally applied. Under a predominantly political and urban artistic patronage, the same artistic idiom was applied indiscriminately in religious as well secular contexts following autonomous aesthetic rather than cultic criteria.

Although the hostility to figural representations, based on hadith rather than explicitly prescribed in the Qur'an, is confirmed in the sacral domain of the mosque and the Qur'anic text, the reality of material culture indicates that its impact was not significant beyond the domain of worship. Figural representations have an uninterrupted tradition with varying emphasis across regions and periods. It has been argued that the exclusion

of figural representations from the religious domain led artistic creativity
to unfold in the direction of abstract and geometric designs. The taste for
abstract rather than naturalistic motifs cannot be explained alone with the
ban of figural motifs in the religious context. After the construction of the
Umayyad mosque of Damascus, with its uninhabited gardens, the genres
of landscapes and still-lifes, which are permissible, did not appeal much to
Islamic artists. The pavements of the desert palace of Khirbat al-Mafjar in
eighth-century Palestine, which is the largest mosaic carpet known to date,
indicates the passion for the geometrical ornaments inherited from the
Byzantine Levant that influenced Islamic art in the following centuries.

When referring to architecture, the Qur'an mentions the ruins of
ancient cities and the vestiges of bygone civilisations as examples of the
futility of earthly life that should serve as a lesson in humility, in the same
sense as the tower of Babel in the Bible exemplifies the ostentatious aspect
of architecture. The Qur'an's disdain for worldly architecture is reiterated
in the hadith. This, however, did not preclude Muslim monarchs, whose
duty was to establish and oversee the religious institutions in their realm,
from becoming major patrons of religious architecture and art. For the
same reasons, some scholars took a sceptical attitude towards ostentatious
monuments and the lavish decoration of sanctuaries, among them Ibn
Hazm and al-Ghazali. However, the mainstream of Islamic culture saw in
the lavish architecture and decoration of the mosques a glorification of
Islam as a religion and as a political force. This attitude is confirmed in the
architectural legacy of the Muslim world.

In absence of any theological dictate, the design of the mosques adopted
a variety of forms, some even inspired from Christian architecture, yet
following regional traditions. The only religious precept to be adhered in
mosque architecture is the orientation towards Mecca.

The words 'Paradise' and 'Heaven' have been used in the last decades in
numerous titles of Western publications dealing with Islamic art, making it a
cliché to associate Islamic art with paradisiacal visions. Although the material
culture and the arts of the Islamic world cannot be reduced to being more
motivated or inspired by the after-life than other artistic traditions, the
tangible nature of the Muslim Paradise, where the believer's felicity is a
sensual experience, mirrors a culture that celebrates the beauty of the form.

BEAUTY PAGEANTS

Nadia Mohd Rasidi

My formal religious education began at the age of six, at the al-Mujahideen mosque in the Damansara suburb of Petaling Jaya, Malaysia. It continued for the next sixteen years until I graduated at 22 as an English Literature major from the International Islamic University Malaysia in Gombak. In the near-decade since, much of what I was taught about religion has fallen by the wayside, by processes of accidental and intentional unlearning. Yet a recurring theme from those lessons that has stuck with me, perhaps because it appealed to the self-obsession of my youth, was the oft-repeated connection between Islam and beauty.

I recall sitting in an Islamic Studies class on a hot and muggy afternoon in 2001 and being jolted out of my early teenage stupor by this phrase from my *ustazah* (female religious instructor), delivered with a smile that bordered on beatific: 'God is beautiful and loves beauty.' For some reason, I was struck and seized by those words and turned them over and over in my mind in the following minutes, hours, and days. In a vague sense, I understood that God's beauty was something beyond my comprehension but His love for beauty, to me, had to be grounded in the tangible world that I lived in. And if God loves beauty, and if, as I then believed, I was not beautiful, what did that mean for me? It wasn't that I thought God didn't love me because I wasn't conventionally beautiful. It's that it was beginning to dawn on me that the beauty I was being told God valued still very much conformed to the parameters of human desire, and so no matter how sweet my words and good my deeds, as a fat person, my body would always betray me to other people through the ugliness of its excess.

In my second year of secondary school, I decided to don the hijab, but only during school hours, when I waded in a sea of teenage girls – my friends – who were growing and blooming in ways I envied with an ache. I strived to keep myself safe from the question: when will I be beautiful?

In time I learned that I could practice modesty all I wanted but my body was constantly slipping out of bounds – I had too much hair, too much fat, too much need. My school already required us to wear a uniform, but the added layer of the stiff white triangle I put on every day granted me more of the anonymity I craved, or so I thought. Beneath it, nobody could see my unruly sideburns growing ever closer to my jawline, in my histrionic teenage mind giving me an unwelcome and somewhat threatening Dickensian aura. Or my sizeable bust, at 13 already a grotesque caricature of womanhood in my eyes and a source of frustration when shopping for clothes and shame in the privacy of my room as I contemplated my matronly figure with dismay.

Looking back, I see how the faux modesty of wearing the *tudung* (headscarf) at school offered a brief respite from such contemplations. Now as an adult Muslim woman, my relationship with the word modesty is, on the best of days, fraught. I have lived in London for most of the last six years as I worked my way through graduate school. On the inaugural occasion of my leaving the house with bare arms, the delight I felt at shedding my hang-ups was shot through with a frisson of fear that I was distancing myself from God in a permanent and irreparable way. This reticence to body-baring is unsurprising given my background and the intractable link forged between beauty and modesty by Malay-Muslim culture. Overt displays of beauty by women are not simply immodest, they are outright immoral and a reflection of bad – and therefore ugly – character.

The first time I thought to myself, 'You don't have to be beautiful,' I was 28. I had spent the three years prior learning about fat activism as I fought to make space for a body that is at once too indelicate to be acknowledged and too unwieldy to be ignored, and until that moment I thought that I had arrived at the end-point of my advocacy: believing that all bodies, no matter how 'deviant', are beautiful. The quiet shock I felt as I disentangled myself from a decades-long belief that beauty should be a goal for everyone soon gave way to, much to my surprise, relief. Fat activism had unbounded my sense of what beauty could encompass but I still clung to the idea that it was not only possible but necessary to find beauty in everything.

Though I had learned to let go of the notion that beauty belonged only to particular bodies, and that appealing aesthetics could be distilled and emulated en masse, it still seemed strange and dangerous to recognise how beauty as a concept, however fluidly defined, no longer served me. This was more than spouting the commonly espoused, Instagram-friendly platitude of 'embracing one's flaws'. It was a personal overhaul and interrogation of how I perceived the imperfections of a thing, and the value I assigned to that not-measuring up. It was hearing the demand made of me by a society fixated on narrowly described markers of beauty to locate the value of my fat and brown body within the context of desirability and responding to this command by saying, 'I reject the demand to be beautiful.' Looking at myself through this new lens felt like a transgression of my femininity and my faith and it has taken time to discern the links between how I thought about beauty and how I have imagined Islam in my own practice. Of specific interest to me as I work through these connections has been the phenomenon of beauty pageants in Malaysia.

The Malaysian relationship with beauty, like many countries grappling with a colonial legacy, is marked by a fixation on fairness and thinness. Advertisements for skin-whitening creams and weight loss treatments dominate the airwaves in implicit recognition that proximity to whiteness makes for easier living. Yet simultaneously, a rejection of 'Western' influences still colours our framing of modesty. This inherently contradictory us-against-them argument reaches its zenith in the beauty pageant industry. We take pride in our women reaching great heights in such competitions, and we have our own yearly competition of dubious prestige, Miss Tourism International, that draws women from across the globe. Yet Muslim women are notably absent from this stage. This is in large part due to a fatwa issued and gazetted on 8 February 1996 under the Administration of Islamic Law (Federal Territories) Act 1993 that prohibited Muslim women from participating in beauty pageants.

Writing about this fatwa sparks an internal conflict. On one hand, the restriction is absurd and discriminatory; on the other, arguing for inclusion in an archaic form of aesthetic assessment undeniably rankles. It raises the question, what do we understand as distinctly Muslim beauty that stands in opposition to non-Muslim beauty? In 2013, four Muslim women qualified as finalists in the Miss Malaysia World competition but were disqualified after their participation gained media attention and the Mufti (state-appointed expert on Islamic law) of the Federal Territories, Wan Zahidi Wan Teh, issued a statement of rebuke, reminding the organisers and contestants of the 1996 fatwa. Although in Muslim jurisprudence, a fatwa only stands as an opinion of a learned scholar, fatwas issued by a state mufti in Malaysia carry the weight of a law, once gazetted. These four women, Sarah Amelia Bernard, 20, Wafa de Korte, 19, Miera Sheikh, 19, and Kathrina Ridzuan, 23, disputed the ban to no avail. The coverage of the controversy was framed by the Malaysian media as a battle between Muslim and Western norms, a question of advocating sin versus embodying good Islamic values. In 2017, a fatwa prohibiting Muslims from participating in beauty pageants was gazetted in the state of Penang. In February 2018, Malaysia's progress in women's rights was reviewed only for the second time since acceding to the UN Convention on the Elimination of All Forms of Discrimination Against Women (CEDAW) in 1995. Ruth Halperin-Kaddari, the vice-chair of the CEDAW committee in Geneva, Switzerland, said that the Malaysian government should state the legality of fatwas and why they take precedence over civil laws despite not being legally binding.

Briefly defined, a fatwa is an answer to a question. But of course, in our contemporary context, its connotations are more complex than being simply explanatory. Fatwas, when issued, seek to address the permissibility of a given practice in Islam – of interest here is the fact that the ones doing the asking and answering in Malaysia are primarily if not solely men. Who then, can we thank for posing the urgent question of whether Muslim women may or may not participant in beauty pageants?

The 2013 incident was not the first time this fatwa reached the public eye. In 1997, two contestants of the Miss Malaysia Petite contest were fined by the Syariah High Court in Kuala Lumpur for breaching this fatwa and were charged under the Syariah Criminal Offences Act (Federal Territory) 1997 which carries a maximum RM3,000 (approximately £560) fine or two years jail upon conviction. In the state of Selangor, three other contestants from the same beauty pageant were brought to trial for violating a similar fatwa. Arrested in a raid conducted during the pageant, the young women were handcuffed and jailed, with their stories making the headlines of the following day's newspapers. Much of the public response centred on complaints about the lack of transparency over a fatwa that many did not even know existed. The then religious adviser to the Prime Minister, Abdul Hamid Othman, asserted that the National

Fatwa Council plays an important role in providing 'guidelines' for 'grey areas' to Muslims.

It is worth considering, however, that in May 2010, the state-linked 1Malaysia Beauty Queen Pageant was held in Putrajaya, a competition that saw its winner, Ann Fiona Phillips, of Bidayuh and Iban heritage from Sarawak in East Malaysia, flanked by two Malay-Muslim runners-up, one of whom competed as a hijabi. A report by local newspaper *Utusan Malaysia* (the *Malaysian Messenger*) makes a point of distinguishing this pageant from 'typical' ones by noting that participants aren't required to model swimsuits but are in fact expected to dress modestly. It becomes clear then, like most edicts issued by men in power, that the fatwa operates on nebulous ground, propelled by a moral code that relies on an unquestioning adherence to shifting definitions on acceptable displays of beauty.

Malaysian religious authorities view the fatwa as absolute, with avenues for the public to participate in discussions notably absent. Malaysia is one of the few countries to make fatwas legally binding. In other parts of the Islamic world, fatwas do not have legal standing – people are not criminalised for going against a fatwa. In Malaysia, however, sin and legality are conflated. Expressing a desire to participate in beauty pageants then becomes not merely a question of morality but one of jurisprudence – the Muslim woman's body on display is not merely shameful but a threat to the state. The idea that women's bodies need controlling is not a new one, and thus to either fight for or against beauty pageants is to wage a war on two opposing but similarly motivated fronts.

Although the forbidding of participation comes from an enforcement of modesty, its strict confines dovetail with the very excess of Western ideology that it purports to combat. The fight for inclusion in a competition that strictly adheres to Western ideals of beauty is well-worn and tiresome.

The history of modern beauty pageants began in 1921 with the advent of Miss America. It was launched as a means to increase newspaper circulation via running photos of the contestants so that readers could judge them before eventually culminating in an in-person evaluation in Atlantic City that assigned value to their personality and social graces. In 1938, the talent portion was introduced, allowing organisers to superficially deflect criticisms of a looks-focused competition. However, that same year also marked the narrowing of eligibility to single, never-married women aged between 18 and 28. These criteria signalled the specificity of beauty that was deemed worthy of award, one that prized a wholesome appeal, whose healthy desirability was predicated on its near-accessibility, the girl-next-door writ large, a head-turner who posed no challenge to the status quo, who was still available to the heterosexual grasp. 'Rule 7' even stated that contestants were expected to be 'of good health and of the white race', though this requirement was dropped in 1940. Pageant winners served the community in the year of their reign through public appearances and charity work, but a large part of the role required the peddling of sponsors' products too.

After four decades of the pageant's increasing popularity on the American stage, 1968 saw it targeted by a radical feminist protest against its inherent misogyny and restrictive notions of beauty. Organised by Carol Hanisch, a member of New York Radical Women who popularised the phrase 'the personal is political', the protest took place on 7 September and spoke out against 'the image of Miss America, an image that oppresses women in every area in which it purports to represent us'. Black feminist activist and lawyer Florynce Kennedy chained herself to a puppet of Miss America 'to highlight the ways women were enslaved by beauty standards'. The women's liberation groups pointed out that in more than 40 years since the dawn of Miss America in 1921, the pageant had never had a black finalist, nor any winners who were Puerto Rican, Mexican-American, Hawaiian or Alaskan.

These women sought to dismantle the pageant and its deleterious effects on American women, and looking back on their attempts 50 years later, little seems to have changed in the way of the disenfranchisement of femmes. Women are still held to impossible standards in our presentations, and the price of failure is not simply emotional but observably financial and physical. As such pageants grew more international, diversity did not follow as it might have. Winners are still primarily white or white-passing. Should I then be happy that I am not able to participate in this pageantry even if I want to? Are Malaysian Muslim women somehow protected from these standards because we have no access to these competitions? Of course not – our competition is every day and it is about survival. The cordoning off of Muslim women in Malaysia is not done out of the progressive interest or out of a desire to protect us from the toxic misogyny that permeates the professional beauty industry, but out of a belief that women's bodies are sites of shame.

The phrase 'modesty culture' has gained traction in Malaysian discourse over the past year, yet what it means still eludes firm description. Its strongest proponents, largely men, claim that it is a way to protect Muslim women from falling victim to the lure of the promiscuous and excessive West. For women, it means an obsession with getting women to cover up, of victim-blaming those who don't, of imposing a patriarchal worldview on those who squirm under it. The shifting definition of 'modest' over the decades in Malaysia fascinates me. Malaysia's participation in international beauty pageants – namely The Big Four of Miss World, Miss Universe, Miss International and Miss Earth – began in 1960 with Zanariah Ahmad representing the country at Miss International. Zanariah served as Raja Permaisuri Agong (the King's Consort) between 1984 and 1989, and her pageant accolade is listed prominently on her Wikipedia page. The competition included a playsuit portion – that is, a swimsuit with a short skirt attached to pre-empt any objections about the revealing nature of swimsuits. I'm reminded of the fact that in 2015, Johor princess Aminah Maimunah Iskandariah quit social media because of relentless online criticism over her choice not to wear the hijab and I try to imagine how many inches of fabric it would take to differentiate between sinner and believer and it seems to go on endlessly.

Though the cultural definition of beauty has widened over the decades, it is still firmly rooted in proximity to whiteness as an unquestioned ideal. The ban on Muslim women participating means that 61 per cent of the Malaysian population is disqualified. What has emerged then is not a predominantly Malaysian Chinese or Indian field, but rather women of ambiguous names and ethnicities that are meant to reflect the country's position of pride as a cultural melting pot. These poreless, porcelain women, with names like Elaine Daly, Deborah Henry, and Samantha James, benefit from being unplaceable, from being unidentifiably Malaysian. If American beauty pageants sought to find the ultimate American princess, the corn-fed girl next door that could symbolise a nation, Malaysian pageants follow suit by demanding an obliteration of ethnic identity in order to go neck and neck with whiteness.

These women are mostly of mixed heritage, having one white parent, which in itself is a boon in a colourist society. I grew up seeing a tube of lightening cream Fair & Lovely hold a permanent spot on my grandmother's dresser, and though I saw little value then in getting any whiter, I grew to love its talcum-like, almost medicinal scent and stole a squeeze whenever I could. As I got fatter, more than a few comments on my weight by relatives were laced with a tinge of reprimand on wasting my relatively fair skin in my slide away from beauty.

These pageants, and who they allow in, legislate the boundaries of beauty and enforce adherence with no leeway. Mainstream beauty pageants have excluded women who are too black or too brown because beauty is unthinkable without 'virtue', and virtue is a trait reserved solely for whiteness. Examining and proving the presence or absence of this virtue is the ostensible goal of interviews, question-and-answer segments, and talent competitions. Virtue is innocence, femininity, submissiveness, morality, and respectability all wrapped into a package often described as the cult of true womanhood. For Malaysian women, being accepted into a mainstream beauty pageant increasingly means showing that you are able to moderate your brownness, to rid yourself of behaviour deemed lewd or uncouth in order to become 'appropriate'.

Interestingly, the Malaysian mass media seem to take little issue with Muslim women of other nationalities and ethnicities participating in beauty pageants internationally. Writing about Somalian American Miss Minnesota contestant Halima Aden, who participated in the 2016 pageant, local online news portal *Astro Awani* was at pains to describe the respect with which Aden's sartorial choices were treated by the judges. The piece quotes one of the pageant's directors, Denise Wallace, as saying that Aden was 'making history tonight'. When not undertaken by Malaysian Muslim women, the project of defying stereotypes is easily deemed worthy. Yet stories like Aden's are outliers.

If participating in mainstream pageants will not work to dismantle white-centric beauty, the marginalised have then sought to create pageants where we are able to frame our own social action and narratives. Step forward the Miss Muslimah pageant.

Beginning in 2011 in Jakarta, Indonesia, Miss Muslimah was initially open only to Indonesian women, but has since broadened its inclusion. It was established by former television reporter Eka Shanty who was demoted after refusing to remove her hijab on screen. The competition enlists 20 young Muslim women from around the world, all of whom wear the hijab. It claims to celebrate not only style and elegance as would a 'typical' pageant but also religious piety, development of humanitarian intelligence, and strength of character, and awards prizes like pilgrimage trips to Mecca and education scholarships. Before they can compete, the 20 finalists are expected to attend a workshop in Jakarta which includes Quran memorisation, and classes on public speaking, humanitarianism, and women's development. One description of the pageant reads: 'A typical day consists of visiting impoverished slums and elderly homes, and speaking with corporate sponsors, all while praying five times a day – and wearing heels.'

A 12-day 'quarantine period' sees the finalists awaken for 5am makeup sessions before spending long days in three-inch heels as they move through a packed schedule which includes visits to deprived communities and networking events. Alongside this is a running tally of their pious acts – for example, on a handful of nights the contestants are also woken up at 2am for additional prayers. The organisers are unapologetic about this gruelling itinerary. 'We're trying to find an excellent personality that can be a role model, an ideal figure to stand on behalf of millions of Muslim women in the world,' says Shanty. Photojournalist Monique Jacques explains her interest in covering the event, 'I thought the contradiction of a Muslim beauty pageant was so interesting and unique. In my work I'm always looking for ways to communicate the experience of young Muslim women to Western audiences. Much of the competition is similar to a pageant in America or anywhere in the West, just with headscarves.'

This explanation stops me short. Is the end goal then, once again, to flatten difference? There is comfort in the familiar, certainly, but such comfort only serves to assuage white and Western fears about the untamed other. Furthermore, I wonder what it means to both deny that modesty is limited by bodily presentations, but also claim that modesty is somehow quantifiable through charity and prayer? There are those who argue too that the attention generated by such competitions, as well as the dressing that demands attention, is not modest and therefore not Islamic. This seems to me a thinly veiled attempt to infringe yet again on Muslim women's fight to define visibility on our own terms. Yet I'm also curious about how Malaysian Muslim authorities would respond to such a pageant if one were proposed in Malaysia. Is there a level of modesty sufficiently achievable for a Muslim woman in public for our bodies to be anything less than a moral nuisance to men? Are these nuances taken into consideration by Malaysian Muslim authorities before doling out fatwas or does it, as is often the case, have nothing to do with the one being looked at but rather those doing the looking?

The fatwa against Muslim women's participation in beauty pageants is about the male gaze. The threat of transgression assumed to take place when a woman reveals herself has no potency without someone on the other end of that revelation. Men are the unasked-for judges, juries, and executioners in the trial of women accused of the unthinkable crime of claiming their beauty as their own. In gate-keeping women's ownership of their presentations, it becomes clear that men want to see the work that goes into performing femininity as much as they want access to the beauty that is a result of that performance. Perhaps pageants are undignified not because they show too much, but because they don't show enough; men want effortlessness but they also want the struggle performed.

On its surface, the fatwa's paternalism is spun as a means of freeing Muslim women from the ritualisation of beauty, from the confines of shallow appreciation and allowing our 'true' selves to be valued. Yet in its limitations it acts as a reprimand to women who approach beauty incorrectly, who dare treat it as something other than a possession that must be surrendered under the shadow of violence.

Deciding, then, that beauty is something I can turn down, can refuse to pursue, becomes a form of solace. I consider using the term empowerment here but I hesitate because it still implies a dependence on external conferment of validation. The way that strength is packaged and repackaged to women is exhausting and still seems to me, besides being ableist, as being another unattainable and nebulously ended goal – who am I being strong for? What am I expected to survive?

The curious topography of life as a Muslim woman at ease with herself means learning to take up space across the boundaries of race, gender, and class. It means confounding expectations to constantly strive towards the most patriarchal version of myself and to veer away from beauty-as-destiny.

The right kind and amount of consumption, the proper volume and intensity of transformation, is sold as a kind of playful liberation when simply buying into beauty-as-destiny turns this play mandatory. It turns being a woman into a game that is played to win without choice in the matter.

As I write about choosing to step away from the pursuit of beauty, I am aware that this decision comes with a significant amount of privilege – I'm a cis woman who is visibly femme, I'm middle-class and educated. For some other women opting out isn't on the table because it has financial and physical repercussions. In 2016, the fatwa was invoked to raid a dinner in Kuala Lumpur organised by transgender women, despite the fact that a pageant was not taking place. I note that the issue of religious authorities not recognising trans women as women was somehow made irrelevant in the former's choice to weaponise sanctioned femininity to condemn a marginalised group. Women are women only when men see us as such.

With all this in mind, who suffers the most hurt when women fight for inclusion in beauty pageants? We are in an age where 'choice feminism' – the notion that something is feminist simply because a woman does it – is deployed indiscriminately as a tool of capitalism. Under these circumstances, it's difficult for me to argue a position which inadvertently lets men remain the arbiters of what is and is not allowed for women navigating their way through their gender presentations. It is still, however, useful to view beauty pageants as a way of laying bare who dictates the terms of that performance in the public sphere: It is not women ourselves but rather a fickle and ever-changing male gaze that demands deference.

EXPERIENCING THE MOST BEAUTIFUL NAMES

Mahmoud Mostafa

Say: Call to Allah or call to the Rahman, whoever you call for Him are the
Most Beautiful Names

(The Qur'an: 7:110)

As I sit with the Qur'an in reflection upon these words, I remember how a moment of insight came to my heart so many years ago that made sense for me of these verses and of my faith. This understanding helped to set things right in my heart and bring me into wholesomeness and surrender to the truth expressed in the Qur'an. 'Call to Allah or call to the Rahman...' I had often wondered why *Rahman* (Merciful) in particular is paired with Allah in this verse? What am I being guided to? The insight came to me when I least expected it, when I was busy with my daily life. Suddenly the words of this verse lit up in my heart and a realisation came to me that was beyond my capacity to formulate or produce by my own logic. I understood how these words were at the core of the message of the Prophet Muhammad.

During my early adult life, I had read every biography of the Prophet that I could get my hands on. I'd read the *Seerah* of Ibn Hisham, and the *History* of Al Tabari, several biographies written in English, and listened to so many conversations and heard so many stories about our beloved Prophet. I thought I understood the basics of his message and the fundamental principles of Islam that he conveyed to his community and was passed down to us through the generations. It seemed obvious to me – Islam at its core was about the oneness of God. No other gods but God. No association of anyone with Allah. All of us know this. The Prophet was the great *muwwahid* ('monotheist'), the unwavering witness to the oneness of God, the idol breaker who purified the Kaaba of its 360 false idols. He was the one who brought back to life the religion of Abraham, the primordial way of our innate human nature.

I have always loved Prophet Muhammad. My earliest memories of him go back to my childhood. Growing up in Egypt my heart was nourished by his presence in our consciousness. His name was frequently mentioned, his character often recalled to remind us of the right thing to do in any situation. It was as if he was alive and with us — it felt like we were mentioning someone who was amongst us. I grew up with so many stories about him, of his loving mercy, his tenderness, his truthfulness, his wisdom, his perseverance, his devotion, his trustworthiness, his detachment from the world and worldliness, his gentle nature, his patience with people, his unwavering commitment to truth and to goodness. My tears flowed when I read about how he chose to live a simple life, his contentment with little, his generous sharing of his meager resources. My heart ached with longing when I read about how he would go hungry for days and how he would sleep on the bare floor and how he said that, for him, this world is like a tree on his path in whose shade he sits for a brief while and then moves on. Whenever his name was mentioned, or a story told of him, my heart would melt, and tears would flow as I felt the wave of love engulfing me. In my heart I knew I wanted to live like him, to be like him. To value what he valued, to be of him.

Growing up Muslim in a majority Muslim country, I was indoctrinated into the prevailing beliefs of my society and family. From my early childhood, I was taught about *tawhid* (the oneness of God). I learned that we were the people of *tawhid* and that what this meant was the pronouncement of the *shahadah*, the declaration of '*la ilaha illa Allah*' ('there is no god but God'). In my imagination, I saw the people of the Prophet's community, the Quraysh, as ignorant people who worshipped statues of false gods. They were caricatures of idiotic men that believed a piece of carved stone had divine power. The Qur'an declared their ignorance in worshipping that which could not harm nor benefit them. They couldn't accept only one God — they wanted many gods for many purposes. We Muslims rejected any other gods beside God. We were not like other religious communities. The Christians had three Gods, or they divided God into three parts. Not us – we were true to only one indivisible God. The Jews also believed God was one, but they had deviated from their faith. Not us – we remained faithful to only one God. The Hindus had many gods – they worshipped idols. Not us – we held steadfastly to only one God. This was the dividing line between us Muslims and everyone else – only one God, and Muhammad is His Messenger. And so, I moved through life, assuming I knew what I needed to know about my faith and that I understood what *tawhid* meant and that I was a *muwwahid* because I said *la ilaha illa Allah*.

Growing up in America in my twenties and thirties, I became more and more drawn to the Qur'an. The more I read it, the more the gap widened between its guidance and what I saw being proclaimed as Islam and practiced by Muslims. The Qur'an's message was universal while we seemed like a closed community, stuck in our conditioned biases, narrow doctrines, oppressive legalism, and repressive rules all enshrined as religion. For me the Qur'an was full of beauty, wisdom, love, and truthfulness while the religion that was being touted in the mosques was full of ugliness, narrow-mindedness, rigidity, and prejudice. I couldn't reconcile my heart to the Islam I saw practiced around me. I couldn't accept the prevailing views about God, about prophethood, about other faith communities, about freedom of consciousness in religion, about women and gender equality, about artistic expression and creativity, about politics, about economics, about war and violence, about judgment and compassion, about our history and its meaning. I felt a real dissonance between what I felt in my heart to be true and what was being presented as Islam. At the same time, I felt profound resonance between what I knew in my heart to be true and what was expressed in the words of the Qur'an. For example, it seemed self-evident to me that every human being has equal access to Allah's *Rahmah* (Mercy) and acceptance into Paradise based on their intentions and deeds, regardless of their religion. It seemed clear that the natural state of humanity is diversity and pluralism. But the prevailing belief around me was that only those who are Muslim can be accepted into Paradise and everyone else is doomed to the fire of Hell and that the ultimate goal is to make everyone Muslim. Yet the Qur'an is as explicit as it can be about Allah's decree and wisdom:

It is not according to your wishful thinking nor the wishful thinking of the People of the Book. Whoever does harm will be requited for it and will not find any friend or support other than Allah. And whoever does wholesome deeds, whether male or female, and has faith, these shall enter Paradise and will not be oppressed by as little as a date stone. (4:123-124)

...to each We have made a way and clear guidance. If Allah willed He would have made you one community but He tries you in what He has given you, so compete in goodness...(5:48)

O human kind! We have created you from male and female and made you into nations and tribes, so you may come to know one another. Truly, the most noble among you in Allah's sight are those of you who are most conscious of Him...(49:13)

One day, these words from the Qur'an filled my consciousness: 'Say: Call to Allah or call to the Rahman, whoever you call for Him are the Most Beautiful Names...' and my understanding of the message of the Prophet and the meaning of *tawhid* changed forever. When this verse came to me, it was in the context of having read and pondered upon the verses in Surah Al Najm (the Chapter of the Star) where the Qur'an takes to task the Quraysh's setting up of female deities:

Do you not see Al Lat and Al Uzzah? And the third one, Manat too? Are the males for you and the females for Him? That, then is an iniquitous division! These are but names you have named, you and your forefathers, for which Allah has not brought forth authority. They only follow conjecture and the vain desires of the egos although guidance has come to them from their Sustainer. (53:19-23)

The understanding that came to my heart was that *tawhid* was the integration of all aspects of the divine, masculine and feminine, into a single reality. Allah is neither male nor female, but He encompasses all masculine and feminine sacred energies. 'Call to Allah or call to Rahman' was the assertion of this truth. *Rahmah* is Allah's prevailing quality in relationship to His creation, the one that encompasses all others, and it is a feminine quality. Prophet Muhammad's message is about ending our fragmented, distorted view of the divine and integrating our fractured understanding into a universal oneness that is of all beautiful qualities.

The Most Beautiful Names represent the integration of all divine qualities into oneness, they hold all of our expressions and experiences of the divine. The oneness of Allah encompasses both feminine and masculine qualities. The Most Beautiful Names are the infinite, interconnected facets of the Divine by which we come to know the meaning of divine unity. It became clear to me that the Prophet's message was about integration, not negation. He didn't come to nullify the beliefs of his community but to integrate them into a more complete wholeness. This was the meaning of *tawhid*; it is the act of bringing our fragmented energies, and our scattered attention to an integrated wholeness. This is the oneness of *tawhid*. *Tawhid* is beyond the theology of monotheism. It is actually a verb meaning to make one, that is, to integrate, to bring to unity that which is fragmented. On the human plane it is the act of realising God's oneness in ourselves.

Tawhid is what leads us to dissolve our fragmented vision of the Divine into a singular, all-encompassing Truth. 'To Him belong the Most Beautiful Names.' The human journey towards spiritual awakening is to come to know the meaning of these divine qualities within us.

There is little doubt in my mind that the message of the Prophet has been distorted by the patriarchy of our society. We have become accustomed to a male-dominated, authoritarian and repressive interpretation of Islam that has all but eliminated the feminine dimension from our spirituality, causing serious imbalances in our lives, our communities and our world.

Even though we Muslims may intellectually accept that God has no gender, our cultural and social conditioning causes us to imagine God as masculine. Arabic, as a gendered language, also leads us to conceive of Allah as a masculine entity. The name Allah is a masculine form, and every other divine name, since it is associated to Allah, is also masculine in form. This leads us to visualise Allah as masculine every time we hear His name or any of the Beautiful Names.

Patriarchy, as an ideology and system in which power is centred on males, has defined the mainstream understanding of our religion. This is a deviation from the *tawhid* that is intrinsic to the Most Beautiful Names. So many of the names represent feminine qualities that bring completeness to our experience of the divine.

The most basic and well-known divine quality of *Rahmah*, which is unconditional love, is the preeminent one that is accepted universally by Muslims. *Al Rahman* is God's best known and most often used name among Muslims. This name comes from the root verb R-H-M and it means 'womb' and this, of course, is a uniquely female quality. God is the Divine Womb that encompasses all things and from which all existence comes into being or is birthed.

It's difficult for us to shift our habitual perspective of God as a He, or male, especially with the limitation of a gendered language like Arabic that defaults to the masculine for indeterminate gender. Yet, if we recall that the feminine embodies such qualities as receptivity, subtlety, surrender, empathy, gentleness, peacefulness, healing, sharing, flowing, reconciliation, loving, tenderness, forgiveness, nurturing, patience, origin and mystery, we will see there are many other divine qualities that are feminine in nature. Among these are Peace *(Salam)*, Faith *(Mu'min)*, Creator *(Khaleq)*, Subtle *(Latif)*, Gentle *(Halim)*, Wise *(Hakim)*, Inner *(Batin)*, Living *(Hayy)*, Bestower *(Wahhab)*, Loving *(Wadud)*, Tender *(Ra'uf)*, Forgiving *(Ghafur)* as well as many others. If we contemplate and reflect upon the Divine Names without our deeply ingrained gender bias, we may open up to understanding the feminine aspects of many of Allah's Divine Qualities. It is evident to me that by invoking Rahman, the Prophet integrated the female gods of the Quraysh into the oneness of Allah, and so the Qur'an proclaims: 'Call to Allah or call to the Rahman…'

The Divine Pairing

We are guided by the Qur'an and the teachings of Prophet Muhammad that beyond any transient existence there exists only the Divine Essence – a pre-eternal, Singular, Indivisible Oneness that is Self-Subsistent. And from this Ever-Existent non-Existence comes an impulse from which all of creation emanates.

A well-known and loved Hadith Qudsi, where the words of God are expressed in the words of the Prophet, that is essential to Sufi understanding of reality is: 'I was a hidden treasure and I loved to be known so I created the universes that I may be known.' Sufis understand this hadith (recorded Tradition of the Prophet Muhammad) to mean that Allah's love is the primal energy that caused creation.

How is creation conceived? What is its characteristic structure? Here are some verses that shed light on the nature of creation:

'We have created everything in pairs that you may remember.' (51:49)

'Allah created you from dust, and then from a tiny drop, and then he made you in pairs.' (35:11)

'He created the two pairs, masculine and feminine.' (53:45)

'When the souls are paired.' (81:7)

Since Love is the Creative Principle, it is no wonder that the structure of existence is relationship through pairings. This pairing is not of opposites, but of two parts that make the whole. We are created in order that the Divine would be known. We say that God sees Himself through Himself in the heart of the human being.

The Most Beautiful Names reflect this Creative Principle in the pairings of divine qualities, for example:

The Giver of Life (*Al Muhiyy*), the Cause of Death (*Al Mumit*)
The Manifest (*Al Zhahir*), The Inner (*Al Batin*)
The Constricter (*Al Qabid*), The Expander (*Al Basit*)
The Abaser (*Al Khafid*), The Elevator (*Al Rafi'*)
The Exalter (*Al Mu'izh*), The Humbler (*Al Muzhill*)
The First (*Al Awwal*), The Last (*Al Akhir*)
The Causer of Harm (*Al Darr*), The Beneficent (*Al Nafi'*)

And then there are others that we tend to not see as pairings, such as:

The Hearer (*Al Sami'*), The Seer (*Al Basir*)
The Judge (*Al Hakam*), The Just (*Al Adl*)
The Living (*Al Hayy*), The Everstanding (*Al Qayyum*)

This pairing is ever present in creation, it is what allows life to flow. It's the motion of existence. It's what enables the turning of the universe.

Life consists of cycles of pairings – in-breath and out-breath, night and day, light and dark, heat and cold, life and death, laughter and sorrow, hardship and ease, expansion and contraction, rising and falling, annihilation and subsistence. And no matter where we look, from the minutest level of existence to the farthest horizons of the galaxies, this structure is evident. At the atomic level we find the electron and proton pair, at the cosmic level we find the dipoles of magnetic fields that allow the movement of galaxies.

Our knowing of the Divine Reality is only possible in consciously experiencing these pairings in our own lives. In the Sufi tradition this is the innate human capacity to manifest the Divine Attributes. This is the Divine knowing Itself through Itself.

So, we come to ourselves, we who are the embodiment of this Divine Pairing, we who are women and men. We who have been endowed with all the Divine Qualities – what do we see? Most of us are largely veiled from who we really are.

Our minds work largely by comparison and we tend to interpret these names as opposites. We often think of death as the opposite of life, for example. When we can transcend our conditioned minds and habitual thoughts and open ourselves to the wisdom of the Qur'an, we may see how these pairings integrate and unify certain qualities into oneness. So, life and death become a wholeness that expresses the nature of existence – one cannot be without the other. Without death there can be no life. If we understand this unity of creation our fear of death may turn into an acceptance and joy with the natural cycles of existence.

Many of us suffer in our current culture because of the imbalance and lack of awareness of this pairing within us. Our modern culture tends to polarise us, not integrate us. The prevalent discourse is one of confrontation and competition. We are conditioned to see ourselves as either/or, not both/and. We are either men or women and our concepts of ourselves are loaded with cultural expectations and restrictions and these limitations veil us from knowing our true selves. And when it comes to the prevalent form of Islam that we suffer from today, this dichotomy of male and female is at an acutely toxic level. The authoritarian form of Islam that dominates our faith today tries to maximise the separation between male and female, and it propagates inequality and prejudice. We are stuck in internal contradictions and we express these in external conflicts.

The either/or paradigm has led us down a path of competition, oppression and injustice. And this afflicts both men and women in different ways and in various degrees. At the root of all this suffering is the ego, the *nafs*, and its tendency towards fragmentation and preference for separation. The *nafs* wants to be in charge and wants to be dominant and wants to be immutable. These desires manifest in our competing to achieve superiority over each other. We are stuck in a cycle of domination and resistance that causes us great suffering. And this cycle perpetuates and is passed on from one generation to the next and becomes enshrined in cultural norms and practices. This was the condition of humanity when the Prophet's mission began, and it hasn't changed since. It has only taken on newer and more formidably sophisticated forms.

It takes a shift in consciousness in order to break away from this pattern. If we can shift our awareness to exploring and understanding our inner pairing of active and receptive capacities and to learn how we can realise these capacities, we would become more integrated human beings. We would know that we embody the Divine Qualities. We would know that our purpose is not to dominate, not to separate, not to last forever and hold on to our position in the world, but to manifest the Divine Attributes within us. Then would we have a chance to come to know ourselves for who we really are, and the Hidden Treasure becomes known.

We can gain insight about our active and receptive capacities by reflecting on the meaning of masculine and feminine. The word for male in Arabic is *zhakar* and comes from the same root as *zhikr*, remembrance. The word for female is *untha* and it means to be fertile, abundant, and soft.

Our active attributes bring us to remembrance, or to the realisation of the Divine Names. Our receptive attributes receive what is remembered with fertile abundance and births these names into manifestation. We need to engage consciously with the active and receptive aspects of our being. If we denigrate or ignore this pairing, we can't know ourselves and so cannot know the Divine.

In the Embrace of the Most Beautiful Names

My experience of the Most Beautiful Names developed as I travelled the Sufi Path. During solitary retreats in which I was given specific Divine Names to invoke for prolonged periods of time, meanings and insights came into my heart to guide me to understanding some profound truths. During one such retreat, my Shaykh guided me to invoke several divine names.

I was in a private room in a house in the San Francisco Bay area. The house was situated in a remote wooded area outside the town of Santa Cruz. I slept on the floor over blankets spread out inside a walk-in closet. It was winter and the room was often cold. I fasted every day of the retreat. I saw no one and spoke to no one during the entire retreat period. My Shaykh would come occasionally to check on me without speaking and he would prescribe for me the *zhikrs* to be invoked until the next time he came. Each day would be spent in long periods of *zhikr* and prayers with brief breaks for naps, resting, reading and keeping a daily journal. I had the Qur'an, the *Mathnawi* of Mawlana Jalaluddin Rumi, the Mawlawi *Wird* (litany of prayers), and the *Wird* of Ibn Arabi with me. Subhana, a fellow dervish who lived in the house, took care of feeding me. She served me a meal at sunset for the breaking of the fast and a late night *suhur* meal. Subhana would leave the tray of food outside the door of my room and leave before I opened the door to take the tray. We communicated by small notes passed under the door of my room. This following is an account of my experience with four of the Divine Names during the retreat.

Ya Halim

Very early during the retreat my Shaykh guided me to invoke the name Al Halim (The Most Forbearing) from early morning until noon. As I started the *zhikr* of *Ya Halim*, I first witness the distractions in my consciousness.

I contemplate what things I am anticipating and desiring. I run through a list that I witness. I want the heat to be set right. I want the house to be empty. I want to be able to read the Mawlawi *Wird*. I think about how thirsty I feel from eating the nuts last night. Slowly I let go of these desires. I ask Allah to take them away from me, to free me for Him.

I enter into the invocation of *Ya Halim*. Not much is happening. I feel some anxiety coming on as I think about the time left until noon. Another anticipation, I remind myself. I seek forgiveness and keep up the *zhikr*.

I doze off for a while. In my sleep I hear people singing songs that I don't know. I see the number 86 (*Al Mujib,* the One Who Responds) on the back of a jersey. I see a bright, strobing light in my left eye that moves to my right eye. Then I see my father seated in a garden smiling, as smartly dressed as ever, sitting in his characteristic style with one leg crossed over another. He's drinking from a cup. I am looking at him from a far and high place and my view seems to narrow in on him as if I am looking at him through a corridor.

I wake up and continue with the *Ya Halim zhikr*. Time is passing and still not much insight. I feel so sleepy. I look at my watch and it is 11:15am, only 45 minutes left to noon! What is the meaning of this name for me?

Suddenly the answer comes into my heart: *Gentleness. Be Gentle. Be gentle with yourself. Be gentle with your words. Be gentle with your ears. Be gentle with your mouth. Be gentle with your tongue. Be gentle with your eyes. Be gentle with your thoughts. Be gentle with your hands. Be gentle with your work. Listen to the birds! Do you hear My Gentleness? Look at the roses, sense their petals, do you feel My Gentleness?*

I plead from the depth of my heart, 'Please, Allah! Teach me. Show me the way.'

Be gentle. Let Me in gently. Be still. Don't count the words. Don't count the beads. Be still. Know My Gentleness.

'Please, take away my harshness. Teach me to be gentle. *Ya Rahim! Ya Halim!*'

Listen to the rain! Do you hear My Gentleness? Feel the air around you, breathe My Gentleness. Look at the sunlight on the leaves! Do you see My Gentleness? This was the Prophet's character. If you are sincere then follow him and learn from him.

Somehow, I know these words are coming through our great Sufi Mawlana Jalaluddin Rumi. My heart bursts open with this insight. Tears pour out like a blessed rain. My whole body is shaking with a release of energy as my resistance dissolves in this torrent of love. My heart feels deep gratitude for this opening. I feel the tenderness in these words and I understand with clarity the intricate harmony of creation. I understand how this attribute can manifest in my being. I am urged to go outside and walk around to see more of this innate gentleness of Life. I take Guzel, Subhana's dog, with me. As we move along the path down from the house I notice that my senses are unusually sharp. I walk very slowly and calmly. I can feel the coolness of the air on my face. I can smell the freshness after the rain. I can hear the leaves and the birds. I can feel the rays of the sun on my skin. I am in an ocean of gentleness. I contemplate the forest and my mind wonders about the violence that is part of nature. What about predators, where is the gentleness in the killing and eating of one another? I think about this question and realise that in nature the killing is fairly swift and comes suddenly. I also realise how infrequently it occurs. And I recall the images of prey and how even in dying there is a strange gentleness, a surrender to death that is part of life. Gentleness is the natural state of life. Violence erupts and ends, but gentleness remains. Even with war this is the case. After all the death and destruction there is an ensuing gentleness. It's as if an irresistible force pulls us back to gentleness no matter how far away we deviate.

Ya Quddus

I return to the room and begin the *zhikr* of *Ya Quddus* (the Most Holy and Pure). I am in such a serene state. I find myself moving into stillness. I am almost completely quiet and motionless. I cannot feel my hands or feet; I cannot feel the usual tension in my muscles. I have the sensation of sinking into a deep ocean, a sense of nothingness. The only movement is when I swallow. The strobing lights in my eyes return and converge into a brilliant flash. '*Allah?*' I ask myself. What a silly question!

I contemplate *Ya Quddus* as I sway with its sound in my heart. I sense that this name has a deep meaning within me, like some ancient, sacred sound. It emanates a profound sacredness, but I don't understand it. I am aware that I'm distracted by this morning's opening with *Ya Halim*. I am impressed with myself. I implore Allah for support, 'Please, cleanse me of myself and keep me moving toward You.'

'Do not be in haste with the Qur'an before its revelation is brought to you. And say, Lord increase my knowledge.' (20:114)

I doze off again. In my dream I see three women, two young ones and one middle-aged one. One of the young ones is dressed in a very short skirt or dress and I am full of lust for her. She is very trusting of me. I am there to hear their complaints against someone who is lusting after them. They think I am pure-hearted, but I know what is inside of me. We walk into the courtroom and sitting in the front is the middle-aged woman with a photograph of herself as a young woman. She was beautiful in her youth. I feel ashamed of myself as I witness my self-serving attention to the younger women and my disdain for the older one. I get close to the older woman and I realise how sacred she is. I understand the sacredness that is in every one of us. I understand how my lusting violates this sacredness.

In another dream I am standing on a high place looking down upon a wooded valley full of minarets and domes. Then I see golden writing floating before me. The calligraphy looks Qur'anic, but I cannot make it out.

As sunset arrives I notice during my prayer how my mind is wandering off toward thoughts of food and eating. Subhana sets a tray for me that is a veritable feast. I eat heartily, filling up my stomach too much. I think it is time to cut back.

I continue with *Ya Quddus*. I know now that it is some ancient holy sound inside of me from some pre-eternal place. It fills me with awe. Its reverberations shake me down to my toes. I feel like a drum and the sound of *Ya Quddus* is my beat. By now I have memorised several verses. I memorised the Light Verse and the two consecutive verses to it. I memorised the beginning of The Star Surah. I memorised part of the Muttaffifun (the Defrauders) and I memorised the last section in Yunus (Jonah). Most of these verses I knew or had memorised in the past but had forgotten with time. It was good to return to them.

Ya Nur

I move from *Ya Quddus* to *Ya Nur* (the Light). I ask Allah to fill me with light. I remember the Prophet's prayer of light.

It's 3:00am, time for the pre-dawn meal. I set the tray of fruits and nuts before me with anticipation, but something stops me after I've eaten the first date. I am being so distracted by food. During my prayers my mind is filled with thoughts of what Subhana has prepared for me. I am praying to the food. I struggle for some time with the thought of not eating anything, or fasting for 24 hours. I see my ego negotiating with me about eating, trying to convince me to just take what is offered. I am tempted by this argument, but something tells me no. My eyes wander over the contents of the tray. Some of my favourite fruits are there: mango, cantaloupe, and strawberries. How can I just let these delicious things go? I want them. Then my ego moves to another argument about disappointing Subhana and rejecting her generosity. My heart tells me that I can be gentle in my turning away of the food. I can be gentle with my words.

I quietly take the tray down to the kitchen. I write Subhana a gentle note thanking her and explaining why and asking her to just offer one plate of food at each meal. As I put the fruits into the refrigerator I notice how the house is flooded in moonlight. I look outside, and I see the moon is full. When I resume my *zhikr* I hear a voice say, 'If you want Me, you can't be waiting for any other.' These words take away my desire for food. *I want You! You fill my stomach with Your light instead of food, Ya Nur.* I feel I've crossed a threshold with this act tonight. Praise be to Allah. I feel a sense of release and I melt in the *zhikr. Be gentle with your killing. Say in the name of Allah and cut quickly. Then let it be a sacrifice for the poor.* I think about my heart and how its light is the reflection of the light of the Spirit that is in me. The Light verse fills my heart as I continue with the *zhikr* of light. *Ya Nur.*

It's 5:30am. Guzel's barking wakes me. Before I dozed off I was very still. I was learning to trust, to give away what I am holding on to. As I lay on my side I see a cylinder of bright light. It is multi-coloured yet white at the same time. I feel the earth shaking beneath me. I sense that my appetite for things has drastically declined. I feel closer. I sense my closeness. *I just want to be near, to know my nearness to You.*

I make the call to prayer and perform the dawn cycle. The room is flooded with the moonlight. The moon is still up. I look to the east and see the day breaking. The sun is rising. I look to the west and see the moon shining as it heads for the Santa Cruz horizon. The sun and the moon are together. Insight floods my heart and my tears shake me. A profoundly loving gift has been given to me. Understanding beyond description engulfs me. A sense of certainty and awareness of what is inside of me move me to my very core. I know what the divine link is that is in all of us.

It finally hits me what all these verses in the Qur'an are about that refer to natural events as signs for 'those who understand'. I now know that it is possible to *know* with the eye of my heart.

How glorious is Allah, the Light of heaven and earth, who favours His servants as He wills with His Mercy. He shows them His signs at His appointed time. In this way He strengthens their hearts and fills them with knowledge and affirms them with the certainty of truth. Blessed is He, the wisest of those who have wisdom.

I see what He wants me to see and understand. The light of the moon is proof of the sun even though the sun may be invisible. The reflection of its light on the moon is proof that it exists. So it is with our heart and Spirit. And at the right time the moon is full in the sky and the sun is rising. The moon and the sun are together. So, there may come a time when both the heart and Spirit become visible. 'Light upon light.' From the depth of my heart I recite these words over and over in a song for the lover and Beloved. I carry on until the moon sets in the western sky. The lover melts and vanishes in the Beloved's light.

'Man is created of haste. I shall show you My signs, so do not be hasty.' (21:37)

I understand that Allah determines the right time and measure. No amount of devotion or effort will bring knowledge or will determine when insight will be gained. It's all His grace. I see it working; I see His grace working. He chooses the time and the duration. It's not mine to reckon, it's only mine to trust and to surrender to His love.

Ya Salam

Towards the end of the retreat my Shaykh prescribes the invocation of *Ya Salam* (the One Who is Peace). I move to *Ya Salam* and it melts my heart and envelops me with serenity and comfort.

During the *zhikr* of *Ya Salam* I begin to shower peace upon my family. *Let them be in peace, let peace be in all our hearts.* I feel a real security in me right now. I asked Allah to make me His Hand of Peace with those I love, and with those I come into contact with in this world.

'Do people think they will be left to say we have faith without being tried and tested?' (29:2)

'Whoever wishes for the meeting with Allah, indeed Allah's appointed time shall come, and He is the Hearing and Knowing.' (29:5)

'And We shall surely guide those who strive in Us to our Ways. Verily, Allah is with those who do beautiful deeds.' (29:69)

Only a few minutes left to sunset. This is my last sunset in retreat, *Alhamdulillah*. I complete the *zhikr* of *Ya Salam* and I invoke it for my wife and each of my children individually. I see the name of Peace surrounding each of them. I envision peace all over them; their heads, eyes, ears, mouths, hands, feet, hearts, stomachs, and groins. Then I envision peace connecting their hearts and my heart, too, together. I ask Allah to fill their hearts with love for one another and to take away all the hard feelings and sorrow between them. I pray for Allah to bless and protect my children. May Allah always fill their heart with contentment and joy. At the end of the *zhikr* I am filled with praise for Allah. As the sun sets I sing the praises of the Prophet and weep as I feel my heart connection with him.

The Beauty of the Most Beautiful Names

The Divine Names are known in Arabic as *Asma'ul Husna*, which means the Beautiful or Good Names. The word *husn* comes from the root verb H-S-N, which is the opposite of ugliness. It carries meanings such as beauty, adornment, goodness, to bring to perfection or completeness, the best of a thing and the opposite of harm.

By the Night that enfolds. By the Day that manifests in glory. And That which created the male and female. Truly your striving is diverse. As for one who gives and is conscious and bears the truth of Beauty, We shall ease him to ease. As for one who withholds and withdraws and denies Beauty, We shall ease him to hardship. (92:1-10)

These verses that open Surah Al Layl (the Chapter of the Night) hold insight to the mystery of our humanness and our relationship to the Divine Names. This relationship is the eternal cycle of self-reflection and discovery that leads us to know and manifest the beauty that is within our souls. Why are Night and Day juxtaposed with Male and Female? Why are these pairs the pathways that bring us to a choice about Beauty/Goodness, taking us towards either ease or hardship, peace or suffering?

As Night and Day describe the experience of the earth in relationship to its own axis and its 'facing' of the Sun, so are our masculine and feminine dimensions expressions of our relationship to our inner axis and our 'facing' towards Allah. Night and Day make up a wholeness, a complementary pairing that expresses the completeness of the earth's relationship to the Sun. Similarly, Masculine and Feminine make up a wholeness, a complementary pairing that express the completeness of our relationship to our *Rabb* (Lord).

This beauty can be experienced when we are able to integrate within ourselves our masculine and feminine aspects – our active and receptive capacities – because in this way we can be more complete human beings with the awareness and self-knowledge to manifest the Divine Names through our being.

The Qur'an declares of Allah that: 'He has perfected/made beautiful the nature of every creation' (32:7). We can come to know this perfection, this beauty that is within us when we integrate our masculine and feminine dimensions. What does this mean on a practical level? For both men and women, it would mean transcending gender roles imposed by patriarchy in the guise of religion or social norms. Men and women can step outside of the confines of what is accepted as male and female interests and behaviours. For men it may mean that we come to know and express our compassion and love more openly. It may mean being more open and honest about our feelings, being able to cry without shame, embracing and touching the people we love, being unafraid of expressing our weakness or doubt. It would mean showing tenderness and sensitivity in our relationships without fear of being seen as weak or effeminate. These are all qualities that were openly expressed and known about the Prophet. There is a well-known tradition of the Prophet where he openly wept over the passing of his son, Ibrahim, and a man who was present expressed his disapproval, saying that the men of his tribe never cry. The Prophet's simple and telling response was, 'What can I do for you if Allah has removed *Rahmah* from your heart?'

Men can learn to express *Rahmaniyyah* in their lives, to be *Rahmah* in the world as the Prophet was *Rahmah* to all the worlds. Women can express their leadership, power, courage and independence without fear of being ostracised or shunned for being too much like a man. It may be that women need to actively pursue their full potential and step beyond pre-defined and limiting gender roles imposed by patriarchy. It may be that women can step up to leadership roles in different aspects of political, social, and economic roles. And it may be that women need to free themselves from the cage of subservience to men that is imposed on them by male-centric interpretations of Islam, and from the exploitation of their bodies as marketing tools to constantly push more and more consumerism upon us.

It is important to be aware of the current pressure to define 'liberation' for women as 'imitating men'. This phenomenon can be seen in today's action and adventure films that depict women as fighters and tough, macho-like characters. This is just another way of denying our inner potential and imposing more male-centric norms on women.

A truly Islamic perspective, based on *tawhid*, would encourage men and women to step outside prescribed gender roles and support the realisation of the inner creative potential in each of us by virtue of our humanness. This creative potential is the Most Beautiful Names awaiting expression through each of us.

A BEAUTIFUL DEATH

Hasina Zaman

In Britain, I am one of a handful of female founders and directors – and perhaps the only Muslim one – of private funeral companies catering to people of all faiths. I am surrounded by death and those in mourning. And I am often taken aback by the negativity, fear and apprehension my clients face upon the death of a loved one. My role involves challenging the common notions of beauty so intrinsically linked with the living and doing my utmost to reconfigure its basis, so that it can erode the negative emotions and experiences which too often envelop the reality of death.

At its core, my job is relatively simple: to fulfil the wishes of the deceased and their bereaved loved ones, whilst striving to ensure that the experience of each funeral rite is one that instils peace in all. Whether that be a Buddhist ceremony, a Muslim burial, or a cremation, I am entrusted with the honour of creating safe passage for the deceased to their final destination, in accordance with their beliefs. Whilst that in itself is a beautiful responsibility, the grief and sometimes outright terror I encounter often compel me to ask: how can we make the subject of death, and the experience of dealing with it, a beautiful one? What foundations must we lay for ourselves and our loved ones to safeguard a beautiful, peaceful death? And how, whilst engulfed by the immensity of pain at the passing of a loved one, can we truly embrace beauty?

The term 'beautiful' is most commonly associated with physical aesthetics – with forms, lines, colours, shapes and movements which are deemed pleasing to the eye. These are, in turn, most commonly associated with life – something living and present which we can reach out and touch. Rarely is the word 'beautiful' associated with death. But for Muslims, taught to strive for beauty in all things, why does the experience of death – for the departed, for ourselves, and for our loved ones – often seem to be anything but beautiful? Why, when we each know the end of our lives is an imminent truth, do we continue to suppress the topic as if it were a harmful afterthought not to be named or discussed?

These are questions I have been asking myself for many years. But at no time were they more poignant than when I was forced to face the deaths of two members of my own family and, through the immense sea of grief and anger felt by my loved ones, develop the courage I needed to confront those feelings so prevalent in my own being.

The first death was that of Maya, my sister-in-law. In 1995, aged only 26, after showing signs of depression and loneliness, she committed suicide. Born into a Sri Lankan Hindu family, she joined, at age 11, her maternal uncle who couldn't have children and who was based in the UK. Maya was educated in a Catholic convent where she became a Christian and, after meeting my brother, became a Muslim. Her death was deeply tragic and my family was devastated following the completion of the identification process with the river police team. The grief felt by my brother and Maya's uncle were harrowing to witness, and yet it took me decades to speak about her death, for the topic always seemed to give rise to hurtful accusations and unwarranted shame.

Suicide of any nature and for whatever reason is a societal taboo, but in Islam it is an especially forbidden topic, making it an infinitely harder experience to process. The lack of care, understanding or compassion by the Islamic agencies involved in laying Maya's body to rest was infuriating, and to this day, continues to beggar belief. Once it was released for burial, her body was prepared by female staff at the appointed Muslim Funeral Directors – each of whom made damning comments about the state of her body, serving only to increase the pain we were all already feeling. An already distressing experience was further heightened by the fact that until the funeral, we had never met Maya's family. Her sister, who had flown in from Paris only to face comments such as those made by the women washing her sister's body, was robbed of any sense of peace or reconciliation with what had happened.

After the *janaza*, or funeral prayer, Maya was laid out for the public to view – and view it they did. The showcasing of her body – so tortured in life and even more so in death – was yet another painful process my brother was forced to bear. He, along with all of us who had loved her, would have preferred for her to be saved from the merciless stares of gawping acquaintances, and for only her closest family members to spend those last precious moments with her. The burial itself was swift, with no mention of who she was or about her family – as if her life and the very fact of her existence needed to be wiped out in a single motion.

As Maya's coffin entered the grave, I walked away, feeling every fibre of my being wanting to scream. As my very first funeral experience, I felt confused, enraged and unsupported by the very agencies whom I believed should have been there to place our minds at peace. There were too many unanswered questions, so many active rejections, of my understanding of God as a merciful and loving being, that I was left with nothing but empty chasms of anger. From the *imam* (prayer leader) who rushed through his reading of verses from the Qur'an to those women who had sullied the holy duty of washing a body with their cruel words, the treatment of Maya and of us as her family was gravely wanting. As I left to return home, I prayed fervently for her past, present and future. I hoped that forgiveness could be the root of our human and holy interactions, which should, at least from an Islamic angle, be geared towards instilling peace in others, not eternal hurt.

It is difficult to even imagine how Maya's death could have been a beautiful one. The despair she must have felt in her final moments, or her desire for the ultimate form of peace, is a heart-stopping moment to fathom. All I know is that her treatment in death should have been reflective of a faith which preaches compassion, empathy and peace, and which, where practiced faithfully, would have yielded a softer, greater gentility in her handling as opposed to the cruel, judgmental one I witnessed.

My experiences of Maya's harsh treatment have informed what I strive for as a funeral director. Over the years, I have had to support families whose loved ones have deliberately committed suicide. And in opposition to my own memories, my company works to support families affected by such a trauma and make the funeral process as loving, comforting and comfortable as humanly possible. We support family members by encouraging them to reflect about their loved one holistically, rather than focus on the manner or cause which led to their ending of life. We give the family the time and tools they need to process the information given by coroners whilst also providing appropriate counsel to the wider communities. In all of these exchanges, we are driven to ensure that the baseline of compassion and integrity lie at the heart of such funerals – just as they would be in so-called normal cases.

What complicates our approach is that mental illness continues to be one of the most prevalent – yet maligned – forms of illness to be acknowledged for the life-threatening disease it is. Despite one in four people across the UK struggling to live with some form of this ailment, it continues to be almost as taboo a topic as suicide. Many communities dismiss any development of it as a curse, a narcissistic tool used to garner attention or, worse still, a signifier of a lack of faith in God. The second and third of these summations lead many people to seek religious leaders to 'break the curse', or to become heavily dependent on prescribed medications. But a great many more live in denial, ignoring the signs and feeling unable to face the social stigma associated with their condition. Maya, despite the severity of her illness, refused to go to the GP and would not accept that she was suffering from depression. This is a trait I suspect many of the 84 men who commit suicide every single week in the UK must share. Yet, despite such horrific facts, little seems to be set in place to help religious communities deal with ailments such as depression, Borderline Personality Disorder (BPD), Body Dysmorphic Disorder (BDD), or loneliness and anxiety. And this results in that missing step that negates a beautiful life – or death – for far too many loved ones.

The second death impacting my life and which served to widen my understanding of our, at times, clinical dealing with death relates to my eldest brother. He passed away in May 2015. It was during Dying Matters Week, an annual period when organisations like mine, linked to the UK's End of Life Care Strategy, try to raise the public's awareness about death so that they can learn how to provide a smooth transition from end-of-life to death. At Compassionate Funerals, we decided to set out and deliver five Death Cafés in East London – a death café being an informal space in which people who have experienced loss or are facing an earlier death can speak about their loved ones and their worries and cares.

We had just finished the second Death Café when a notification popped up on my phone – I had 22 missed calls from my brother's hospital. He had died from heart and kidney failure after being in hospital for three months, amidst discussions about whether he would have a triple by-pass or a heart transplant. He wanted neither and was terrified of any medical procedure.

At the hospital, the doctor who last saw my brother informed me of his death in words that I will never forget: 'I'm so sorry we failed in our work.'

In that moment, I felt most keenly for the doctor. I sensed his distress about 'failing' and struggled to find the words to tell him that none of this was his fault, that this was a natural end we all had to face one day, and that it was simply a part of the life cycle with which God had blessed us. After all, there was nothing surprising or dramatic about my brother's passing. Life had been touch-and-go for him following the development of a grievously weak heart and kidneys which could function only minimally. His rock and roll lifestyle as a musician was something he had never altered, even when those first signs of ill-health had crept up on him.

To this day, I remain astounded at how medical professionals, and other workers who are charged with the immense responsibility of keeping people healthy and alive for as long as possible, are blamed by others – and themselves – for deaths that occur under their care. It is, I believe, in great part to do with medical philosophy, which places a grave onus on the saving of lives, whilst viewing death as a signifier of failure. This, in itself, is rooted in our wider communal fear of death. It's about our societal distaste for a fact we all seem to accept on the surface, but probably view as a secret disease to be avoided at all costs. As the children's author Lemony Snicket succinctly puts it:

> It is a curious thing.... We all know that our time in this world is limited, and that eventually all of us will end up underneath some sheet, never to wake up. And yet it is always a surprise when it happens.... It is like walking up the stairs to your bedroom in the dark and thinking there is one more stair than there is. Your foot falls down, through the air, and there is a sickly moment of dark surprise as you try and readjust the way you thought of things.

Fear, guilt, denial, assigning blame, shock – all are accepted markers of grief. Yet I left the hospital that day thinking how different the experience could have been, for both my family members and the doctor had looked for the impossible, had we changed the modus operandi of our thoughts on this one topic.

Following my brother's death came the next step – arranging the funeral. I now recognise that, like many of my clients, I was living in denial. Like most women charged with leading a family as well as a company, I was also on autopilot mode. This was ruptured during my Fajr (dawn) prayers one morning, when a harrowing grief set upon me for a whole twenty minutes. Only then did I allow myself to cry deeply from my heart and soul and to fully feel the pain that life without my big brother presented. I was left feeling hollow, shell-like and depleted. But life had to go on – especially when it involved four children, a husband who was feeling the loss as keenly as I did, and a deeply saddened family.

The test was heightened as my father also became my client – something I had never envisioned as a possibility. So, like many of my loved ones, I turned to the reassurances gifted by the Qur'an and the promise that: 'Allah does not burden a soul more than it can bear' (2:286). This verse was on permanent 'repeat' in my mind and tongue and enabled me to focus on serving my father's wishes and caring for the rest of my brother's music family. Looking back, I can acknowledge that my brother had a beautiful funeral, but neither a beautiful nor peaceful death. As his heart had begun to fail, the Crash Team's efforts to revive him by CPR for 45 minutes was something I know he would never have wanted. Only later did I learn that being only fifty, there was no DNR (Do Not Resuscitate) legal order in place – a reminder that the lack of knowledge about even the smallest technicalities can impede a peaceful ending.

My brother went on to have a Muslim funeral and was buried according to Islamic funeral rites. After the *janaza* at East London Mosque, we went to view him and say our final goodbyes. The burial process was one of the most difficult I faced. As an act of self-preservation, I had gone into robot mode, making sure everyone was in the right place and that my family were fully involved and their wishes respected at every turn. My father wanted my brother to have a shroud burial to keep in line with Islamic funeral rites. Once at the grave side, however, he changed his mind. Not wanting to see the outline of his son's body, he suddenly told me that he wanted my brother to have a full coffin burial. I informed him, as gently as I could, that as the grave had been prepared for a shroud burial, a coffin wouldn't fit. The acute pain felt at this moment, and as my brother's body was taken out of the coffin and gently lowered into the earth, is something only those who have witnessed the burial of a sibling in the accompaniment of a parent can truly understand. Moments of solace were found in the sound of the imam's voice – a friend – as he recited verses from the Quran whilst the men, women and children began to surround the grave. On this beautifully sunny day, and in the presence of two hundred people, my children covered the grave with rose petals. My brother loved roses.

Afterwards, I asked my siblings and my brother's friends if I could host a Death Café in his living room. A week later, I did so, with ten people present and a friend from Sweden via Skype. The session began with us tucking into my brother's favourite food – a plate of Bengali staples comprised of rice, dhal and fish cakes, followed by *mishti* (Indian sweets). Emotions were raw, and anger and sadness prevalent, as my siblings spoke honestly and frankly. Meanwhile, my brother's friends steered the conversation towards trying to understand the journey of the soul following death and tried to fathom where my brother's soul might have been at that moment. For many of them, it was the first time they had spoken of death so openly and asked questions in relation to fears and superstitions and stories that they had long waited to ask. As always, it was a bittersweet tribute to the loved one who had compelled us to gather, and as the discussion moved from initial feelings of loss towards theories of existential states of being and other universes, to being shallowed up by the 'light' of the cosmos, I found myself out of my comfort zone. This Death Café was personal and, in many ways, the publicising of a personal grief. But I knew I had to do it – my instinct served me well. The growth that emerges from acknowledging grief and the beauty of the person being honoured outweighs the discomfort instilled within us by our communities when we speak of anything related to death.

The ways in which we deal with grief can manifest in a thousand and one ways. Most methods of coping are viewed by others – including our employers and colleagues, or friends and families – as negative. Meanwhile, only those deemed closest to the deceased in Islam are given the mandatory forty days respite to confront their emotions and accept God's takings. But what about everyone else? What about the neighbour who was helped by the departed? The best friend at work? The kindred spirit who grew up together and the friends who forged a part of the life now gone? Negating them from the equation of grief or giving them but a brief sharing of it, our general societal attitude seems geared towards suppressing and silencing grief and reprimanding those unable to 'move on' or 'get over it' in the time allotted to them. Grief remains a discomfort

— a state we should do our best to leave as quickly as possible so that we can feel, look and be 'normal' again.

In Britain, the stiff-upper-lip nature of dealing with death seems to have seeped into roots of many Muslim communities dealing with death, to the point where it is no longer normal to speak of the death of a loved one beyond a timed remit. To speak every day of the person that has passed, to remember them through photos and memories shared, to celebrate their lives and continue daily works in their names — these are not seen as healthy ways of grieving, but of clinging onto something which should be left behind. But, I believe, attitudes that make death an impossible fact for many to deal with become the basis for addictions to food, alcohol, prescription drugs, and even sex, which are used to mask unresolved grief. The expression of grief continues to be treated as a mental illness rather than a natural process which plays its part in the lifecycle of birth and death. The author and grief counsellor Elisabeth Kübler-Ross, who established the Kübler-Ross model on which the now infamous five stages of grief were founded, reminds us that following a death, 'we're expected to go back to work immediately, keep moving, to get on with our lives. But it doesn't work that way. We need time to move through the pain of loss. We need to step into it, really to get to know it, in order to learn.'

Too often, the clients coming through my office door have a grave need to share the pain and stories that surround the death of a loved one. These words need an outlet and a larger response than a sympathetic pat on the back and a silent nod. Whoever the person, and however close or far their link with the deceased, the bond must be acknowledged, and the interwoven nature of lives and loves celebrated, not hushed. My response to this need has deepened over the years and has altered from silent sympathy to a verbal reassurance that love is an enduring emotional currency. Love does not end with the demise of the physical presence and beauty of a soul. We feel 'negative' emotions — including anger, denial, and despair — because of the love, connection, and time we spent with the person who has died. There are many brilliant grief theories which can help all of us, from children to the elderly, to understand our personal grief cycles. But again, too often, these are hardly spoken of, explored, discussed or even made available to the vast majority of communities. This begs the question – how can any of us find peace or beauty in a loved one's passing if we are not even permitted the gift of grieving?

I recall most vividly the second funeral I ever arranged. George, my client, was 26 years old and came from Hungary, after his partner David had died from lung cancer at the tender age of thirty. A month after the funeral, I caught up with George to see how he was managing life without David. I was aghast to hear that George's manager had told him to 'move on and find a new partner'. The words had cut like a knife, leaving George horrified and in disbelief at how anyone could be so insensitive. George wanted to keep the memories and feelings of his partner 'alive' for a long as possible – as both his life and death had been so beautiful. This was reflected in the funeral service, in which David's loved ones had all arrived wearing his favourite colour (a deep purple) and had been surrounded by a selection of photos of him smiling and playing jokes on his friends, whilst listening to his favourite songs. The funeral had ended with the release of thirty eco-friendly purple balloons: a surreal and beautiful send-off of a man whose life I had only come to learn of and love following his death.

Whereas George was able to embrace and celebrate his loved one's life post-death and found solace in his grief, for many, being faced with grief – or a grieving person – can instil a numbing fear. Silence, a loss for words, awkward sentences, the wringing of hands, uncomfortable pats on the back, finding any excuse to run away – all are tools of self-preservation and an active barrier to acknowledging and soothing the grief on display.

Terror management theory suggests that 'terror' is a construct created by the trifecta of society, media, and politics. Creating a fear-filled and helpless mindset is required by commercial enterprises to ensure human beings take advantage of consumer-led, competitive, and commercial values – in other words, paying someone to do something too frightening for the rest of us to take care of independently. The negation of understanding that a healthy cycle of life incorporates the birth-life-death process as part of our shared unity (reflected in the Islamic concept of *tawhid*), continues to plunge people into a need to get rid of their grief as quickly as possible. This is aggravated further because over the last hundred years, life expectancy has increased. With people living longer and healthier lives, death – excepting death from accidents, natural disasters, murder, or suicide – is something that we only face when we are much older. Meanwhile, post-death care, once the sole responsibility of the immediate family and community, has been industrialised and meted out to mosque services or to professionals like me. At the same time, media platforms – and the reality of political warfare, ongoing genocides and violent hostilities – make sure that we continue to be bombarded with images and headlines which instantly link death with terror and horror, and a need to look the other way.

Fear, of confronting death on a daily basis and of accepting it as a natural step in each of our lives, is a self-inflicted negation of peace. Even the imagining of 'The End' of our time on earth is a task many people feel incapable of. As part of my work, I also run a Death, Dying and Bereavement course for carers – many of whom are the first to arrive on a scene of death of an elderly or vulnerable person. On one such course, the carers I was teaching, all of whom were Muslim, were charged with exploring the notion of a 'Good Death'. Many were perplexed by the idea and, when called upon to close their eyes and imagine death, eighty per cent said they had imagined themselves drowning in the sea – lonely, scared, and terrified. Each carer, it seemed, had slanted towards envisioning a devastating and painful death. Only after many questions, which asked them to imagine themselves bedbound and to describe their ideal surroundings, were the majority able to describe a Good Death. Many said they envisioned an end in which they were not in hospital or in a care home, but in their own bedroom, on a sunny day with windows framed by open curtains, and the Qur'an playing in the background.

The capacity to imagine a beautiful end is a rare and courageous gift, but it can only be given to ourselves when appropriate examples are provided and the criteria to safeguard it have been met. For many of my Muslim clientele, a lack of thought and real, honest, and fearless conversations about death – including all the steps we need to take to prepare for it – means few are, in reality, ready for it at any level. This is especially true for those whose perception of death has been defined by the most traumatic of human-made inflictions, such as war.

My own encounter with someone whose understanding of death had been shaped by war came in 2015. I had been contacted by a local hospice and asked to support a wonderful woman called Sara, who was actively exploring her decision of whether or not to be buried in East London or to be repatriated to her home country, Albania. Sara was terminally ill with an aggressive cancer and had been given just a few weeks to live. Split between her loyalty of being put to rest in her home country and her children's urges for her to be buried in the UK, where they could pray beside her grave and attend to it, Sara decided to be buried in East London. But as she had never attended a funeral in the UK or been to a cemetery, I offered to take Sara to a variety of cemeteries and burial grounds.

Used to seeing big Ottoman headstones as opposed to none, Sara wanted a place that felt more akin with her roots. So, as we continued to explore options, Sara began to speak openly of divorce, of domestic violence, of leaving Albania and the racism she and her three children had faced. I asked her if she had ever been to a funeral. The question led to her describing the 1997 Albanian Civil War, in which over 2,000 people were killed. Sara said the only funerals she had ever been to 'were mass burials were people died from the war…they were buried without the proper Islamic Funeral Rites of washing and shrouding…an image I can't get out of my eyes'. Sara was still traumatised by the inhumanities she had seen and survived. As with all survivors of atrocities, she had gone with the general silence which followed, unable to 'share this with anyone'.

Following her death, Sara was buried at West Ham Cemetery, with her wishes for a full and simple Islamic funeral honoured. She had been ready. Her presence and passing were as surreal and yet as beautiful as she had been. I will always carry the gift of the immense honour, trust, and privilege she had placed in me to look after her and to be entrusted with her death care and funeral. Her *janaza* took place at Friday Jumu'ah prayers, and on this day, the Friday *khutbah* was given by special guest scholar, Shaykh Yasir Qadhi. Shaykh Yasir spoke about Surah Kawthar in the Qur'an – the Chapter of Abundance – and the infinite beauties and joys gifted to mankind. One of which can, if we strive for it, include a beautiful end.

Whilst death is a reality, which we as Muslims remind ourselves every time we read the Qur'an or stand at the hem of our prayer mat, my role has exposed a truth which must be confronted. It is that for too many of our communities, the truly difficult conversations about death, its reality, our legacy, and our funeral wishes have yet to occur. That death itself still brings fear and terror to those who should be reassured, instead of an opportunity and reminder that we are all commanded to leave this world in a better state than we arrive in it. Only by changing our views on the fate we all share – and raising awareness of the steps we can take to bid adieu to our time here, in a manner befitting the honour of having been alive – can we make our lives and deaths truly beautiful.

BEAUTIFUL (POP) SOUNDS

Jonas Otterbeck

Once, I was in a discussion with an *'alim* (Islamic scholar) who claimed that true art cannot be ugly, and that this is written in the Qur'an. I was puzzled. What I heard was Plato, not the Qur'an. I never really grasped his *'tafsir'* (exegesis), and he probably thought I was way off mark. Plato claimed, or maybe more correctly, others have claimed that Plato thought that only the beautiful, the morally perfected, is of true value, contrasting it with the ugly and vulgar that has no value, and may even be considered destructive to society. This is not a mere judgement of taste. Rather, the conviction is entwined with concepts such as perfection, the good, the essence of an idea, while the opposite is associated with flaws, sins, deception, corruption of ideas and a contempt for the pleasures of the people. Becoming well-versed in Islamic thinking and then engaging with Plato must be a remarkable experience for anyone. As is well-known, many intellectual rationalisations and responses to the foundational texts in Islam throughout history contain elements of Platonic and neo-Platonic thinking. Thus, the position of this *'alim* is not unusual and can be found both in history and in our day and age. Indeed, Platonic conceptions of beauty have become an integral part of the discussions about *al-fann al-hadif*, art with a purpose, over the last three to four decades.

My discussion with the *alim* happened in 2013 in Oxford, England, at a closed meeting about art and Islamic ethics. I was invited because of my work on Islam and music and the invitation probably came because I had become acquainted with Sharif Banna, CEO of Awakening, a thriving media company specialising in Islamic products, particularly music. Banna, at the time pursuing a PhD at al-Azhar University in Cairo and simultaneously running an expanding world-wide company, had a key role in finding the participants for the discussion. Apart from the *'ulama'* (the scholars of Islam) and me, he had managed to engage Ruh al-Alam, the

London-based designer and artist, and Zarqa Nawaz, the witty writer of the Canadian comedy show *Little Mosque on the Prairie*. The atmosphere was relaxed but discussions were lively, with much disagreement in the room.

The recent appropriation of modern art expressions by Islamic intellectuals, in contrast to the condemnation of them during most of the twentieth century – such as the genre of popular music – is a remarkable and noteworthy development. It parallels, not least, Christian and Jewish art discussions – and oddly enough also Marxist ones – but has its own internal, discursive logic, a logic that can be explored by looking into the relation between Islamic pop music, ethics and aesthetics. But how do you create and market pop music that has the explicit aim to come across as Islamic?

Awakening

For a number of years, I have closely followed the Islamic media company Awakening, especially its work in music production. The company's amazing ability to generate superstar artists like Sami Yusuf and Maher Zain is impressive in itself, but I have been particularly curious about how the balance between Islamic ethics and consumer society marketing is managed and how this affects aesthetic expressions. I first encountered Awakening in Rotterdam in 2008. I had been invited to give a talk on music and Islam at an Islamic conference celebrating *id al-fitr* (the festivities after Ramadan). British singer-songwriter Hamza Robertson gave a concert attended by a seated, observant, and very quiet audience – well, apart from the three teenage, hijabi girls who suddenly, in the middle of the concert, all cried out at the top of their voices and then scurried giggling out of the room when all rows in front of them turned their heads and looked at them disapprovingly. I was sitting right behind them and remember thinking: 'Now, that was something new!' Afterwards a presentation and a question-and-answer session with Sharif Banna and the singer was arranged. I talked to Banna and exchanged contact cards. (Later, he was to become the gatekeeper who first allowed me in to the field. One often does not plan these things – they just happen.)

Strictly speaking, I had already encountered Awakening without noticing. I had picked up a CD issued by them a few years back, actually – Sami Yusuf's debut. Ever since I started to travel frequently to Egypt in

1987, working as a tour guide for a Scandinavian company, I had tried to follow the many trends in Arab music with the help of some music connoisseurs working as cassette vendors in the bazaar district of Khan al-Khalili. As I have always been eclectic in my taste of music – to the point of treachery according to some more puritan friends – I had no problem diving into and enjoying the colourful sea of Arabic pop. Islamic pop, however, triggered my scholarly instincts.

Awakening was founded in 2000 by four young men wanting to create contemporary Islamic media products appreciated for their aesthetical quality. One of the company's first successes was a book with translations of the *Al-Ma'thurat*, a litany composed by Hassan al-Banna, the founder of the Muslim Brotherhood. Because of its quality paper and fine design, it was noticed by many and is still in demand in reprints, also available as an audio CD and recently as an app.

In 2003, Awakening decided to make a contemporary English-language *nashid* record, inspired, not least, by the music of Dawud Wharnsby, Zain Bhikha, Yusuf Islam, and Raihan. The word *nashid*, in Islamic contexts, implies a song of praise, traditionally with only vocals, possibly accompanied by drums. But commercial recordings during the twentieth century had seen the growth of three different *nashid* trends – one Sufi (at times with large orchestras), one Shi'ite, and one vocals-only (related to Sunni Islamic resurgence groups). The artists mentioned above – Wharnsby, Bhikha, Islam, and Raihan – created a fourth trend, with devout Sunni *nashid* detached from the resurgence movements it was most closely related to. Awakening's idea was to take production and songs relating to the fourth trend to the next level. With Sami Yusuf's debut album *al-Mu'allim* (2003), a modern classic was born. When I spoke with the Canadian singer-songwriter Dawud Wharnsby, he remembered that when he first heard Sami Yusuf at a concert, he thought to himself, 'Oh, so this is where it's going now!', amazed by the quality of the production and the songs. At the time, making records using only vocals and drums were the standard, and *al-Mu'allim* was no exception. What was extraordinary was the creative and frequent use of digital vocal pads enlarging the sound of the production, making it sound more like regular pop.

Sami Yusuf has since left the label and new artists have been signed, for example the already-mentioned Maher Zain, Mesut Kurtis, Harris J, Raef, and Hamza Namira. To date, Awakening has produced more than 50 music video clips, more than 400 songs, arranged more than a thousand gigs and sold more than five million albums. Further, the official YouTube channel of Awakening celebrated one billion views in 2016. In the company's self-presentation, issued as a book in 2014, CEO Banna presents Awakening's music as a countercultural product: 'Music is at the forefront of a cultural conduit which reaches and impacts millions. It is everywhere. Faith-conscious Muslim artists are now producing "Islamic music" as an attempt to provide an alternative to mainstream pop culture.' Awakening aims to offer moral and meaningful songs in contrast to hedonistic pop and rock, love for Allah, the Prophet and mankind, in contrast with sex and drugs and rock 'n' roll, or rather metal, R&B, or hip-hop, to contemporise the metaphor. To be able to market a modernist popular culture phenomenon such as pop music as Islamic, the music will have to communicate the beneficial and the beautiful, not the beastly and the base. How is this done?

Ethical sounds

The production values of Awakening songs are clean yet rather contemporary. Think Lionel Richie meets Taylor Swift. Distorted sounds or dark atmospheres are not part of the soundscape (but let's not get into auto-tune, which I do consider a distortion, regardless of what its advocates argue, because it lessens the individual character of a voice). Musical instruments, with the exception of drums, were not used at first. These recordings are called vocals-only. This was essential at the time as Islamic legal ethics rarely found stringed and wind instruments acceptable. Since Sami Yusuf's debut, digital sound pads have been used extensively. These pads may consist of, for example, sampled voices producing a required type of sound texture, in this case the imitation of a choir or even different instruments. Pads are also used to provide vocal basslines and swooping synthesizer-like chords, creating much larger sonic landscapes than previous recordings of the genre. Almost all mainstream pop productions of today make extensive use of pads. However, around 2003-05, opinions started to change among Islamic intellectuals and artists and in the coming years several artists that used to produce vocals-only recordings started to add instruments, including such seminal artists as Yusuf Islam, Dawud Wharnsby and Awakening's own Sami Yusuf.

Following this initial success, Sami Yusuf recorded his second album, *My Ummah* (2005). A decision was taken to let the multi-instrumentalist artist use his skills and the record contained all kinds of instruments. To please an audience preferring a more restricted attitude to instruments, a vocals-only version was recorded too. Eventually, vocals-only has become a trademark of Awakening, but not a preference of the artists who like to record with actual instruments. Thus, the company now produces a fully instrumentalised version of songs and then turns to a studio specialised in vocals-only production to produce equivalent voice-only arrangements, replacing the instruments, but only for their more popular albums.

The overall soundscape of Awakening pop music is recognisable from, not least, American, Turkish and Arabic pop. Pop genre expectations about the length of a song (3–4 minutes), the structure (intros, verses, chorus), complexities of melodies, and musicianship are met. The topics of songs are however different, focusing on the love of Allah and the Prophet, the promotion of Islamic lifestyles, or the wonders of nature. When the odd cover is recorded or played live, sometimes lyrics are changed, like when Raef, during an October 2017 charity tour in UK, played John Lennon's 'Imagine', changing the line 'Imagine there's no heaven' to 'Imagine we're in heaven', and the line 'and no religions too' to 'and no divisions too'. The latter was a smart reference to the religious divisions in this world, both within Islam and beyond. Further, as heaven is a recurrent topic of the song, 'division' possibly also refers to the end of days when the division of Islam into seventy-two sects (plus one rightful one) finally ceases. The actual music of the covers is not given an 'Islamic' guise, but is rather rendered straightforwardly.

But let us return to the beautiful sound as an idea. In classical times, philosophers like al-Farabi (d. 950) or the group Ikhwan al-Safa (active in tenth century Baghdad) thought the perfectly tuned and built instrument was capable of reproducing cosmic sounds and expressing the perfection of the idea of music, and thus the beautiful. For those among intellectual Muslims who did not consider music as the Devil's lure for humans, the philosophers' ideas held true. Music was perceived as inherently powerful and, used in the right way, it could elevate the soul, not least in the opinion of those inspired by Sufi mysticism.

However, at the dawn of the commodification and commercialisation of music in the early twentieth century, very few Islamic intellectuals ascribed any value to recorded music. Rather, the opposite was true – they associated musical recordings with the cultural colonisation of the local elites who willingly adopted the so-called high culture of the Europeans and (later) Americans. Though the Egyptian Muslim Brotherhood, for example, experimented with (but soon gave up) religio-political theatre in its early days, it was not until the early 1980s that a discursive change came about with *al-fann al-hadif* discussions. The idea was that if popular culture, including music, could express Islamic values and propel people, not least youth, into action, then these forms of popular culture could be considered *halal* (allowed). This happened simultaneously in Shi'a and Sunni circles invested in political Islam, but eventually became a much broader discourse. It is impossible to conclude whether the change required an Islamic minded Muslim middle class, ready and able to consume popular culture; or the enabling discourse from some lenient Muslim intellectuals; or a change in the media landscape through the introduction of satellite channels; or a digital revolution in recording and social media; or simply the surfacing of the right creative individuals. The repositioning of popular music in Islamic thinking is probably indebted to all of these factors and more.

Some artists make edgier music produced with the pretention to be perceived as Islamic, like German-Turkish Islamic hip-hop group Sert Müslümanlar (Tough Muslims) and Indonesian Islamic metalband Tengkorak (Skull), making it difficult to please more than a handful of fans. Some US jazz and hip-hop artists – like Yusuf Lateef, Public Enemy or Fugees – have successfully, over time, incorporated rather coded Islamic-themed lyrics but the more outspoken acts have remained fairly marginal apart from a few, like Native Deen. In comparison, Awakening's choice of a clean production has become a popular alternative to mainstream pop. Setting lyrical content aside for now, the production aesthetics of Islamic pop resonate with a modern Islamic consumer culture whilst strengthening an ethical narrative about the artists and their songs.

Beautiful video clips

Contrary to mainstream video clips thriving on sex, directed with short sequences and fast movements, Awakening videos are fairly slow-moving and blunt sexualisation is avoided altogether. The people populating the video clips are generally kind to others, caring and smiling (Maher Zain's 'Ya Nabi, Salam Alayka'). Muslim couples of different ethnicities and ages feature frequently, lovingly paying attention to each other (Maher Zain's 'For the Rest of my Life'). Other popular tropes are beautiful historical mosques and places (Sami Yusuf's 'Hasbi Rabbi'), situations where people practice traditional culture (Mesut Kurtis' 'Burdah') or simply, the beauty and miracle of nature (Irfan Makki's 'I Believe'). Some video clips appeal to traditional calligraphy as an expression of Islamic authenticity and beauty (Maher Zain's 'Mawlaya'). The photography is generally of the highest quality and talented directors like Lena Khan from the US and Hamzah Jamjoom from Saudi Arabia are engaged.

The video clips offer other Islamic realities than those frequently represented in, for example, news or popular culture – in both Muslim-majority and non-Muslim countries. In those, Muslim life is stereotypically related to war, terror, political and humanitarian crises, and situations that are generally problematic. As such, the clips are intentionally made – and clearly consumed – as Muslim pride. The lyrics of the songs support this interpretation, even though topics span more widely than just Muslim pride. Environments in the video clips often signal upper middle-class or possibly a tight-knit fellowship of traditional culture. In Sami Yusuf's 'Al-Mu'allim', the home interior is stylish, the car and camera of the artist is expensive, and so on, clearly intending to associate the artist and Awakening with the burgeoning middle and upper classes, or the ones aspiring to this kind of social mobility. When trying to discuss this in an email interview with US-based Lena Khan, one of the directors, she misunderstood my interest as a questioning of the authenticity of a Muslim middle class. When that was sorted out, she stressed the importance of representing the growing Muslim middle class and their lifestyles and life worlds to an audience. And by all means, judging from general stereotypes, she is entirely correct.

At times, social or political problems are addressed in videos, like in the cartoon video clip made for Maher Zain's 'Palestine Will be Free' in which a tiny but dignified young girl takes a stand against an Israeli tank. Those environments are not as stylish, of course. However, such politically charged video clips are rare.

In a discussion in the tour bus engaging a number of people involved in Awakening, the question arose about the 'beautiful and slow' video clips and the possible need to do something more daring. It was a discussion filled with wild ideas and laughter but it also touched a nerve; to leave the established aesthetic ideals would risk challenging the authenticity and seriousness of Awakening's ethical engagement. While lyrics have taken on new topics, not least some pressing social issues, and instrumentation has changed, the video aesthetics have not quite moved beyond the ethical boundaries established early on in the company's history. The company is part and parcel of powerful discursive practices that establish the very ethics considered to be 'Islamic' in this field, in these times. Awakening is in dialogue with scholars; indeed, CEO Banna is a scholar in his own right. Awakening's ways of making and marketing music and tackling aesthetics is monitored, copied or rejected and affects discussions about the legality of music in on-line forums and among scholars.

Handsome, ethical men

As the attentive reader might have noted, all artists mentioned thus far are men. This is because, up until the launch of the artist Iman at a charity gig in London in late October 2017, Awakening had not signed any female artists. This discounts a children's album recorded by Egyptian artist Mariam Elhiny issued through Awakening some ten years prior to that. The reason was, as Sharif Banna confessed, that the company had no idea how to promote a woman artist, fearing her sexualisation and potentially negative exposure. But as the Islamic pop scene evolved and as women *nashid* singers nowadays are recording and singing on stage in many countries, Awakening decided that now is the time.

Banna's worry about a woman artist was, however, based on how the male artists they had launched were received. As Sami Yusuf became a superstar, the audience proved difficult to control. Even at Islamic gatherings or charity concerts, some members of the audience transgressed expectations about female modesty and tried out the role of screaming fan-girls or danced in the aisles or in their seat rows. At a show in Manchester in 2014, Maher Zain took the stage and encouraged the audience to 'enjoy themselves', adding a 'in a halal way, of course' with a broad, charming smile. A little later he admonished the crowd with a polite 'please sisters, no screaming'. A couple of years later, in 2017, he didn't bother although the spontaneity and shouting-screaming and dancing had rather increased. The popular singers are consumed as pop idols and poster boys by a substantial part of the crowd, which begs the question: how are the Awakening male artists performing their masculinity, and with what consequences?

Awakening markets its stars much in the same way as other pop stars are marketed. The company commissions professional photography and video clips, making their artists appear handsome – at times boy-bandish cute – yet ethically sound. The artists seldom wear Islamic garb in images for public consumption. Rather, dress is 'modern, yet modest', to paraphrase the Iranian gender historian Afsaneh Najmabadi's discussion about Muslim women taking part in modernity. Preferred colours are brown, black, white, green, grey, and orange – earth-tone colours. Sweaters, t-shirts, scarves, hats and caps, trousers, shirts, and jackets, at times suits, are the preferred apparel. Most artists have a casual stubble. Performers display a fashionable modernity appealing to fans of Islamic pop who don't want to consume the unfashionable but the modern – in an 'Islamic' form.

The artists often move slowly in directed music videos (Maher Zain's 'Ramadan'). They walk slowly and gesture slowly. They change their body posture slowly. Movements in time with the music are rare and it is quite common for artists to sing sitting down, making dance-like movements unnecessary. However, in Maher Zain's 'Medina' video clip from 2017, he is actually moving in time with the music, if not really dancing, and in the 2018 'Ramadan is Here' video clip, Raef is moving and jumping to the energetic music.

Looking at live performances, a similar pattern emerges. The artists seldom move their bodies in time with the music. They rarely mark the beat of the songs, not even when songs are rhythmical, apart from encouraging the audience to clap in time. Dance is extremely rare: I have only seen one fan-posted clip containing dance. It was from a concert in Lebanon when Maher Zain has *dabka* dancers on stage – for a short while he joins in the dance.

The performers come across as handsome and charming in front of the crowd. Their mild-mannered appearances, handsome faces and downplayed body presence present a model for the modern, Muslim male to be held forth in contrast to the stereotypical male Islamist with his specific 'anti-Western' dress and angry visage. The scholar of Jewish history Michael Berkowitz makes the inspired argument that the Zionist movement in the beginning of the twentieth century profiled itself by its handsome and manly leaders, contrasting them with anti-Semitic caricatures. Zionist leaders appeared on images looking virile and strong – according to Berkowitz, this was a crowd-puller. In a similar fashion, Awakening's artists can be endorsed with pride and admiration, something that cannot go unnoticed at a concert.

The artists also serve as possible alternatives to other pop artists marketed through sexuality not least in music video clips, a very common phenomenon worldwide. Being able to engage 'poster boys' like Sami Yusuf, Maher Zain or Mesut Kurtis makes the Islamic organisations and conferences that book their acts more appealing and attractive as alternatives in the marketplace of ideas and leisure time activities. Going to an Islamic meeting might actually be fun and up-to-date. During the charity tours in the UK, I met with many teenage volunteers who thought raising money for a good cause (such as for schools in poorer countries) and getting a free ticket to see Awakening's artists was more than a fair deal. Many who are fans of modern Islamic pop music are eager to point out that the artists are role models and good people to be proud of, people who help the fans to keep, engage in, and develop their faith – not small tasks to shoulder.

Awakening artists are engaged in charities apart from more regular concerts. Maher Zain is a so-called high-profile supporter of the UN's Refugee Agency, UNHCR, aiding in the organisation's work with Syrian refugees in Lebanon. Harris J has initiated an acting career in an Indonesian youth television show taking a stance against cyber-bullying. Raef has a Ramadan-themed programme in Indonesia that includes him travelling around Indonesian islands experiencing and narrating Indonesian history and meeting featured guests of the show. This trait of being a mild-mannered, caring, curious and modern man is essential as the persona of the typical Awakening artist rests on being perceived as ethically Islamic.

Due to the development of social media, artists are increasingly active on Twitter, Instagram, Facebook and other platforms. Maher Zain is followed by no less that 26 million people on Facebook and 3.7 million on Instagram. While I do not know if he is the one updating his Facebook account, I know for a fact that he controls his own Instagram account, which is very active. While travelling the UK on tour, the long hours on the bus were, at times, spent communicating directly with fans. Maher Zain was trying to answer their questions while filming himself and others (including me). This immediacy changes the rules of self-presentation. In such social media, artists are both forced to – but also expected to – present themselves in another manner than when being marketed. On the bus, in a hoodie, joggers and a woollen scarf, Maher Zain is not arranged for a photo session. Because of this, Awakening has to let go of its image control to a certain extent. This has given room to a frequent flow of images of the artists working out at the gym or eating and clips of them laughing, singing, and generally horsing around. It has also introduced the artists in Islamic dress more often, for example, when visiting key religious sites in Saudi Arabia or just praying.

At times, the frequent use of social media challenges the ethics of the persona. When Harris J published a snap of him and a stunning female cousin – leaning his head on her shoulder – some just had to comment on their supposed breach of traditional Islamic morals. Others defended him, pointing out that cousins can be like sisters – give him a break. The playfulness and casualness become yet something else to manage ethically for artists.

Commercial, religious art

Producing commercial art – in this case music – with the ambition to come across as Islamic, or more precisely, as ethically and aesthetically Islamic, requires thought-through strategies and honest engagement. The music of Awakening provides a fascinating case. Its artists have contributed to changed attitudes to musical instruments among many, transforming the *nashid* trend into Islamic pop music without losing track of the original elements of the genre, especially with lyrical content. Further, they have succeeded in their ambition to create a global alternative to more hedonistic commercial music. Even though it remains a countercultural phenomenon, Awakening's music has sold well – in excess of five million CDs in total – and is played on mainstream radio in some countries (not least Malaysia and Indonesia). Journalists and anthropologists frequently make reference to Maher Zain's songs when writing atmospheric descriptions in their articles. People are getting married to the music of Maher Zain ('Barakallah') or Raef ('You are the One'), and they break the Ramadan fast by partaking food *and* by putting on Islamic pop music to get into the right mood.

According to general celebrity culture logic, every scandal is a good scandal. Many high-profile artists have used this and tried to take control over the news by feeding mass media their so-called scandals, even seeking out the scandalous to be able to remain relevant to the supposedly celebrity-crazed masses. Religious authority and authenticity does not follow that logic. Religious celebrities have to be more consistent, they cannot cultivate an ethically responsible stage persona and divert from this privately, caving into their lusts and desires.

Awakening markets its artists as responsible men or youth. It has also, through aesthetic values about beauty, accentuated the ethical Islamic-ness of their commercial music. This understanding of beauty ties into ideas about the morally good as beautiful. This has affected the way that the music is produced, how promotional material is developed, which artists have been contracted, lyrics, video clips, stage performances, social engagements of the artists, and even their private lives.

Obviously, social media's immediacy poses a possible threat to the presentation of the artists, but is, all the same, experienced as crucial for marketing in modern consumer societies. The possibilities of artists with a religious persona (as well as anyone seeking religious authority) to communicate vastly increases, but the risks of being exposed as inconsistent or a charlatan increase infinitely. Awakening trust their artists to be the real deal. When Maher Zain was signed he was first called down to Cairo for a full week where the Awakening leaders talked religion and ethics with him. When they decided he was devout in the right way, they started to discuss music. With background checks like that, Awakening can afford the intimacy of social media.

The aesthetics of modern Islamic pop music, presented with all available means in contemporary consumer societies, is interlaced with ethical Islamic values about the acceptable and thus the beautiful, echoing Islamised Platonic ideals. Through creativity and entrepreneurship, Awakening and its artists have actually contributed to the ethical debate in Islam and mapped out new paths towards future expressions of the faith. Who said pop music cannot change the world?

WELLNESS

Irum Shehreen Ali

If ever there was a slippery concept, it's inner beauty. What is it? How is it manifested? Is it inherent or can it be cultivated? If so, how? In a completely unscientific survey of my friends and colleagues, inner beauty had two components: qualities that defined it, 'what we are', and actions that manifested it, 'what we do'. Those who possessed inner beauty had highly prized traits of kindness, thoughtfulness, authenticity, openness, self-awareness, hard work and generosity. They were also engaged in activities that enhanced these qualities: outward-focused altruism and inward focused self-reflection and improvement. Some argued that the very act of making it a named concept and pursuing its cultivation made one less inwardly beautiful. However, many more thought that purposefully nurturing inner beauty was an essential aspect of personal evolution and the path to greater self-awareness. Now more than ever, people want to balance purpose and contentment, to still the voices that simultaneously say 'be more' and 'be good enough'.

This life of wellness – the multidimensional process of pursuing mental and bodily health that we crave – is a symptom of the world we live in. If the life and body we want is achievable by design, so why not our inner selves? For those who are beyond the survival stage, and let us be very clear, this is a first-world problem of the most first-world kind, the idea that without inner peace there cannot be any peace in relationships and work-life attainment is becoming deeply embedded. While it is factually true that we live in the most stable and prosperous times historically, the 24-hour news cycle constantly highlighting the destabilising socio-political and economic atmosphere makes us feel less secure than ever. The current capitalist status quo doesn't engender balance or fulfilment, and in order to wrench back some sense of control from The Man, The Politicians and The World at Large, we focus inwards. We engage in the quest for inner wellbeing through an endlessly interlinked and stackable number of practices that focus on food intake, mental health and spiritual growth, physical activities and lifestyle choices. The outside is a reflection of our insides, and to glow without is to be enlightened within. Enter the wellness industrial complex: now that the goal of self-actualisation is considered a legitimate aspiration, companies and individuals can sell us an endless array of the holistic, wellbeing, and life-coaching products and services that help us in the quest towards becoming more beautiful from the inside out.

But does seeking a narrative of internal redemption make us feel happier, more balanced, more fulfilled and indeed more beautiful on the inside? It is not problematic in itself to want to be more mindful, have better work-life balance, feel more purposeful, eat food that is more nutritious and be more cognisant of the influences on our mind states. Understanding that living a worthy life takes serious and continuing self-inquiry can reap profound benefits. Engaging in all or some activities like eating a healthier diet, practising yoga and working towards self-improvement can lead to better mental health, bodily wellbeing, and interpersonal connectivity. However, when these practices become expensive, restrictive, rigid and exclusionary codes of behaviour, the pursuit of inner beauty comes at a heavy cost to both the person and society.

What many of these practices have in common is that they encourage us to look inward and not engage outwards with the world to find nourishment for our souls. While this message feels profound, is it merely selfishness dressed up as spirituality? When fulfilment comes at the cost of retreat, are we truly living 'our best lives'? This intense self-focus promotes a denial of greater economic and socio-cultural forces that intersect to create the inequality, discrimination and negative working conditions that lead to poor mental health and wellbeing outcomes. The onus is placed on the individual, in most cases, the woman – as the default subject in the wellness industry is female – to ensure her own success and happiness while not challenging the societal norms and institutions that limit her. The knowledge that the wellness industry sells us is freely available: eat in moderation, take time to move your body and be mindful of stress, but it is now packaged to create new fears and pathologies. A rise in disordered eating and failure to follow evidence-based medical advice has been linked to the advent of clean eating and restrictive diets. In the eternal pursuit to 'live our best lives', we are constantly afraid of failing to do so. In the effort to escape the capitalist system, we become the perfect capitalist subjects, convinced we would be better, wiser, happier and more at peace if we bought into one more thing. Thus, practices that seem outwardly radical only serve to reinforce the very system they endeavour to escape and reinforce the social distinctions that they seek to rise above. For those who sell us the solutions to our existential woes, this is a massive branding opportunity for people who want to exert control in an uncontrollable world by controlling themselves.

In today's world, food has become a complex problem for many in a way that modern medicine has been slow to acknowledge and even slower to meaningfully address. Research shows that current Western diets that are high in sugar, processed meats and far too low in plant-based food are linked to many poor public health outcomes like soaring rates of type 2 diabetes, obesity and cardiovascular disease. Mainstream scientific advice on unhealthy food has flip-flopped over the decades: first it was fat, then it was sugar and now it is processed meat! People are understandably confused as to what they should be eating, how much and when, with tools such as the food pyramid and nutritional information on food packaging being difficult to use in daily life. If we can't trust the scientific experts, whom can we trust? For women the complexities around health and food are even greater. Research has shown that ingrained sexism in mainstream medicine means that women presenting with pain symptoms are offered less medication, have to wait longer for it, are more likely to have their symptoms dismissed as hypochondria, and are more frequently misdiagnosed. Conditions that affect women more than men such as fibromyalgia and endometriosis are more likely to be thought of as having psychological sources, with even autoimmune diseases like multiple sclerosis being diagnosed. This makes women particularly susceptible to the welcoming, sympathetic and assuring claims of the wellness industry, where the default body is female and the default attitude is that we are listening to you.

A combination of living in uncertain times and in a social media maelstrom heightens feelings of being inadequate and out of control. We are constantly fed images of perfectly curated lives that are better than ours, yet tantalisingly just beyond reach. A raft of recent academic research has shown that the use of Facebook is negatively associated with overall well-being. The longer users spent on the site, the less satisfied they were with their lives and bodies, and the more anxious they felt. The wellness industry tells us that the secret to a better and more balanced life is an upgraded inner world. Then we too can show off on social media with posts about awakenings, life changes and colourful bowls of super foods. In this landscape where internal beautification is a moral imperative, its definition grows ever wider. The scope of what can be sold to us now includes not only the old hardware of external beautification, i.e. make-up, food and exercise, but also software of internal beauty, i.e. mental wellbeing. If mainstream food and medicine can no longer be trusted, then we are on a hunt for alternatives. The sellers, the gurus and the marketeers sell us interlinked and stackable sets of lifestyle practices and accessories for this purpose. We can now buy the peace of mind, the food, access to the physical activities, and the lifestyle that will make us happier and more at peace.

The core elements of the wellness juggernaut are food and diet, mental and spiritual health, and physical lifestyle practices. Consumers are turning to self-care techniques like meditation, exercise and dietary changes to mitigate the effects of stressful lives. In late 2016, Women's Marketing, a global marketing consultancy called wellness the next trillion-dollar global industry, with fitness and mind-body exercise being a US$390 billion share of it and diet and nutrition worth US$277 billion. For customers, wellness is a desirable new status symbol. For brands, integrating a wellness dimension into their products, or 'Brand Wagon-ing', can provide big returns. While Millennials (those born between the early 1980s and mid-1990s) spend twice as much as Baby Boomers (born between the mid-1940s and mid-1960s) on self-care and personal improvement, Generation Z (born between the mid-1990s to early 2000s) also perform strongly as wellness consumers. The dissemination of wellness practices and products is via social media and online tools such as Instagram, Facebook, smart phone applications and YouTube.

One of the primary entry points into wellness space is through mindfulness activities for mental peace and clarity. Mindfulness is described as the quality or state of being conscious or aware of something and mindfulness meditation is a technique in which distracting thoughts or feelings are acknowledged and detachedly observed to create awareness.

There are many free and subscription-based mediation apps such as Headspace and Calm. Headspace, the highest ranked of these, has been downloaded more than 11 million times, with 400,000 paying subscribers, an annual revenue of over $50 million and recent Forbes valuation of $250 million. Businesses such as Google, LinkedIn, and Thrive Global offer it to their employees, Spotify subscribers can stream their Headspace subscriptions, and seven airlines offer Headspace meditation on their flights. Bringing mindfulness to the masses is clearly a thriving business. Video and audio resources in the form of Instagram posts, podcasts and YouTube channels are growing by the minute, with thousands of led meditations available online. If practising inner peace with other people is more your thing, meditation classes run everywhere from gyms, yoga studios, community centres and even in work places. There is also the growing popularity of holistic and spiritual approaches to mental health and healing such as crystal therapy, acupuncture, reiki and Ayurveda to name a few. Again, dedicated Instagram accounts and YouTube channels have an unimaginable amount of information and clickable links to purchase the associated paraphernalia.

The battle for inner beauty begins with food. If we truly are what we eat, then it's never been more important to eat the right way. The inexorable rise of clean eating, detoxes, elimination diets, gluten and dairy intolerances, and highly specific eating habits (for example, intermittent fasting, the 80/20, the Ketogenic diet, Paleo, and Whole 30) are just some examples of recent health trends. Large supermarket chains are increasing their offerings of ethical, organic, 'free from' (gluten and dairy), fair trade, and vegan food. As of 2014, the UK gluten free market was worth £175 million. One of the earliest and most popular doyennes of clean eating, Ella Mills, sold 32,000 copies of her first book in the first week of release in 2015. In 2016, 18 out of the 20 Amazon UK top sellers in the food and drink category had a focus on healthy eating. Sales of avocados, beetroots, courgettes, spiralisers, Nutribullets and many other accoutrements of healthy eating have shot through the roof in the past few years.

Yoga is now firmly in the mainstream, with yoga studios populating the high streets of many major cities. Knowledge of the various types of yoga, e.g. ashtanga, hatha, Bikram, power, and vinyasa, is becoming popular knowledge. The long understood physical benefits of yoga are now being sold alongside the spiritual practices that form the other parts of traditional yoga practice in India, such as meditation, breathing and philosophies. The latter is but another device for the enhancement of inner peace and excavation of the true self that so many are seeking.

What all these tools in the pursuit of inner beauty have in common is that the way we access them is overwhelmingly via social media and mobile technology. YouTube lifestyle and health channels are among some of their most profitable, with thousands of channels devoted to every type of diet and spiritual practice imaginable. Along with Instagram, it has enabled countless of young men and women 'content creators' to become successful and wealthy entrepreneurs by sharing with their devoted audiences their chosen lifestyles, wellness practices and, most importantly, product and lifestyle recommendations. There is an inordinate amount of money to be made in clicks, views, likes and comments. Top yoga and wellness bloggers can make up to US$25,000 for a sponsored brand partnership. The channel Yoga With Adrienne, with a community of nearly 3.5 million subscribers, provides a hundred yoga practice videos that allow the viewer to develop an in-depth at-home practice. The unstoppable rise and rise of Instagram has been a salutary lesson to heritage brands and marketeers on how many and how far you can reach with a well edited picture and heart-grabbing caption. It is now the medium by which food, health and lifestyle companies and individual vendors sell their wares. These products can be anything from the services of a lifestyle coach or spiritual healer to food supplements, cookbooks, exercise regimens, and apparel. On Instagram, the top-paid posts by food bloggers can generate up to US$10,000 per sponsored post and even bloggers with smaller followings (100,000 followers) can make up to US$5,000 each time. Generation Y, inherently suspicious of large corporations and their monolithic approach to selling, responded early and in droves to the seemingly authentic product recommendations of lifestyle bloggers long before they had that title. People are clamouring to be shown authentic journeys, transformations and achievements: real people living real lives, eating real food, overcoming their real problems and using products in everyday settings. Subscribers and followers are incredibly loyal to content creators and invested in their lives. They want to see, in perfectly square boxes on their phones, that in this world of uncertainty, inner peace is not only attainable, but maintainable.

Now that the wellness backlash is in full swing it feels pertinent to ask: are millions of mindfulness and yoga practicing, plant-based-diet-eating people wrong? To some degree, of course not. At a time when so many are struggling with stress, the ill effects of a poor diet and the unrelenting pressure to conform to restrictive standard norms of beauty, there is a genuine need for better eating, mental and physical practices. The wellness movement has contributed greatly towards making people aware of the food they eat, the benefits of physical exercise and highlighted the need to focus on self-care and slowing down in a fast-paced world. When we are so often concerned with the external, looking inside oneself is to be lauded. The fact that people are finding connection, company and encouragement through social media to engage in these practices is heartening and positive. Those on a journey to a more balanced and healthful lifestyle find that sharing those journeys with their fellow online denizens creates encouragement, accountability and support that they often don't have in the real world. For the current generation of digital natives, living out their internal health, mental or otherwise, online, feels natural.

The democratisation of knowledge by the Internet is empowering individuals to be accountable for their own choices around health and inner wellbeing. Given that mainstream medicine has been slow to understand and educate the public about the huge impact of diet on health outcomes, people have often felt that they have to take things into their own hands. Government campaigns aimed at improving health practices are often preachy and ineffective. In a country where the majority of people eat diets low in vegetables and high in sugar, a more holistic way of looking at food that marries it with inner wellbeing is a positive step. Many wellness approaches start with the basic premise that we should eat more vegetables, and less sugar and red meat, all of which are sound nutritional principles. If clean eating has educated thousands of people to the benefits of eating more greens, grains and whole foods, then it is surely a positive thing?

For many women, especially, who have often been ill-served by mainstream medical professionals, the welcoming embrace of wellness practitioners has positively contributed to their quality of life. Having someone who understands the seriousness of chronic pain or gynaecological concerns is a lifeline. Apps like Flo Living that educate women about their menstrual cycles and hormonal flows, and suggest ways to relieve symptoms and make more educated fertility decisions are empowering women. The benefits of meditation such as increases in both short- and long-term emotional wellbeing, better stress management skills, improved patience and tolerance have been recognised in scores of reviewed scientific studies. Mindfulness is being touted by the NHS, which has its own suite of videos and techniques, as a key tool in improving not only general quality of life but in the management of chronic pain and long term illness. By the same token, recent scientific research has shown the increased physical (lower blood pressure and blood sugar levels, improved lipid profiles, overall fitness), and mental (increased calmness and lower stress levels) benefits that accrue from regular yoga practice to be extremely beneficial in combating anxiety and depression. It is even being used as a complementary intervention for patients with cancer and heart disease. Thousands of dedicated yoga teachers, both in real life and online, are bringing a beneficial practice to a wider audience who are reaping its benefits. Subscribers' comments left on Yoga With Adrienne's YouTube channel often speak of how having a yoga and meditation practice that they can do at home for free has resulted in huge improvements in mental and physical well being. From the branding, selling and marketing side, the wellness industry has allowed many female and younger entrepreneurs to harness technology and social media to reach other women who may have felt that they are being ignored by traditional brands. As we become more and more aware of the damage that we are doing to the world around us, many feel the need to live a more environmentally conscious and lower impact lifestyle. There are countless resources online that teach us how to live richer lives with fewer and more environmentally friendly clutter: the minimalism, capsule wardrobe, zero waste, low carbon and small house movements are just some examples. Inspired by others online, people are actively pushing back against the impetus to purchase their way to happiness, by buying less and doing more.

However, the danger lies in the fact that many in the wellness industry use people's antipathy towards mainstream medicine and food culture and the nebulous nature of wellbeing to spread and sell misinformation to a susceptible public. In the pursuit of inner beauty, people are leaving behind decades of evidence-based medical and nutritional practices in a way that can leave us feeling the very opposite of well. While an awareness of how we are treating our bodies and minds is no bad thing, the wellness industry is guilty of selling philosophies, products and promises that are at the very least borne of debunked ideas and pseudoscience, and at the worst actively harmful to people. In an atmosphere of anxiety regarding food, clean eating philosophies offer reassurance that if you follow the rules of this holistic way of life, you too will be healthy and whole. As a result, thousands are obsessing over chemical toxins, using coconut oil for every ailment, going gluten free despite not having coeliac disease, adopting ever more rigid and inflexible patterns of eating. Many doctors and scientists have shown elimination diets to be based on bad science. Writer Bee Wilson notes that faced with conflicting nutritional information and an overwhelming array of unhealthy food, clean eating is 'best seen as a dysfunctional response to a still more dysfunctional food supply: a dream of purity in a toxic world'. Chef Ruby Tandoh's much shared article on this phenomenon notes the paradox that almost all wellness proponents think of white sugar as the devil, yet tout large quantities of expensive unrefined forms of it. There is also the much-derided love of expensive vegetables like avocados and 'super foods'. She rightly notes that if 'health food advocates take us down only the most expensive and exclusionary paths to health, we ought to question their integrity'. These ways of eating are often too expensive, and impossible to follow, even for the largely middle class audience they are aimed at. More and more, people are losing the joy in eating a variety of foods, and equating healthy eating with restrictive eating. Rather than just a way of eating, for many it has become a belief system where food is 'good/bad' or 'pure/impure'. The functionalism of the body and eating has become moralised, and to eat food that is not pure is to not be pure.

As many commentators have noted, clean eating is diet culture dressed up as health and wellness. Many doctors, nutritionists and dieticians like Renee McGregor have recently noted the rise in patients with body dysmorphia and orthorexia, the preoccupation with 'good' and 'bad' foods that leads people to severely restrict food intake. The entire wellness conversation as it relates to eating is shot through with the fear of fatness, despite branding itself as a movement that cares about how one feels and not how one looks. Recent academic research in Australia and the US has shown that Instagram is the worst app for mental health, and that scrolling through health and fitness images for as little as 30 minutes can make women more anxious and unhappier about their own bodies. Given the societal pressures women are constantly under regarding their appearance, the wellness gurus' promises that their way of eating comes without guilt has a deep pull. The people selling us wellness look like the women society wants us to be: slender, conventionally beautiful white women with Instagram-perfect lives. The underlying message here is the same as all aspirational advertising: if you do like me, you'll look like me too. This overwhelming whiteness highlights a serious problem in the wellness space: a lack of diversity in voice and representation.

Not only are women and men of colour often invisible in wellness spaces and platforms, it can also feel like they are not welcome. Looking at the most popular women's health and wellness magazines and online platforms highlights a sea of white faces, and inside them is more of the same. Writer Salma Haidrani notes that of the past 27 covers of *Women's Health*, only two have been non-white, featuring bi-racial actresses. A survey of the current best-selling wellness, mindfulness and lifestyle books shows an equally predominantly white array of authors. Of all the recent clean eating superstars like the Helmsley sisters, Amelia Freer and Madeline Shaw *et al* who have hit explosive social media fame and the app, book and lifestyle sponsorship deals that come with it, not one is non-white. Non-white content creators have spoken about how they are bypassed for commercial opportunities for 'not having the right look', even when their following is as big or bigger than some of their white counterparts. It is particularly interesting to note this phenomenon in light of the fact that ethnic foods and spices taken out of their traditional cuisines – such as dates, tahini, za'atar seasoning, harissa, chipotle, turmeric, and ginger – have been aggressively promoted by the clean-eating movement as 'novel' ways to inject healthful flavour into dishes. It would seem that these ingredients are only acceptable in the mainstream when aspirational white faces present them. The very success of an exclusionary practice depends on appropriating from those it excludes.

Despite yoga's origins in India as a multi-faceted practice that prepared the body to attain deep states of meditative awareness with a goal of union with the divine, the form it mainly takes in the UK today is very far from it. As currently marketed to us by studios, apparel retailers, yoga magazines, blogs and Instagram accounts it is a practice of aspirational physical postures by slender, white and already fit women. In its myriad new forms such as 'power' and 'high energy' it is touted as the perfect way to reduce stress and get fit to function better in our modern lives. However, many long-term practitioners of yoga in India and in the West have argued that the appropriation of what is a cultural practice, stripping it of its context and repackaging it as a lifestyle to sell more leggings and energy balls is akin to colonisation. They argue that it is an inclusionary meditative practice that is open to everyone, with a complementary focus on the physical *asanas*. The exclusion of those who do not conform to a certain body type or ethnicity is itself an act not compatible with yoga's foundations and aims. Recently there has been a robust discussion about yoga's lack of inclusivity, with practitioners like Dana Falsetti and Jessamyn Stanley vocally advocating for yoga studios, retailers and platforms to be welcoming and to showcase body and ethnic diversity.

The wellness movement has been heralded by a wave of social media life coaches who promise to help us uncover our true purpose and by doing so lead us to happier, more productive and balanced lives. Each sun-washed, millennial pink-hued Instagram post of long tanned limbs from a beach in Mexico promises that if we breathe deep, write gratitude journals, make visions boards, align work with purpose and do more yoga, we too will be living an amazing life. And downloading their 10 Step Plan to an Amazing Life for the low price of £499 is the key to this. The goal of all personal development coaching should be to improve the life that their clients already have by generating inquiry, action and empowerment, not to promise perfection. The problem is that many prominent life coaches are selling their own lifestyles, rather than the coaching services that can add value to their customers. Add to this the vast amount of pseudo-scientific philosophies, services and products that are sold to complement this industry – I am looking at you and your incredibly expensive death/medicine/common-sense denialist nonsense, Gwynneth Paltrow – and we are being sold many faulty bills of goods. There is no amount of crystals, angelic healing and US$38.00 'Brain Dust' that will 'align you with the mighty cosmic flow needed for great achievement'.

Wellness is essentially a philosophy of selfishness, dressed up as spiritual awakening. It also locates the entire onus of inner wellbeing and happiness on the individual and ignores the problem of oppressive cultural norms. It is an especially deep form of denialism that essentially tells people that living anything less than their 'best possible life' is a failure of their own making. It does not take to task the classism, misogyny and capitalist practices that are culturally ingrained to make people feel unfulfilled and stressed. We are all now 360 degree billboards for our own personal brands. Social media is the new marketplace for ideas with short, attention-grabbing visuals that document every journey of hitting a wall and finding redemption – usually through some combination of yoga, mindfulness, following a highly restrictive diet, and engaging a life coach. The story now goes that we no longer have to accept what we are born with; we can sculpt it, both outside and inside, especially the latter. We are constantly being told we are sacred and unique and the way to find inner peace is to just redefine the ways in which we think about ourselves. While the message is ostensibly to engage in continuous acts of gratitude, it is difficult when constantly confronted with a visual account of the lives others posses. The cocooning of the self to feed the need for inner beautification and wellbeing conversely has to be documented in the most public of ways: witness the thousands of pictures of vegan brunches, impossible yoga *asanas* and screenshots of meditation statistics. Generation Y, to whom self-documentation is as natural as breathing, sees no contradiction in being told to put down their phone and go meditate by a YouTube video or Instagram caption, and then putting up a meditation mirror selfie to be validated by their followers. An ostensibly internally driven conversation is being played out in an external space. It's hard to miss the irony lit large: corporations telling us that to be more beautiful on the inside, we need to nourish it from the outside with their products and on their platforms.

Food activist and academic Michael Pollan provides all the advice we need: 'Eat food. Not too much. Mostly plants.' In a world where we are becoming ever more atomised, overwhelmed and afraid of what we eat, what could be more beautiful than sharing time, love, fresh air and food with those around us?

TAMING THE BARBARIANS

Henry Brefo

The rise of Islamophobia has coincided with widespread commodification of Muslim culture. Muslim cultural aesthetics, fashion and iconography are taking centre stage in the visual economy. The American street artist Shepard Fairey, in one of his political paintings, turns his gaze on the Muslim woman, reframing the hijab within the searing landscape of New Age feminism, as an exotic signifier of diversity. A Muslim woman wearing a headscarf decorated in the American flag beams at once provocative and, at the same time, smacks of protest overkill. Tenderly preened in a radiant light skin and adorned with seductive red lipstick, she is transformed into a politically decorated femme fatale – absolutely ravishing for the male gaze.

Beyond the realm of art, a Nike commercial features the 'hijabi' as a common fixture of the mainstream, yet never losing the peculiar sensation of the foreign, to be tamed and normalised into multicultural Britain. The deliberate positioning of the hijabi performing strenuous athletic feats may have been well-intended. Perhaps initially envisaged by the curators as a bold celebration of Muslim women's liberation. Interestingly, the centrality of the light-skinned Muslim women along with the emphasis on gender in relation to the 'hijab' raises several questions. To begin with, do all Muslim women wear hijab? And is the hijab the only measure of one's religious devotion or the only cultural symbol of true 'Muslimness'? And wassup with the saturation of light-skinned images? Are all Muslim women light-skinned or are these just the ones that meet Eurocentric norms of beauty?

Yes, we have our right to admire these images as positive steps towards diversity and cultural representation. But beware confusing objectification for representation. Indeed, ethnic minorities have desired to see reflections of their diverse cultures within the mainstream as much as they have spurned essentialist depictions. One does not need to bring any intellectual weight upon these questions to ascertain that, once again, there is an insidious interplay of race and capital at work. At the helm stands the corporate beast, making a mockery of deep social, political and cultural concerns – all for pure financial euphoria. For the past few years, black feminism has bound hip to hip with women of colour and other groups that face intersecting oppressions – especially lesbian, gay, bisexual, transgender and queer (LGBTQ) people – to affirm the heterogeneity of gender struggles. This point goes amiss with the emerging 'white feminist' representation of Muslim women's liberation in the media today. The Canadian Muslim journalist, Tasbeeh Herwees, in her article, 'Stop using Muslim women to sell soda', condemns Pepsi's recent commercial for using Muslim women as a signifier of 'diversity' and 'vague resistance' to exploit and defang protest for commercial gain. She maintains, 'a light-skinned Muslim woman in a pretty headscarf is not threatening to the status quo, especially when she, already perceived as subservient, shares a Pepsi with the police. It would be lot more difficult to conjure that image if that Muslim was Black.'

As a member of the Socialist Workers Party (SWP) during my undergraduate days, I witnessed how the keffiyeh (the chequered, black-and-white scarf) was transformed overnight, from being associated with Arab terrorism in 1980s Hollywood action flicks to acquiring political currency as an expression of solidarity with Palestine and the rest of the Middle East. It was, in fact, a sign of political protest, mainly worn by the politically astute and those in tune with the dissonance of geopolitics. The upheaval in the Middle East has in no way waned – Palestine still stands on the precipice of fear of extinction; Lebanon is in turmoil; Saudi Arabia is experiencing apical conflicts amongst the aristocracy. Meanwhile, Iran keeps the hairs of Western leaders up and the ghost of Iraq haunts neoliberal democratic projects. But the keffiyeh has remained triumphant, brokering a peace deal where everyone else failed, leaving the sites of protest and war behind. On the streets of London, the keffiyeh flaunts its acquired panache with an indiscriminate pedestrian verve. In the endz (as the youth would say), it has made a splendid entry into yardie fashion. The hard-washed, ripped, skinny Diesel jeans are completed with keffiyeh shrugged around defiant shoulders. Similarly have the images of newly converted Man Dems or homies clasping the Qur'an in one hand while massaging a keffiyeh in the other become part of the repertoire of urban geography. Today, one can pick up a *keffiyeh* at H&M for perhaps a fiver or a tenner. On rare occasions, stick-thin women in heels have been spotted in the distance modelling the *keffiyeh*.

So, high fashion is catching up. Muslim sensibilities have descended upon the world of couture, bringing modest fashion into vogue. Who would have thought that in the era of body positivity, an invention like a burkini would have been a conceptual reality? First created by Aheda Zanetti in 2004, the burkini has courted controversy. In 2016, the then French Prime Minister Manuel Valls pushed for a ban on burkinis, describing them as 'the affirmation of political Islam in the public space' and denouncing their usage as an 'enslavement of women'. Zanetti responded, declaring, 'I made the burkini to give women freedom, not to take it away.' Despite her clarification, the burkini remains banned in several beach resorts and public pools in France.

Eastern influences in Western fashion date back to the sixteenth century. Some accounts, however, put the emergence of Islamic aesthetics in the west as early as the twelfth century. Particularly, in religious and scholarly dress during the First Crusade, coats of Turkish and Arabic provenance in the form of the kaftan made an appearance amongst English monks and clerics. The prevalence of the adoption of Eastern fashion nonetheless became limited to the aristocracy and monarchs during the sixteenth century. A famous portrait of Henry VIII from around 1542, at the National Portrait Gallery, shows the King donned in an elaborate gown reminiscent of his contemporary, the Ottoman ruler, Sultan Süleyman the Magnificent (1520-1556), except for the headgear. In Samuel Pepys' diary, he recounts visiting Sir Phillip Howard and finding him dressed 'in a gown and turban like a Turk'. Commerce between the Eastern and Western world during this period laid open the floodgate of Islamic cultural influence in music, philosophy, architecture, theatre, and military ideas.

We must also not forget that the works of renowned Greek philosophers, which laid the foundation to Western thought and knowledge systems, would have been lost to the world at large if not for Islamic scholars in the ninth and tenth centuries. It was in Baghdad that Caliph Harun al-Rashid (763/6-809) set up the House of Wisdom, devoted to the preservation of knowledge. Having receded into the barrenness of time, its magnificent edifice must be imagined. The walls would have been decorated with intricate Islamic calligraphy and geometric patterns, seamlessly interlaced by dazzling ornaments. The grand gothic doors would have been opened to weary minds coming to quench their thirst for knowledge. Scholars and adventurers alike would have agitated over all manner of questions pertaining to the ancient world and ultimately the origin and purpose of humankind. Under the direction of Caliph Abdallah al-Mamun (786-833), son of Harun al-Rashid, the works of Aristotle, Plato, Pythagoras, Hippocrates, Euclid, Galen and Plotinus were first translated into Arabic before making their way into Latin. It was in this sepulchre of knowledge that the notion that the earth revolved around the sun, and not vice versa, was first conceived by the translator and philosopher Ibn Qurra. Six centuries after Ibn Qurra's postulation, Nicolaus Copernicus (1473-1543) made a similar observation. One wonders whether the latter ever stumbled on the work of the former. It is certainly difficult to prove this assertion given that the House of Wisdom was destroyed during the invasion of Baghdad by Mongol forces under the leadership of Hulagu Khan in 1258. The sacking of Baghdad delivered a fatal blow from which the Islamic world never fully recovered.

By the eighteenth century, as trade between the East and West deepened, resulting in cultural exchanges on both side, the Islamic world increasingly won the fascination and interest of Western observers. This engagement was accompanied by an emerging mode of thinking about the Islamic world, now referred to as Orientalism. In his ground-breaking monograph, Edward Said explains that Orientalism served as an ideological criterion, a lens, praxis, or a way to deal with the otherness of Eastern cultures, their customs, beliefs and traditions. From philosophers' couches to the bureaus of colonial administrators and the studios of artists and writers, the 'Orient' was given form, meaning and presence. Held under the Western gaze, the Orient could only emerge as its polar opposite, arousing intense cravings for the exotic. At worst, Orientalism stirred up deep fears and a macabre anticipation for Armageddon. In the works of artists and writers throughout the eighteenth and twentieth centuries, the presence of the Muslim was reconfigured within a shifting tableau. The image that materialises is more of an inchoate collage of fantastical imaginings. From the works of Eugène Delacroix, Gustave Flaubert, Benjamin Disraeli, Rudyard Kipling and EM Forster, the Muslim is delivered as a temptress, a beguiling Adonis, a royal *file de joie*, and last, but not the least, an unruly urchin of terror. The litany of representation is too broad and constantly altering to build a coherent picture.

Said's critique has been met with resounding applause and has offered a subsequent generation of cultural critics a fitting language to articulate Western imperialism and the construction of 'the native'. Though profound, rich and dense in its analysis, *Orientalism* left out the role of the market in shaping a cultural economy of Otherness. The representations of the Orient were not mere facsimiles of white self-gratification, designed to prop up a Western sense of cultural superiority. On the contrary, they were also facilitated by the expanding capitalist economy, which played a crucial role in engineering consumer tastes and sensibilities and facilitating a supply chain of Orientalist aesthetics.

But whilst projections of the Orient vary, one thing has endured – the fractured visage of the Muslim, vast but disembodied, yet now reducible to the phenomenon of multiculturalism. In recent times, multiculturalism – as an ideology and practice – has exploded from the oratory of politicians and pages of newspaper tabloids, providing an ideal type through which the Muslim is to be seized upon, captured, defined and understood. Practices of multiculturalism within the mainstream border on farce, or damp squib, if you ask me. The so-called celebration of diverse cultures, if examined closely, gradually descends into a performance of exoticism. For multiculturalism, irrespective of the moral grandstanding of the state, does not in any way reflect the daily confluence of diverse cultures, blending, and intermingling in the free-flowing pools of understanding, reconciliation and unity. Rather, it is erected on the national theatres as a cultural spectacle, circumscribed to Western desires, tastes and sensibilities. Multiculturalism is acceptable so far as it conforms to the norm, even within the realm of fantasy. The celebration of Diwali, the Hindu festival of lights, must always involve a troupe of Indian women dressed in traditional garb, gyrating to public delight. This suggests that the city must once again be graced with native sexuality for the benefit of subsequent generations, who no longer have the Empire at their disposal. Africa Day can be summed up by a cacophony of colours and sounds, all too insufferable to your average UKIP voter hankering after a post-Brexit, white utopia. Black History Month is one of the very rare moments when

debates on race do not have to placate white discomfort. Even this cannot
be guaranteed for long, as the cries of 'what about White History Month'
and 'don't white lives matter, too' get louder and louder each year.

This is not to say that the celebration of cultural diversity on a national
scale is completely bonkers, but that national expressions and
performances of multiculturalism have engendered within racial minorities
a double consciousness, whereby they tend to emphasise and showcase
cultural difference by accentuating on their otherness. Peculiarly, though,
this otherness must correspond to Western stereotypes of the Other. One
can definitely concede that cultural diversity takes on a form of negotiation
and compromise between dominant and minority groups. It would,
however, be facetious to conclude that both groups have the same level of
agency. And thus, the outcome of this interaction privileges cultural equity.
Multiculturalism in Britain today is truly a wholesale enterprise of
internalised exoticism, wherein minority cultures unwittingly display their
constant otherness. This is largely because the ubiquitous presence of the
foreboding white gaze is intimately felt – what Malcolm X characterised
as the Man. Under the watch of the Man, Muslims are declared a fixed
nation, floating in some amorphous ether and timeless space. Irrespective
of their place of birth, cultural and social orientation, or political
affiliation, be they Pakistani, Afghan, or Iranian, or British, Conservative,
Liberal, or Fascist, it all balls down to their Muslimness. As if being a
Muslim underlies a singular essence of being. Louis Armstrong once sang,
'My only sin is in my face – what did I do to be so black and blue?' Muslims
could equally squall that their only transgression is their faith.

This brings us back to the question of the representation of Muslim
culture in the mainstream. Under the guise of multiculturalism and
inclusivity, portrayals of Muslims have mainly centred on the woman in
hijab. The hijabi is to be afforded the same freedom accorded to the
modern-day, white Western woman, except that the former must offer her
struggles as a political sideshow to Western liberal propaganda in order to
be worthy of her new-found freedom. She must prove that she is like the
Western woman in many senses. For starters, she must be fair of
complexion, and her public appearances must make a statement on
Muslim-hood. In this sense, she is to carry the burden of representing the
deeply diverse and heterogeneous Muslim communities and cultures in the

West. To achieve this, she would have to play the role of the good immigrant and comply with the dominant narrative of the docile, oppressed Muslim woman, waiting to be saved by the West. She would also have to come to accept that Western culture is not the enemy but her liberator. The complete absence of the Muslim man in contemporary depictions of Muslims in the arts and media renders her free game for the instrument of Western propaganda. For the Muslim man in dominant visual representation has his rightful place in medievalesque scenes of barbarism, war and terror. The Muslim woman's culture and aesthetics must be stripped of any religious or political connotations that detract from the narrative of secularisation. Any political message associated with the hijab must be seen through the prism of the Western gaze. In short, the hijabi is to be apprehended and remanufactured for mass consumption.

In this vein, multi-national corporations such as Nike, Pepsi and others have come to see the value in appropriating the hijab for financial gains. They claim it is to capture an emerging market and to put diversity on the top of their agenda. On a superficial level, this may ring true, but it is not just a forgotten demographic that they hope to reach. Even if we were to cut them some slack and assume good intentions, such depictions unconsciously produce narratives about Muslim women subjectivities that reveal a great deal about Western attitudes towards Muslims in general. The hijab in Western political discourse is loaded with so much meaning. Since the invasion of Iraq, it has become almost impossible to speak of Muslims and Muslim culture without mentioning the hijab. It has become a site of ideological warfare, a re-arming of the Empire. Muslim women have been caught in crossfire, with their bodies to be served as spoils of war for the victor. No wonder the fair hijabi must be delectably served to Western audiences as an icon of the sublime and beautiful. Whilst several European countries have banned the niqab and burka on the basis of national security, it is only a matter of time that the hijab is dragged into the ongoing fray of bullish Trumpism and Western ethno-nationalism.

Within the Muslim community as well, the hijab possesses multiple meanings. It is multivocal, polysemic and performs different functions. It forms part of the ongoing discursive tensions on faith, culture and tradition in a postmodern era. To treat the hijab in such a wanton fashion by distancing it from deep political, social and cultural concerns, for the sole purpose of appeasing white fear of the veiled Muslim, reveals a casual disdain for Islam within Western society.

It would be absurd, however, to suggest that the commodification of Muslim cultural aesthetics and fashion stems solely from Western domination of Eastern cultures. The tenacity of the hijab in confronting mainstream prejudice as a declaration of self-determination suggests that convergence between the hijab and the market cannot be explained away through conventional socialist or anti-capitalist paradigms. Neither is it only a case of bad corporations appropriating Muslim fashion for gains – that would be too simplistic and reductive. The reality as usual lies somewhere in the middle. After all, the debate on hijab in mainstream media has, for a long time, featured Baby Boomers and Generation X, in the form of writers, academics and other odd mixes of media personalities. Yasmin Alibhai-Brown, a British Muslim journalist, fervently condemns the hijab and all the claptrap that goes along with it. She writes in her book, *Refusing the Veil*, 'Cloaks, scarves and masks degrade women by degrading them primarily as sexual creatures but severely controlled ones.'

To her dismay a new, fresh, bold and vibrant millennial generation, unashamedly British, brazenly Muslim and downright fashionable are rocking the hijab with remarkable aplomb. You will certainly not catch them on mainstream media, for these Instagram glams prefer to tell their own stories rather than to be worked into someone's else prime-time set. They have their own YouTube channels and some are bloggers and vloggers. For these modest fashion vloggers, the hijab takes on multiple interpretations – for some, it is a religious symbol of modesty, for others a cultural expression, and some consider it to be a vehicle of self -expression. Their hijabs come in a range of intricate styles, designs and dazzling colours, highlighting its multivalent function and conflicting meaning. This is where fashion meets religion, coolness finds modesty, and piety embraces self-emancipation – express your Self!

As we are already aware, however, not all Muslims wear the hijab. The former Miss Universe contestant for Great Britain, Muna Jama, a British Somali, explains in an interview with *Glamour* magazine, 'when the media focuses so much on those who wear the hijab, they can forget the diversity of thought among Muslim women. I love wearing a headscarf on certain days and, at other times, practice my modesty entirely differently. That may be wearing a kaftan, owning the catwalk at Modest Fashion Weeks around the world or simply by being a considerate and compassionate person.' Back in 2017, Jama caused a sensation by refusing to wear a bikini at the finals, opting for a kaftan.

Jama makes a good point, since the homogeneous representation of Muslim culture in the media and arts further reinforces the psychological conflict of being and belonging within the Muslim community. After all, if the Muslim in the state's multicultural vision is really British, the hijab would not be seized upon as the singular expression of Muslim identity. So, if these multimillion dollar corporations are keen on representing diversity in their marketing campaigns, then the representation of the plurality of cultures and genders that constitute Muslim identity is a healthy start. Historically, Muslim fashion and aesthetics have been integrated into Western styles, ironically with very little appreciation for Muslim or Islamic philosophical traditions. Even the concept of modest fashion, deeply rooted in Islamic thought, has entered into high fashion not as a Muslim contribution to the Western world of fashion, but a Western discovery of nouveau couture. It's like the locating of Lake Victoria by David Livingstone – his 'discovery' was something long known and referred to by the Ndebele people as Tokaleya Tonga: Mosi-oa-Tunya, (The Smoke that Thunders). Livingstone's bland designation – Victoria – is what sticks in popular memory. For now, it seems that the absorption of Muslim style and fashion in the West is a function of the commodification of the exotic as part of some national programme for cultural domestication. To borrow from Shakespeare: it's about the taming of the barbarian.

SKIN SHADES

Yovanka Paquete Perdigao

As a child growing up in Dakar, Senegal, I remember playing a guessing game with my cousins. Whenever we saw light-skinned women in the street, in telenovelas, or in movies, we always looked attentively at their elbows, knees and hands. If any of these body parts were distinctly darker than their overall complexion, one of us who would call it for what was: *khessel*. In other parts of the world, they simply call it skin lightening.

A phenomenon that is as old as the advent of colonialism, skin lightening is a multi-billion-dollar beauty industry that persists in many parts of the world, despite its serious health implications. Indeed, there is a long list of side effects of using skin lightening products: permanent skin bleaching, thinning of the skin, uneven colour loss leading to a blotchy appearance, redness and intense irritation, dark grey spots; skin cancer, acne, increase in appetite and weight gain, osteoporosis, neurological and kidney damage due to high mercury levels, psychiatric disorders, asthma, liver damage, and severe birth defects in children born to mothers who abuse these creams. However, that has not stopped many women but also men from going to great lengths to acquire lightening products. In Ghana, some women are even using pills to lighten their unborn children's skin colour. Whilst many may frown upon such practices, they are very common and pervasive. Skin lightening is deeply embedded in the historical legacy of colonialism and colourism, or shadeism, uncomfortable words that many are reluctant to acknowledge, let alone discuss. I still remember, in my last year of undergraduate study, becoming irate when a fellow Caucasian student dismissed skin lightening as just another trend, like tanning. He refused to see the difference between the two, despite me pointing out that no people of colour had colonised and brutally ruled Caucasian people and installed a meritocracy based on skin colour. It is precisely within European colonialism that the obsession with skin lightening began.

Colonial exploitation often had elements of slavery or forced labour. Beyond political and territorial control, the colonisers had to find a way to assert and maintain their dominance over the people they subjugated. Western colonialism employed a variety of tools to capture minds and souls and instil shame and erase traditional practices and other religions of the people they colonised. One instrument in this arsenal was the use of interracial relationships to cement alliances. 'The relationships with local women,' writes Carina Ray, the historian of Africa, 'were not merely a matter of basic survival, they also allowed European men to cement profitable commercial and political alliances with local families, whose social, political and trade networks were opened only to trusted strangers whose loyalty could be assured.' Interracial relationships resulted in children of mixed heritage that could not be ignored by colonial powers. These children came to have a variety of names, such as Métis, half-caste, mixed-raced or mulatto. Interestingly the latter is used both in Portuguese and Spanish speaking countries and is believed to be derived from the Galician word *mula*, meaning mule – the hybrid offspring of a horse and a donkey. A mule is sterile – it cannot reproduce unless paired with a purebred. To me, this is an interesting but tragic irony that reflects the colonial perspective on interracial relationships and children of mixed heritage. Such relationships might have been arranged or sought after, but the truth was that such unions were seen unfavourably by colonial societies and their fruits virulently regarded as a travesty that did not belong in civilised white society.

For colonial societies to survive in this new racial set-up, however, a fresh discourse had to emerge that reflected this emerging 'diversity'. Children of mixed heritage were conceived to be the perfect intermediaries – historically known as 'middlemen' – between 'rational man' and 'irrational man', between civilised and uncivilised. They had the insidious blood of their darker parent, 'tempered' by the white man's blood, therefore were superior to their jezebel mothers who had brought them into this world, or the fathers who had lingered too long in a white woman's garden. They began to fulfil the roles that were too elevated for their darker skin counterparts but too lowly for whites, such as working in massa's house or low-ranking colonial administrative stations.

Western colonialism enshrined colourism by dividing the colonised, the colonisers and 'middlemen' in categories within a racial system often codified within colonial legislation. This meant that for many colonised people, skin tone truly was the determinant of one's opportunities in life. For example, in Senegal, many female descendants of Senegalese women and white colonial officers enjoyed a relatively comfortable life because of their skin colour, compared to their darker skin counterparts. These women came to be known as the Signares. They dominated Senegalese history and imagination for decades for their cunning beauty and savvy in controlling trade networks in Saint-Louis, Rufisque, and the infamous island Gorée, the largest slave-trading centre on the African coast from the fifteenth to the nineteenth centuries. The Signares even exerted influence in the English, Portuguese and French courts. Their success and riches were largely due to their racial ambiguity and their ability to use their 'middlemen' position to move through colonial societies unrestricted by the rules that suffocated others of darker skin tone.

It is no surprise that in many postcolonial countries, skin tones are often associated with power. As Neha Mishra, a legal scholar, and Ronald Hall, a professor of social work, point out in relation to India, 'being subject to a succession of white(ish) overlords has long associated light skin with power, status and desirability among Indians. Today, the contempt for brown skin is embraced by both the ruling class and lower castes, and reinforced daily by beauty magazine covers that feature almost exclusively Caucasian, often foreign, models'.

In her edited volume, *Color Matters: Skin Tone Bias and the Myth of a Postracial America*, Kimberly Jade Norwood reveals that in African continent alone, the following proportions of the population regularly use skin-whitening products – 77 per cent of Nigerian women; 60 per cent of Zambian women between the ages of 30 and 39; 59 per cent of Togolese people; 50 to 60 per cent of adult Ghanaian women; 52 per cent of women in Bamako, Mali; and 35 per cent of people in Pretoria, South Africa. This is hardly a surprise when beauty adverts constantly bombard us with ideas of fair skin as beautiful, with celebrities endorsing these harmful campaigns. In Nigeria, pop star Dencia was lambasted for launching a skin cream called Whitenicious in 2014 – the promotional pictures of her showed a jaw dropping transformation of her skin to almost-white. The advert by Dove shared in October 2017 is another example, showing a black woman appearing to become white after using the brand's lotion. In

2011, Dove had another advert of three women, in progressive paler order, standing in towers under the labels 'before' and 'after', suggesting that the use of Dove products ensured lighter skin, or luminous skin, as they put it. While Dove apologised and drew much praise for its other campaigns with 'real women', its parent company is Unilever, which also owns Fair & Lovely, a company that produces skin whitening products in India. Many Bollywood actors have been featured in high-profile ad campaigns for skin lightening cosmetics, such as Vidya Balan, Shahid Kapoor, Deepika Padukone, Sidharth Malhotra, Sonam Kapoor, and Shah Rukh Khan.

As our societies and economies have become consumer led, more women and men are prepared to go to great lengths to alter their physical appearance. According to the anti-racist activist and feminist sociologist Meeta Jha:

> Eurocentic beauty ideals, valorised in beauty pageants and Disney films, exer-
> cise social control over female bodies generating fantasies, inspiration, injury
> and inequality. Women can train or approximate this beauty ideal only if they
> can mould, sculpt, manipulate, and reshape their body according to the cultur-
> ally validated norms.

The belief that is being sold is that achieving such beauty ideals is only possible through consumer practices, such as more clothes, more skincare products, more gym memberships, trips to the hairdresser and, for those willing to go all the way, surgery. The rise of the latter has increasingly concerned feminist thinkers, such as Jha, who have throughout the years called this a 'gendered psychological and physical health epidemic'. Women's bodies have historically been a site of violence controlled by religion, and national and political institutions. Beauty companies survive on creating illusions of what beauty ought to be and, through patriarchy and capitalism, enforce these ideals and profit from them by driving women to succumb to them. Take, for example, razors designed for women in America. Jean-Jacques Perret designed the first real straight razor for men in the 1770s, but it could also be used by women. It was in the 1800s that a safer razor was created by King Camp Gillette – in 1915 Gillette created the Milady Décolleté and launched the campaign 'The First Great Anti-Underarm Hair Campaign'. This advertisement campaign suggested to women that armpit hair was unattractive, but with Milady Décolleté they were one step closer to being beautiful. Even fashion magazines were claiming bare underarms to be a necessity, as shown by an ad in *Harper's Bazaar* in 1915. The 1940s and 1950s were another turning point where women were encouraged to shave their legs. With World War II at the door of American women, there was a shortage of nylon, meaning women couldn't wear stockings and had to go bare-legged. This further encouraged women to shave their legs in order to be deemed socially acceptable. Shaving one's armpits and legs was never a necessity but was conceived to be so in order to drive sales, with a dose of the politics of respectability.

In the Muslim world, beauty is, like in the West, just another capitalist business that is deeply rooted in racism, class, ethnicity, and caste. Those who possess fair skin and Eurocentric features are usually the most prominent ones to represent the Muslim world and to receive preferential treatment. Consequently, there is a prevalent negative view towards those who are more melanin-rich. Jha's argument remains as true in many Muslim contexts as in the West, when she maintains that:

> The white standard of beauty created a hierarchy of humanness with Europeans at the top of racial hierarchy.... The institutionalisation of Eurocentric, white beauty norms of skin colour, body size, shape, hair texture, physiognomy, and facial features in beauty pageants the world over has spawned a global beauty industry devoted to skin lightening, skin-bleaching creams, corrective cosmetic surgery, dieting, and fashion.

The Muslim beauty industry is also plagued by such colour bias. In 2017, Dubai Modest Fashion Week (DMFW) only invited one black model, Halima Aden, who is the first hijabi model to be featured on *Vogue*, and one influential black blogger, Chinutay. This sparked an online fury with prominent black Muslim beauty and fashion bloggers becoming vocal about the lack of representation in the Muslim beauty industry and the intra-Muslim discrimination they faced. On her YouTube channel, beauty blogger Shahd Batal suggested that the lack diversity in the DMWF was simply a reflection of the Muslim beauty industry's attitude to black people. Many Muslim spaces were inherently racist, she said, despite profiting from the labour and success of prominent black Muslim personalities. Amidst this controversy, British black Muslim Najwa created the hashtag #BlackMuslimahExcellence. Black Muslim women around the world joined in, posting their pictures on Twitter and showcasing black beauty, excellence, and refusal to conform to the establishment's anti-black attitude. Indeed, looking through the hashtag, black Muslims are cognisant of the Muslim world being partial to fair skin and more European-like facial features, and are aware of their own invisibility in this world.

The message perpetuated by the Muslim beauty industry seems to be that to be a Muslim excludes anyone of a darker skin tone. It is then no surprise that in African, Arab, and South-Asian communities, skin lightening products are a huge business and representation of darker skinned people is scarce. People of darker skin are looked down upon, marginalised, and even enslaved.

In Arabic, the word *abd* is frequently used to describe African and dark-skinned people but it also means 'slave'. This is despite the fact that a significant part of the African continent speaks Arabic and shares many traditions, customs and history with the Middle East. Even within the Middle East, dark-skinned Arabs are at the mercy of social and institutional racism. Hanna-Johara Dokal writes of the bias she has faced as a Yemeni:

> When I have had the opportunity to explain my Yemeni heritage, I have been met with grunts and dismissals because 'Yemeni' is the wrong type of Arab to be. It is the seventh poorest country in the world and many inhabitants are dark-skinned with coarse, curly hair. The Al-Akhdam tribe of Yemen are deemed the lowest class, because they are black. This is not the Arab to be in the Arab world…. My grandfather often tells the story of how he was chosen to be the worker out of his twelve siblings. He was not the eldest, the strongest or the dimmest; he was, however, the darkest. He told of how he often helped his brothers with their homework even though he had not been allowed to attend school, but they had. He had instead been sent out to work for the family although he showed much academic promise.

Similar views and treatments of dark-skinned people can be observed in African Muslim communities. Slavery is still a vivid reality in Mauritania, where descendants of black Africans captured during historical slave raids are called Haratin and often serve as slaves to the lighter-skinned Berbers or mixed Berber-Arabs. Mauritania was the last country in the world to abolish slavery in 1981 but had no laws enshrined to offer the Haratin people protection. It was only in 2007, under much scrutiny from the international community, that Mauritania passed a law that allowed slaveholders to be prosecuted. But in a country ravaged by corruption and abuse of power, many slaveholders are not brought to justice. The Global Slavery Index estimated in 2015 that there were 43,000 slaves in Mauritania and SOS Slavery believes that the more accurate number would be 600,000. Slavery in Mauritania is one of the most severe for many reasons – the majority of slaves are illiterate and poor; they depend on masters to provide them food and clothing; and it is difficult for many to run away. Because of these factors and more, the Haratin have ingrained the idea that their destiny is one of servitude. The government has continued throughout the years to turn a blind eye, subverting any criticism as manipulations by the West.

Somalia, which has been plagued by civil unrest, is one of the few countries in Africa that is ethnically homogenous and united mostly by Islam. The root of conflict in Somalia has sometimes been attributed to its clan system. Somalis are divided into various clan groupings, brought together by important kinship ties that play a central part in Somali culture and politics. Belonging to a clan is key, as this represents the highest kinship level – some clans even own territorial properties and are typically led by a clan-head or Sultan. The northern clans have Arab ancestry and tend to be fairer, with Middle Eastern or Eurocentric features, whereas southern clans have more prominent African ancestry and tend to be darker. Consequently, the northern clans dominated Somalia prior to its disintegration and despised the southern tribes who had ancestry that was mixed with African slaves from the Arab slave trade.

More recently, in October 2017, the maltreatment of darker skinned people has been brought into sharper focus in Libya. Black migrants attempting to cross to Europe often have to make the journey through Libya. Many of them were cheated or captured by Arab Libyans with the nefarious intentions of selling them to slavery. A report by CNN found that thousands of people were thrown in detention centres, abused, and sold for as little as US$400. It is no coincidence that the slave traders were of Arabic descent and whiter skin, and those trafficked of darker skin tone.

The younger generation have started to push back against toxic beauty standards and are campaigning against the use of skin lightening products. Poet Aranya Johar went viral for her YouTube video, 'A Brown Girl's Guide to Beauty', reaching 1.5 million views. Her spoken-word poetry was a call to arms to reject Eurocentric beauty standards, with lines like 'forget Snow White, say hello to chocolate brown; I'll write my own fairy-tale'.

More women of colour are now campaigning against the beauty industry that encourages this harmful discourse. In India in 2012, the brand Clean & Dry began advertising for a new wash to lighten women's genitals with an ad comparing vaginas with coffee. The ad caused major controversy, with feminist activists calling for the Advertising Standards Council of India to intervene. Ultimately, they issued guidelines stating that 'ads should not reinforce negative social stereotyping on the basis of skin colour' or 'portray people with darker skin [as] inferior, or unsuccessful in any aspect of life particularly in relation to being attractive to the opposite sex'.

The entertainment industry in India has also begun to change its stance towards skin lightening products. Bollywood actress Nandita Das, unlike many of her peers, has been actively campaigning against the skin bleaching industry and is the face of the Dark is Beautiful campaign, launched in 2009 by Women of Worth. In an interview with the International Women's Media Foundation, she stated that the South Asian media always emphasise her skin tone by using words such 'the dark and dusky actress'. Since becoming a rising star in the industry, she faced pressure to lighten her skin or play lower-caste roles. Actress Priyanka Chopra revealed in an interview with *Glamour* magazine that she once used lightening creams and was in a commercial for a brand but quickly regretted it:

> When I was an actor, around my early 20s, I did a commercial for a skin-lightening cream. I was playing that girl with insecurities. And when I saw it, I was like, 'Oh shit. What did I do?' And I started talking about being proud of the way I looked. I actually really like my skin tone.

In neighbouring Pakistan, Fatima Lodhi launched the country's first anti-colourism movement, Dark is Divine, and visits schools to raise awareness amongst the younger generations about skin-colour discrimination and self-esteem issues. In the African continent, huge debates have been sparked in protest at celebrity endorsements of skin-bleaching products and bold advertisements by cosmetics companies. In Senegal, a cosmetic company had a high-profile campaign for a new cream called 'Khess Petch', or 'all white' in the local language Wolof. This gave rise to a movement called

'Nuul Kukk' which means 'all black', prompting campaigners to put up their own posters all over Dakar. Senegalese celebrities lent their support, such as rapper Keyti, the stylist Dior Lo, and women's rights activist Kiné-Fatim Diop. And in the United States, a group of students launched an Instagram campaign called #unfairandlovely which featured darker-skinned people sharing their pictures and rejecting colourism.

Beauty is truly skin deep. But until we decolonise our minds and beauty aesthetics, skin bleaching will remain an option in stores around the world.

NOSE JOBS, IRANIAN STYLE

Nima Nasseri

Seven days following his surgery, Parsa was preparing to remove his nose bandages. He had undergone a nose job, following his mother, sister, two aunts and his cousins, thereby continuing the family tradition of cosmetic surgery. He said, 'Fifteen years ago, if a man or a boy would have had a nose job, everyone would have thought that there was something wrong with him and they would laugh at him and tease him, but now it's very normal. Lots of boys and men are having their noses done.' Parsa, an engineering student with a rich father involved in construction, then told me about his friend Saman who works in a cosmetic and makeup shop in a busy area of central Tehran. Saman had his nose job last year and had to sell his car in order to pay for the surgery. His main motivation, Parsa explained, was to improve his appearance and to attract more customers. 'Every day he has to deal with a lot of women and girls coming to him for cosmetic products. That's why he has to look good and stylish.'

Later that day, in the consulting room, Parsa's consultant, Dr Mahmoud, highlighted the point that beauty standards in Iran have shifted towards 'Western' ideals. 'Iranians are naturally very beautiful. They have very strong facial features like strong cheekbones, thick arched eyebrows and beautiful almond shaped eyes, but the size of the nose mostly lets them down,' he said, grinning. Asked about men's cosmetic surgery, Dr Mahmoud explained that in comparison to fifteen to twenty years ago, men have become much more preoccupied by their looks. They choose to have cosmetic surgery for many reasons but one thing for sure is the increased influence of social media on men's perceptions of their appearance and how they look. A lot of boys and men are taking nice pictures of themselves and sharing them on social media outlets such as Facebook and Instagram. Therefore, they are constantly feeling the pressure to look good. 'Cosmetic surgery has also become a fashion for many boys who compete against each other over girls or middle-aged men trying to keep up with their younger wives or girlfriends,' said Dr Mahmoud, adding that in current Iranian society, being beautiful has become a value – undertaking cosmetic surgery has therefore become a priority in life for both sexes. Dr Mahmoud said he mainly does four operations (ear, nose, face lifts and eyelids) and his calendar is full for the whole year. But what's remarkable is that increasingly his patients are Iranian men. 'You must have thought a country that is governed by Islamic ruling and principles would consider such actions as an unnecessary act and would disapprove and condemn cosmetic surgery, especially for men, as a whole. Not so.'

Dr Mahmoud has a point. On the surface, one would think that cosmetic surgery, mostly viewed as materialistic and superficial, would be incompatible with Islam, often portrayed as a proactive force for spiritualism and divinity. But Iran, a Muslim country, is not only home to various surgical interventions such as sex reassignment, in vitro fertilisation, sterilisation, and the transplantation and selling of organs, but cosmetic procedures are also commonly accepted and sometimes considered to be essential. As implied by the Islamic jurists interviewed by Marzieh Kaivanara during her ethnographic fieldwork in Tehran, it seems that being beautiful is not wrong for women but rather a necessity within their relationships, or towards marriage or future careers, or both. Women's natural beauty is admired and those who do not aim to 'rectify' their physical 'faults' using different cosmetic procedures are harshly criticised.

The Rhinology Research Society of Iran carried out joint research with Johns Hopkins University in the US which demonstrated that the rate of nose jobs per capita in Iran is seven times that in the US. According to a report in the reformist *Etemad* newspaper, published in Tehran, more than 200,000 Iranians have cosmetic surgery each year to reduce the size of their noses. This is astounding for a self-proclaimed Islamic Republic and, according to a story in *The Guardian* in 2013, it is not only limited to upper class and wealthy people but also many office workers, university students, shop keepers, and even teenagers who choose to spend their savings or risk going into debt for such procedures. For foreign media outlets, such an increase in demand for cosmetic surgery in Iran is very surprising and unusual – how could this be happening in a country that is supposedly governed by Islamic rules and whose leaders are mostly hostile towards 'Western' culture? Anything that refers to 'Western culture', including beauty operations, is not supposed to be advertised on public billboards or promoted on national state-run television. As a result, it is mostly through social media and the illegal, but extensively consumed, satellite channels that the latest surgical technologies and 'Western' ideals of beauty are promoted and advertised.

Nose jobs aside, the push for physical beautification amongst men and women in the Islamic Republic has made Iran one of the leading countries in the world with regards to plastic surgery. Such cosmetic procedures are not only limited to the capital, Tehran. Some of the biggest beauty clinics and hospitals for cosmetic surgery are in Mashhad, the country's second largest and most important religious city, as well as in other more cosmopolitan cities such as Isfahan and Shiraz. The majority of clients are women, but men's interest in such practices has increased greatly in recent years. Men account for about one third of all cosmetic operations undertaken in Iran which, in comparison to the rest of the world where men share the total cosmetic surgeries of fifteen per cent, is a relatively high proportion. According to *Hamshahri Online*, the online version of the Iranian daily *Hamshahri,* cosmetic surgery in the Islamic Republic of Iran is as common as it is in Brazil. Seeing Iran listed among the countries with the highest number of cosmetic surgeries including Brazil, in which public bodily display is endorsed and perceived as a 'right', is remarkable. In Iran, undergoing cosmetic surgery is not just about gaining beauty. Stories about young Iranians placing plasters on their noses without even having a nose job or keeping the bandages on for longer than required following surgery suggests that cosmetic surgery is considered a socially valued procedure. To many Iranians, such display makes perfect sense as it demonstrates their good financial position which, for many, is preferable to having a naturally small nose.

While laws in Iran forbid any reference to eroticism, news of a well-known British porn actress from Essex, who travelled to the Iranian capital Tehran in 2016 for a nose job, sparked controversy on social media and amongst Iranian officials. The actress revealed her trip with a photograph of herself on Instagram in the back of a taxi wearing a hijab (headscarf), worn Iranian style. 'My nose was not straight and they are the best in the world in nose surgery. I had my nose done,' she wrote. What's amusing about her photo is that although her eyes are hidden behind sunglasses with a scarf partially covering her blond hair, she looks a lot like Tehranian 'hot chicks', with her small straight nose, thick and full eyebrows, a tanned skin-tone that matches her blonde straightened hair, and lips that have been augmented, puffed and enhanced with shiny lipstick. Many Iranians commented on the photo, pointing out the fact that they were unable to distinguish her from glamorous women on Tehran's streets. A social media user known as Professor Balthazar posted: 'We have so many girls with a porn-star look in Tehran. We missed that a real porn star literally came to Iran.' Another user, Dom Iman, tweeted: 'A porn star travelling to Iran is one of the benefits of nuclear deal between Iran and the West.' Her post received thousands of comments and the story proved particularly popular on Farsi chat apps such as Telegram. What was most surprising for many on social media was how she had managed to get a visa for Iran.

In an interview with the online magazine *Cairo Scene*, the porn star praised the quality of cosmetic work being done in Iran. 'It's very common for models to visit Iran for surgery, especially facial, as they do it the best,' she said. In fact, she may just be one of many taking advantage of the country's low-cost cosmetic surgery, with the cost of a nose job in Iran being around sixty per cent cheaper than in the UK. Furthermore, due to the high publicity of this case and the extreme reaction of the conservative parties and hardliners, the foreign ministry was forced to defend its decision on granting a visa to a British porn star. The Iranian Deputy Foreign Minister Hassan Qashqavi explained that it was exactly because of the high moral standards of the Islamic republic that officials had not known who the porn star was. 'Our colleagues are not supposed to know that kind of women. It would be counterproductive if they did.'

This is not the first time that social media debate has been provoked by such reports from Iran, nor will it be the last. Although there are a lot of humorous and paradoxical reactions aimed at both men and women who have had cosmetic surgeries, beauty plays a highly significant role in all aspects of daily life. Those deemed less attractive often find themselves disregarded and penalised for not taking better care of themselves or their appearance. For instance, Iran's education department sparked anger online after publishing a long list of requirements for incoming teachers, apparently prohibiting 'ugly' people from entering the profession. The list published by the *Fars* news agency excludes individuals with a wide range of illnesses (including female infertility, cancer, and bladder stones) but also bans people from teaching based on their physical appearance. Individuals with severe acne, burn marks, unsightly moles, and those with fewer than twenty teeth are among those prohibited by the Ministry of Education. Cross-eyed people and women with facial hair also fail to qualify. Yet, since teaching is referred to as a highly respectable career and often described as 'the job of Prophets' by the administrators of the Islamic regime, one would expect less emphasis to be placed on the physical appearance and traits for those wishing to become teachers and more importance on other teaching criteria such as personal experience, knowledge and professionalism. Iranian journalist Omid Memarian pointed out that under such restrictions, the prominent physicist Stephen Hawking would not have been able to get a teaching job in Iran. Meanwhile, journalist Sara Omatal called the measures a 'definitive violation of basic human rights'. After some criticism on social media, a special assistant to President Hassan Rouhani said the matter would be investigated. Such policies are just a few examples of the many laws that marginalise those who do not fit within accepted norms, are considered physically unattractive, or do not follow conventional social standards.

Many of the men and women I spoke to agreed that it is natural for women to be concerned about their appearance and beauty. This can be seen by the growing number of beauty parlours and shops and the large-scale import and use of cosmetic products, in addition to the increasing number of practitioners and plastic surgery clinics around the country. Sara, a 26-year-old student, explained that you have to be attractive in order to get good jobs and have better salaries. She declared, 'Being pretty attracts money while being unattractive inclines you more towards hardship.' Furthermore, surgery for women can be a response to the restrictive rules of compulsory hijab. Since in Iran women are not allowed to display most of their bodies, hair styles or tattoos, what has become prominent is their faces, the only body part they can openly display in public. Sahar and Samira, two sisters from north Tehran, both working as freelance artists, both complained that the Iranian regime won't let them show their beauty. 'It's only natural to want to attract attention using a striking figure and gorgeous hair and skin … but wearing the hijab does not permit that. As a result, we have no choice but to display our "art" on our faces,' said Sahar, the older sister.

The majority of people I spoke to were not that committed to Islamic piety, including the observance of hijab. This, however, does not mean that religious people don't opt for cosmetic surgery. Sara, the 26-year old student, comes from a religious family that supported her decision to have a nose job. She explained that encouragement from her friends and family was one of the main factors that convinced her to go through with cosmetic surgery.

Similar to many other social and cultural changes in Iran, such increasing trends towards improving physical appearance can be explained in what the sociologist Asef Bayat refers to as 'quiet encroachment'. The notion of quiet encroachment illustrates the silent, protracted, but pervasive advancement of ordinary people on the propertied, powerful, or the public, in order to change their lives and social values. Their advancement is marked by quiet, mainly atomised and long-lasting mobilisation with periodic collective action – open and fleeting struggles without apparent leadership, ideology, or structured organisation. Quiet encroachment takes advantage of spaces that authoritarian states cannot fully control. Within these spaces, a different public order, which is mostly outside the state-controlled sphere of formal politics, is established by the citizens. Quiet encroachment is not centrally organised and cannot be considered a social movement, thus Bayat refers to it as a constellation of social 'non-movements'. Overall, a non-movement refers to the united actions of people who do not consciously organise collectively. For instance, the Iranian people's obsession with physical beauty and the consequently large number of people (religious and non-religious) opting for cosmetic procedures has had the effect of normalising and legitimising behaviours that are otherwise deemed illegitimate or wrong. Although such acts of physical beautification are contentious and against the ethics of the Islamic regime, the large number of people opting for such procedures has weakened the effective governmentality of the state machinery. This can push the regime towards more compromise or conflict, or both. Some religious and pro-government websites that might have condemned such acts of physical beautification are now publishing guidelines for those who have had undergone cosmetic procedures on how to perform their religious duties such as *wuzu* (ritual ablutions) while still having their bandages on.

When discussing men's cosmetic surgery, however, the general public's response is much more diverse. Most believe that women's interest in beauty is natural and to be expected. Some, however, deem that there is 'something wrong' with men who chose to undergo plastic surgery. They argue that men should care only about their health and not worry about facial beauty. On the other hand, some claim that men like beauty in the same way as women do and many men have natural physical imperfections, so why not use cosmetic surgery to improve their features? Talking about men's cosmetic surgery, Arman, a music teacher from north Tehran, who had undergone plastic surgery, said he thought that due to changes in society, men chose to have surgical procedures as they do not have the opportunity to show their 'true' masculinity.

I accompanied Arman on a visit to his doctor, Darius, a well-known beauty consultant in North Tehran. While waiting to see Dr Darius, I could not help but think how busy the waiting room was and how everyone was meticulously dressed this early in the morning. I spoke to Ali, a 45-year-old engineer who visits Dr Darius regularly to receive Botox injections. He explained that it was around three years ago when he was encouraged by his wife to get Botox injections and he happily complied. 'It has boosted my self-confidence greatly. We were brainwashed from childhood to believe that men should be masculine and rugged and not to take care of their looks,' he said. Later, Dr Darius told me that there is no difference between men and women in the desire to look youthful. If women like to stay and look young, then so do men. He explained that a lot of older men attend his clinic for facial fillers in order to treat their laughter lines and rectify any signs of aging (such as wrinkles). Younger people mainly opt for chin and cheek implants to alter the underlying structure of their face. Dr Darius said that in the past three to four years, the number of men visiting his clinic for beauty procedures has equalled the number of women. He also pointed out that such beauty procedures are not just popular amongst Iranians living in Iran but also amongst Iranians abroad, who are influenced by the culture in their home country. Value for money with regards to procedure costs are much better in Iran compared to other countries across the world. For example, cheek implants in the US start at around US$5,000, while in Iran the same procedure would cost you a maximum of US$1,000. This is why a lot of overseas Iranians travel from America and Europe to alter their faces. For many Iranians, both men and women, such procedures are not only an indication of physical beauty but also imply a certain status with regards to wealth and social prestige. In some cases, the desire to undergo surgery is not due to vanity but more about the wish to be Iranians who have a European appearance, travel, read American literature, and live Western lives. Dr Darius explained that the criteria for the ideal Iranian face have altered. Ironically, removing the Persian bump (a distinctive aspect of the Iranian 'hooked' nose) now adds to a person's perception of Iranian identity. He maintained that although surgical alteration of the nose changes a distinctly Persian aspect of a person's facial features, the decision to undergo surgery is very much an Iranian decision. Dr Darius saw cosmetic surgery as a positive thing. He suggested that cosmetic surgery in men can boost their confidence and increase their sense of satisfaction, therefore allowing them to experience more joy in life. 'It is well known that if you believe that you look good, you are more likely to feel good about yourself. Evidence has shown that personal appearance and self-confidence are inter linked.' The rise in cosmetic surgery among Iranians verifies that confidence is lacking in both men and women and the traditional patriarchal system has now had an impact on the male gender, obliging them to follow unwritten beauty standards. It could be said that abiding by cultural standards of beauty has become a 'must', otherwise individuals may not be accepted by the wider community.

One could argue that Iranians are most attracted to smaller noses found in the 'West'. In other words, a cultural preference for a 'Western' appearance has led Iran to its current obsession with nose jobs. Looking at the majority of Iranians who have had a nose job it can clearly be seen that they modelled their noses on the typical shape of a white Euro-American nose rather than that of other racial groups – they requested that their noses be made smaller with a slight curve and a fine tip. One woman I spoke to told me that she was always jealous of European noses. She had undergone nose surgery about twenty years ago. 'European people are so lucky because naturally they have beautiful noses and don't need surgery. This however, does not mean that all Iranians like to copy European noses completely. They mainly look for smaller and more natural noses,' she said. Both Iranian men and women modify their noses for different personal or social reasons. Nevertheless, an unspoken desire to look more 'Western' unites them. Mohsen, a maths teacher from the west of Tehran, explained how obsessed he is with noses:

> I find the European nose most appealing, particularly people from Scandinavia. The smaller the nose the better it is. This is mainly because it would draw less attention to itself as possible. Ideally when someone looks at you, you want your eyes, cheeks or lips to draw their attention. But if you have an extra-large nose or a nose that does not fit the rest of your face, then people's attention will mostly be on your nose. Such a distraction cannot be flattering on their overall opinion of your attractiveness.

When I asked whether small noses are naturally beautiful or whether they are made more attractive due to Western cultural influence, he was sceptical. Yet he argued that even in a hundred years' time, a smaller nose would be deemed more attractive than a larger, broader nose.

Dr Darius also emphasised the important effects of social media outlets on young people's decision to undertake cosmetic surgery. 'When you post a selfie on your Instagram page, it's not only to show people what you have been up to but also it's a continuous reminder of the way you look.' Social media has become a place to share your life. Hollywood actors and actresses and many other celebrities post pictures of their before-and-after cosmetic operations. People tweet about going in for Botox injections or blog about their breast implants and post pictures on their personal online pages. Undergoing cosmetic surgery has become something to be shared. As a result, attractiveness is no longer under a person's control and beauty standards are being promoted through social media and, to some extent, being dictated by fashion.

I also spoke to Shahrzad, Dr Darius's wife. Well dressed in a sophisticated, beaded lace blouse with designer-ripped skinny jeans and without a headscarf, she was a true advocate of her husband's work, having undergone the majority of plastic surgeries available. 'We have a lot of young men turning up here with pictures of their favourite actors or celebrities wanting to look like them,' she said. Johnny Depp, Antonio Banderas and Jake Gyllenhaal were amongst names I recognised. 'What is also becoming a trend is that people are bringing in their digitally altered selfies or photos of themselves in a favourable angle and demanding to look like that.' Asked about whether they get any odd requests, she responded, 'We get a lot of strange and weird requests, for instance men asking for cheek and lip augmentation, eyelid surgery and brow lifts all at the same time.' 'All they need then is just whiskers to look like a cat,' the secretary shouted from the corner of the room. 'Our response is *khoda shafat bede* (which can be translated as "I hope you get well soon" but also means "You are out of your mind!"),' Shahrzad added. The secretary continued, 'Gone are those days when men had to look manly and rough. Now they all are waxing their chests and using lip augmentation.'

According to Shahrzad more than sixty per cent of their patients (mainly men) are advised to have fewer injections as most of them attend the clinic to exaggerate certain parts of their face. 'To look like a panther with big cheekbones,' said the secretary while laughing. Shahrzad added:

> But, generally speaking I think it's a very positive trend and like fashion, it is an important social and cultural component of Iranian society. People can now look more beautiful due to the advancement in technology and medical science so why shouldn't they? I think it's good that both men and women are more prepared to welcome change and construct their most beautiful self, but you will always have people who will take things too far.

Given the high demand for cosmetic surgery, it is not surprising that illegal clinics have mushroomed. Indeed, many operations are now being carried out by unprofessional and dishonest surgeons. A recent report, published by the pathology research group of the Arya Strategic Studies Centre in Tehran, stated that out of 7,000 cosmetic practitioners in Tehran, only 157 are licensed cosmetic surgeons.

The obsession with physical beauty amongst many Iranians is a long way from the revolutionary ideals of the Islamic republic, which encouraged people to focus on inner spirituality. The Iranian Revolution was based on Islamic ethics and values that maintained that humility and sincerity were of greatest importance. After 1979, this philosophy was extended to unwritten social rules – wealth and affluence were frowned upon, whereas poverty and hardship were praised as symbols of godliness. With regards to fashion, clothing, and looks, simplicity and modesty were the order of the day and anyone not following such stereotypes could risk being ostracised or labelled an opponent of the Revolution. However, almost forty years after the Revolution, things have changed dramatically. Both the more affluent and 'middle class' populations enjoy purchasing fashionable clothes made by Western retailers, with some saving for months to buy their desired outfit. Others are undergoing cosmetic surgery with the sole aim of gaining their desired features or emulating the faces and bodies of actors and actresses they admire in Western films and satellite television programmes. To many observers outside Iran, the increase in cosmetic surgery would seem like a surprising story. But in Iran, such acts of non-movement, conscious or unconscious, are part of a wave of clandestine dissent against the country's conservative and hard-line laws and social principles.

ARTS AND LETTERS

NIGHT JOURNEY AT THE END OF THE WORLD
by Alev Adil
EGYPTOMANIA *by Yasmin Desouki*
WOMEN WRESTLERS *by Ricci Shryock*
FIVE POEMS *by Mustafa Abu Sneineh*
POEMS *by Brandino Machiavelli*

NIGHT JOURNEY AT THE END OF THE WORLD

Alev Adil

1. Moon-water and the moon

Here, at the End of the World, the end of her world, a woman disappeared. She hid in her library, then she slipped through the pages of a book and then she wasn't there at all. Later a shadow appeared, two thousand miles away from the Metropolis, in a dead-end street, in the Occupied Zone, in the legally unrecognised territories, the streets left unnamed on the maps of the legal Republic. No longer a woman, now only a shadow, a rumour reflected in a well, they only saw her at night, walking the tangled back streets of the old Turkish *mahalle*. This shadow, the ghost that appears at night, is Moon-water. Her mother looked into her slate grey eyes and called her Aysu. Moon. Water.

She does not speak but the moon hears her, the moon reflected in the stone trough of water:

I am in the dead
of night, the living dead
of the moon remembered
full then pared to a crescent
on dark water
the moon remembered
reflected in the deep waters
of a well

and this all happened in a dream
that's all there was

and the whispering of the palm
the scent of orange blossom

there was something I wanted
so much
to say
that is to say so much
I wanted more than I could say,
bear, more than I could bear
losing so much
more
and still wanting
long after waking

I have to believe in many times
a love story for each name
and all the ninety-nine names
that would return
the beloved to the lover

at the end of the world.

2. The little yellow flower and the moon spell

Astragalus brachycalyx, commonly known as Persian manna, is a perennial
deciduous bush with needle like leaves and small butter-yellow flowers
that grows on rocky mountain slopes in Asia, from western Iran and
northern Iraq to Turkey. The sap is drained from the root of the plant and
then dried. It has a variety of medicinal purposes and can also be used as
a thickening agent. The gum seeps from the plant in twisted ribbons or
flakes. After harvesting, this can be powdered and then later again be
mixed with water and stirred into a paste. Reputed to have many health-
giving properties the gum doesn't taste of anything, although many find
the scent repugnant.

Had there been years and years of waiting?
She had been shot

and I kept running but bits
kept flying off
feathers, petals, silk scarves and sequined things,
skin, fat, fairy dust,
until there was
less and less.
You kept erasing the layers
unpicking the threads of thought
skeins of words
more surface than meaning,
more meaning than
language can bear,
less and less
of Her.
A worn-out fresco,
you are rubbing your cheek
on the sun-warmed wall
the gentle plaster impression
of yourself as a ghost,
returned to streets
with names no one cares to know,
blue jasmine dancing gently over
the padlocked gates.
Was there something I could have done
otherwise
so that...
No, there is no point in regret.

Aysu leans over the stone trough in her little garden under the full moon.
She is mixing the powdered sap of Persian manna, three teaspoons to a
gallon of distilled water. She adds a little rosewater, and her tears, although
conventional recipes do not call for roses or tears. She mixes the brew
until the gum has dissolved completely. Then she leaves the mixture to rest
for two days. The moon hides in the noon day sun and returns a little
thinner and hides again and returns slimmer still. An old witch had advised
her years ago to cast spells for that which you want to grow when the

moon is waxing, that which you want to be free of when she wanes. Aysu waits two days for the gum to dissolve fully, for the water to acquire a viscous sticky density. She wants her love to wane, to be free of it.

3. From A to Z, victory and destiny

Aysu met Zafer at a seminar on paper marbling and bookbinding in Florence in 2003. She had been invited by Maria, descendent of the Giannini family, purveyors of gorgeous marbled stationary since the 1850s, to deliver a paper on the history of Safavid and Ottoman paper marbling. Aysu had met Maria when she first visited Florence as an undergraduate on a field trip, twenty years earlier. Whilst her peers sought out Botticelli and Boccaccio in galleries and churches, Aysu couldn't tear herself away from the beautiful marbled paper she discovered in *Giulio Giannini e Figlio*, that renowned shop directly opposite the Pitti Palace, which seemed to her not so much a stationary shop but rather a small corner of paradise.

The conference attracted an eclectic crew, a fat Dutch historian spoke about the history of smuggling marbled paper from Amsterdam to London in the nineteenth century, to avoid the exorbitant import duties excised in England at the time. A literature professor from Oxford, with fluffy white hair and a huge coral necklace, discussed Elizabeth Browning's *Casa Guidi Windows,* which had been bound by Giulio Giannini. A wan, beautiful but inaudible, Japanese artist in lilac showed examples of her *suminagashi* practice. A panel of academics from China, Iran and Turkey had a heated discussion on the origins of paper marbling and couldn't agree on anything. A Turkish academic in the audience insisted that it was an essentially Turkish art form and called on Aysu to corroborate her nationalist rant. It was autumn, the light dancing on the Arno was quince gold and Aysu longed to leave the conference and to wander through the streets of the city. She abhorred the panel's appropriation of culture for nationalist purposes, especially the Turkish academic's screechy objections but she understood them too. They were all on trips paid for by their respective governments, their careers and promotions depended on such nonsense. They were there to build careers really, not to discuss the art. 'As you have discussed, Ebru derives its name from Farsi, *ebri*, meaning cloud-like,' Aysu said, 'and in Chinese it is *liu sha jian* , meaning drifting sand... it drifts, it flows. Clouds and sands have no passports, know no borders.' Aysu didn't have to please any government, she worked designing stationery for Liberty's at the time. She could afford to rise above such territorialism. She had a well-paid job. Her job was to produce beautiful paper. This was before the economic crisis.

She had a headache by the time Zafer gave his paper on the importance of water tension, not just in paper marbling, but also in engineering design. She was barely aware of what he said, although she can still remember that there were a plethora of slides on the study of biofilms and monolayers, and how they might be harnessed for constructive purposes in sewage treatment plants, oil spill habitat cleanup and biomedical products. Zafer had just embarked on a doctorate at Imperial College in London, he told Aysu later, at the conference dinner. His parents lived in Alexandria, his brother ran a bar in Brussels. He seemed too serious, stern, a little lost, lonely even.

The next day they walked up the hill to a cemetery full of family crypts and kitsch monuments to death. The place was creepy but the view breathtaking. She still remembers the scent of cypress and wild basil that seduced her much more than his rather lugubrious and formal manners. Or so she thought. Looking back, later, they both agreed that's when they fell in love. Although he was far too young for her, she told him, back in London, over sushi, after they had been to see *Battle of Algiers* together in Bloomsbury. 'Ah, you can be my Khadija,' he had joked.

4. Ox bile

Once she has prepared the water with the *astragulus* gum (salep, orchid root, may also be used) and left it to rest for two days Aysu prepares the dyes: two teaspoons of powdered pigment to a cup of water, she shakes the mixture up with ox bile in a glass bottle.

Gold for the sunlight,
green for the waters of the river.
Should she add a touch of red?

His lips. She found his lips irresistible long before they kissed.
Had there been years and years of waiting?
She had been shot
and I kept running but bits
kept flying off
feathers, petals, silk scarves and sequined things,
skin, fat, fairy dust,
until there was
less and less.
You kept erasing the layers
unpicking the threads of thought
skeins of words
more surface than meaning,
colours dappled
marbled feelings
more meaning than
language can bear,
less and less
of Her.
Drifting sands and passing clouds
you are yourself
as a ghost,
returned to streets
with names no one cares to know,
blue jasmine dancing gently over
the padlocked gates.
Was there something I could have done
otherwise
so that...
No, there is no point in regret.

The gummy water is then poured into a metal container. Aysu places the
tray into the old stone trough in the garden. The moon is thinner but it is
still bright enough, or does the work form the colours of memory? Be sure
to wipe the tears from your eyes, she tells herself, and to dispel any
bubbles from the surface of the viscous liquid. You can shake the tray or use

a stick. Begin with the darkest colour, sprinkle with a brush, or tip it in.
This is where the art lies.

How to be better,
a better sentence,
with a happy ending.
Had there been years?
Years away. Years that now
seem submerged and underwater,
heavy water,
just an extra molecule of hydrogen
it's the full moon in the well
that makes it look like mercury.
All night the fires burnt
the whole city burnt
and I stood amongst the ruins
part animation, part film,
part reconstruction from old photographs,
an approximate depiction.
I looked out to sea.

No, too much green, and then far too dark, far too much red. Blood.

It ended so suddenly, after twelve years.
Twelve trees would make a small orchard,
twelve men disciples for a would-be god.

'This relationship has reached its conclusion.' He told her. A clean break he
told her. Clean. 6 October 2015. And then he disappeared, completely.

I cannot get my bearings
there are no pavements and the narrow streets
curve and coil back upon themselves
become more confusing and familiar,
their strangeness, random meanderings
undiminished but interrupted
by constant jolts of déjà vu.
I take photographs of the dark,
a silent record of a dog's almost bark

more of a query than a threat.
Is this now my fate?
These uncanny streets in the heart
of a bulging ugly little town by the sea,
is this my home?
I have an official card to confirm I belong.
My heart is a toad in my mouth,
a terrified fat thing, breathe,
breathe, I tell it, myself,
the shadow of a tree.
Twelve trees.

She thought she might die of the heartbreak. They tell you one can't die of a broken heart these days and when you do they blame cigarettes, or cheese.

Zafer had resigned from the university, wound up his financial affairs, closed all his social media accounts. Her emails bounced back. Why, how, such useless questions in the face of lovelessness. Why had he left? How had she felt so loved when he must have been planning to abandon her for months? Years? Could love end so suddenly as he had claimed? Could love just disappear in an instant, a stray cat disappearing over the garden wall?

Not Khadija then. No.

Now take a needle and draw it across the surface of the water, to create ripples, if you choose you may make images, a flower perhaps.

Aysu paints a crescent moon.

Once you have manipulated the dye, place the paper on the surface of the water carefully.

Two months after he had left her so abruptly Aysu went to Brussels, searching for Zafer's brother Omar, but she wasn't sure if she found the right bar. It was boarded up and no one would admit to having known him. Then someone in a nearby grocery store said they thought he was dead. Brussels and all its citizens were taciturn and sullen, the city seemed to be under martial law. There were tanks on the streets. Bataclan, Bataclan, an ugly murmur everywhere.

Gently lift the paper, now marbled with your design, and leave to dry.

I hoped I could build a new,
small life, a stroll by the sea,
coffee in the harbour,
a walk past the castle, the old Ottoman tombs,
the ghosts are much quieter here,
but ever present nevertheless.
I thought I could,
I could build… I told myself,
a life I could.
But I cannot and I do.
Still running then,
for who else would choose such a fate,
who would choose to live in
a legal no man's land
in an occupied zone
unless they had been shot
and had to keep moving,
moving enough to make a new story,
if you want a story
full of ghosts and fools.

Ebru paper was often used as the background for Islamic calligraphic arts.

Yesterday eight corpses spewed out by the Syrian civil war washed up on the Cypriot shore further up the coast.

I am no calligrapher, but if I were I'd transform these words into a white stallion with a beautiful woman's face. The stallion would charge across the stormy green sea, under the bloody moon, off the marbled paper, away from all this violence and cruelty. If this was my story and not Aysu's nightmare I'd have her fall in love with Buraq, not with Zafer, for after all, this is her night journey.

You did not build this ancient city,
left nothing more
than your heroic statue,
but you were my conqueror,

who knew the easy trick,
the way to feed a village
to the moon
dark precursor bitter sweet
on my tongue.
I gave my state your name
my love,
despite its long history
that predated you,
all the rituals, customs
and knick knacks,
small glass bottles
to catch my tears
and razor blades
for bloody Christmases past.

What did you do though?
And how? I had not thought.
There was so much
left undone, unsaid.
And then you lit the fuse,
pulled the pin,
left the room,
my punishment
for loving the soldier
in you.

and still long after waking
I have to believe in many times
a love story for each name
and all the ninety-nine names
that would return
the beloved to the lover

at the end of the world.

EGYPTOMANIA

Yasmin Desouki

Barbara Walters: Who would you like to see playing you in a movie?
Anwar Al Sadat: Robert Redford.

Televised interview, aired shortly after signing of the
Camp David Accords in 1978

The beginning of cinema was arguably marked by acute insincerity. Early pictures were the domain of bourgeois values, and it took some time for the medium to come into its own as an art form for the masses. Audiences rightly experienced a sense of wonderment at the new technology that could capture a facsimile of reality so well, and bedazzlement with fantastic imagery was all the rage. The Lumière Brothers' work quickly evolved from shooting an oncoming train or factory labourers leaving work *en masse*, to filming exotic locales throughout the world. In 1897, Alexandre Promio – one of the Lumière company's most notable cameramen – arrived on the shores of Alexandria, with the duty of completing *Les Pyramides* (1897), a 50-second short capturing the Sphinx and the Nile for posterity. Other major film companies, such as Edison and Pathé, would follow suit. And while countries as diverse as Turkey, Tunisia, Russia, and Japan featured strongly in a global audience's fantasia of strikingly beautiful imagery, Egypt's landscape held a particular fascination in the imperial imagination.

This is due in part to the popularity of moving images coinciding with the curious phenomenon of Egyptomania – an obsession with all things Pharaonic that dates back to the Victorian Age and which reached a fever-pitch with the discovery of King Tutankhamun's tomb in 1922. The silent cinema adored the glamorous mystique of Ancient Egypt, and Hollywood celebrated it through the splashy production of numerous films. Likewise, the first Egyptian features resurrected Cleopatra and mummies *ad infinitum*, although little of this work survives today. The imagery was potent, and early filmmakers tried their hardest to seduce Egyptian audiences with the new spectacle of cinema. However, film did not become truly celebrated as an emotionally powerful and commercially sustainable force till the advent of sound. And even more so, the iconography that film traded upon was deeply emblematic of a national consciousness, one that was undergoing tremendous revolutionary change throughout much of the twentieth century – the mummy, the ancient vixen, the Bedouin, the poor but industrious young man, the rich bully, and so on.

The extent to which these representations echo their Western counterpart's interpretation of history is a rather fraught proposition. This is true, at least, up until a certain moment in time, when films became more 'sincere' and thus reflected the plight of their largely working-class and middle-class viewers. With Egypt being the key centrepiece in long imperialistic struggles – and the country's subsequent fight for independence – the opposing narratives are more interwoven than they first appear. Egyptian cinema's ghosts are a multitude, and it is frequently haunted by the state's active proposal of icons to follow, as the varying governments understood one thing to be true: image is everything. So, when President Anwar Al Sadat offered his deadpan response to Barbara Walters in the late 1970s, it was understood by the West as a marker of his razor-sharp wit. Egyptians, however, duly noted that the glibness hid a deep love for the cosmetic, and an understanding of the visual power entailed in a strong chin.

Ancient Decadence and Hollywood Glamour

Florence Nightingale's writing on Egypt is both beautiful and superfluous, as many of the travelogues produced in the late 1800s are wont to be. Her silk handkerchief floating in the desert, staring with open awe at the vacant landscape before her, waiting for history to be written upon it – this is the hallmark of most imperialist impulses. It's a syndrome – *the page I found is blank till I scrawl all over it.* But what it lacks in political awareness it makes up for in dreamy mysticism, and indeed has influenced much of the literature and cinema to emerge later. Early moviegoers the world over watched films as though they were entering a quiet tomb, about to embark on a séance to conjure ghostly images for the screen. Sorcery was synonymous with ancient cultures and, later on, film. The colonial project in Egypt fed these twin perceptions, as images of the pharaohs and hieroglyphics flooded much of Europe and America, culminating in the debut of slinky belly dancing (the term itself a distinctly American moniker) in 1893 at Chicago's World Fair. Egypt was seen as the gateway to the Orient, a country whose history was so mixed ethnically and religiously, presenting an amalgam of cultures and histories, that it somehow invited a sense of familiarity in the British and French colonial imagination, rather than complete disconnect.

The iconography of Ancient Egypt was a raging fascination, and it made its way even further to the United States, where it informed modern attitudes regarding race and sexuality. The 1920s arrival of the Vamp is almost impossible to understand fully without acknowledging the obsession with ancient cultures, both Egyptian and otherwise. And its exemplification of questionable sexual mores was best embodied by the kohl-rimmed eyes of Theda Bara, the silent-film star whose iteration of Cleopatra in 1917 proved to be a watershed moment in early moving-image history. By that same token, Hollywood studios were eager to bankroll projects depicting the pharaohs, in a move that is now seen by some historians as a clarion call to African American audiences. It acknowledged their viewership, if only tangentially, by linking their interest in thinkers on racial theory such as Frederick Douglass and W.E.B. Du Bois to the on-screen imagery, which was often presented as racially ambiguous.

The West's mania with all things ancient Egyptian throughout the late 1700s and early 1900s is rather easy to understand. Especially when this fascination is projected against the backdrop of incredible archaeological discovery, beginning with the Rosetta Stone in 1799 to the unveiling of King Tut's tomb in 1922. But what is recounted far less often is how Egyptians themselves considered these findings, and the ways in which the country's moving-image history – actually home to one of the oldest industries in the world – captured this notable element of its past. The shadow of a mummy lurking around the corner, a dancing Hatshepsut in the desert, and an ancient Egyptian maiden rising from the Nile like a phoenix with a twinkle in her eye – these are not images from Hollywood movies but, rather, mainstream Egyptian films. Was the visual iconography debuting in Egyptian cinemas bowdlerised versions of a deeply American view of Ancient Egypt, or another beast altogether? Did they alter the ways in which modern Egyptians viewed their own history, or was there stagnant alienation rather than startling recognition? The truth lies somewhere in between.

Two of the most important film producers throughout the 1930s and 1940s were Ibrahim and Badr Lama, Chilean-born citizens of Palestinian descent who made Egypt their home in 1924. Both originally cinematographers, they joined the society of *Ansar al Sowar al Motahareqa* (Champions of the Moving Image), which later became MENA Film, and eventually started Studio Lama in 1930. Badr, being an actor himself, was completely taken by the desert epics produced by Hollywood during this time and was a fan of Rudolph Valentino's work in *The Sheikh* (1921) and *The Son of the Sheikh* (1926). Ibrahim would direct many epics starring his brother, in films that at first glance seemed to be carbon copies of their sensationalised American counterparts. Most notable is the 1943 film *Cleopatra*. Unfortunately, there is no surviving print, but the filmed version had roots in the theatrical tradition, while borrowing heavily from Pharaonic iconography which informed so much of early Hollywood silent film. This Egyptian version, however, starring the formidable theater actress Amina Rizk, was filmed with sound.

Indeed, early Egyptian cinema primarily focused on the powerful imagery afforded by Bedouin love stories, desert epics, and melodrama. Only Mohamed Karim's 1930 work, *Zeinab*, offered a change of course, by making class struggle a centerpiece of the film's central plot. However, the black-and-white dichotomies posited by the Palestinian intellectual Edward Said's interpretation of Orientalism don't always work in accurately portraying the power structures and audience dynamics in Egyptian viewership of early cinema. On one hand, it is true that the works of the Lama Brothers and other important players within the industry borrowed heavily from glitzy Hollywood films. On the other hand, it is also true that the works produced in Hollywood themselves borrowed from Egypt's own visual culture – a pantomime that renders interpretation of this history all the more convoluted, especially since neither the American nor Egyptian versions of *Cleopatra* exist in their entirety today. Further, a number of the country's early film producers were not necessarily Egyptian-born, as in the case of the Lama Brothers. With that being said, this was at a moment in Egypt's history wherein nationality meant precious little. And, as fraught as the term 'cosmopolitan' has become, it can be said without reverting to cheap nostalgia that Egyptian society (at least, in the major metropolises) was deeply pluralistic during much of the early twentieth century. Thus, there are no definitive answers. Instead, what can be precisely ascertained is the popularity of these films with Egyptian audiences, and that they provided an Egyptianised version of Americanised versions of their history. The looking glass mirrors the other looking glass, and the copy becomes the original.

This is not to say that these early works in all their symbolic potency were not actively challenged for their alleged 'authenticity' by the country's intelligentsia at the time. Rather, they were part of a broader discussion regarding Egypt's sense of agency and place in world events, and the nation's newly emerging cultural and political consciousness. Having recently been free of British colonial rule in 1922, these images – be they in print, contemporary art, or film – became incredibly vital in answering the question of 'Egyptianness'.

The country's first truly independent filmmaker, Muhammed Bayoumi, who initiated the newsreel Amun Film in 1923, was onsite and camera-ready to film Howard Carter and the treasures he found in King Tut's tomb. This occurrence seems to have been glossed over in the history books, as though the only Egyptians at the tomb were Lord Carnarvon's and Carter's personal handlers. Perhaps, when viewing this period of history, copying or stereotyping is not the worst offense. Sometimes, being invisible is a far more terrible fate.

WWII and the Fallen Woman

The dawn of World War II arguably served as another turning point in the culture's broader awareness of the image's inarguable power. Foreign newsreels were being screened in Egypt at a remarkable pace, introducing audiences to what is now commonly understood as a form of 'propaganda'. They pointed to the country's geographic importance to the conflict, with Egypt being crucial to both the Allied forces and German troops and getting caught in the middle. Opulent Hollywood films were also screened frequently, if not for the sake of the cinema-loving locals than for the troops now landing in droves in the country. As a result, the back-and-forth of cultural influence continued in perhaps an even more direct manner. For instance, the remarkable photographer Van Leo, born to a family of Armenian descent, began his work in the shadow of WWII. His first clients were soldiers posted in Egypt. He borrowed heavily from the ultra-glam portraiture churned out by Hollywood but inflected them with his own incredible understanding of light and shadow and the local culture, especially when it came to capturing major Egyptian film stars.

While every film actor or starry-eyed performer would eventually be photographed by Van Leo – especially throughout the late 1950s and 1970s – working class heroes and heroines, peasants, gypsies, and wise-cracking ne'er-do-wells dominated the silver screen. The 1940s ushered in an era that is now commonly viewed to be the country's golden age of cinematic production. The advent of sound enforced a new malleability in the images projected on-screen, as producers rushed to make films that resonated with a growing audience eager to see a reflection of themselves beyond the more bourgeoisie fare offered to them at the beginning of the century. While pharaonic history was viewed with considerable pride by establishment artists and the government, it offered little to modern cinematic audiences beyond comedic segues. These audiences wanted more than mummies sneezing themselves to life to the horror of the film's bumbling heroes. In a country that continued to undergo seismic change, the anachronistic nature of the ancient no longer fitted – for a film to be emblematic of heritage was to be out of step with time.

The new stars of Egyptian cinema consisted of simple labourers trying to make ends meet. There was the hilarious working-class comedian Ali El Kassar, whose attempts to navigate the upper echelons of society were met with incredible empathy by audiences. Meanwhile, his slightly darker skin tone was meant to invoke both Nubian culture and a history of workers slaving away in the sun, unlike the majority of his cohort. His dramatic counterpart was resident tough guy Farid Shawky, whose burly physique and righteous battles with evil businessmen made him one of the biggest stars of Egyptian cinema, particularly in light of the 1952 revolution. He was subsequently referred to as *Malek al Terso* (King of the Third Class), a reference to the third-tier movie theater seats bought by members of the working class who eagerly came to see his films.

On the other side of the gender spectrum was the idea of the gypsy, best personified by the free-spirited dancer and comedienne Naima Akef. The iconoclastic peasant or farm girl would appear on-screen from time to time but did not come to have symbolic resonance till Nasserite politics appeared on the stage in the late 1950s.

The 'gypsy' Naima Akef

Running parallel to the resonant images depicted in commercial cinema were artistic movements that eventually – if somewhat indirectly – influenced popular culture tremendously. These included the Egyptian surrealists, led by Inji Afflatoun, Georges Henein, and Abduh Khalil, amongst others, whose group was called *Art et Liberté*.

They advocated for an art that was less calculated than their European equivalents and more socially engaged, drawing upon local symbols that would be familiar to Egyptians. However, they steered clear of nationalistic imagery, preferring not to fetishise pharaonic elements in the same manner as state-sponsored artists. When the country's ancient heritage did feature in their work, it was more often than not with a keen sense of humour, poking fun at the past's austere elegance.

It is also worth noting that the surrealists fought virulently against what they saw as a fascist tide encroaching upon the public sphere and Egypt's vulnerability to the movement. Britain's reluctance to allow the country a true sense of autonomy in its own affairs rendered divisive figures such as Mussolini rather appealing. In this sense, the surrealists were deeply aware of the state apparatus' attempts to drive home a specific picture of Egyptian identity for the populace to emulate. Their art was a direct challenge to state narratives, and they brought to light issues which were not frequently addressed by other collectives.

When WWII was at its height, both of the country's major metropolises, Cairo and Alexandria, saw a tremendous influx of soldiers – by some estimates nearly 150,000 in just one city. This inevitably led to a surge in prostitution, which brought with it disease and other forms of abuse to Egyptian women. The drastic change in the city's tone and character, the stark shift in power structures, wherein the foreigners were no longer seen as friendly equals to their Egyptian brethren, infiltrated much of the surrealists' works. Emaciated or disfigured women floating in swirls of dark paint, entirely robbed of eroticism, became a key image, particularly in Inji Afflatoun's feminist work, namely *Girl and Monster*. Cairo's cabarets pandered to their new audience at night; the belly dancing felt exaggerated, at times vulgar. The dance's artistry instead became a coded invitation for paid services, and the coarseness of sexual violence reverberated in the Egyptian surrealists' paintings. Something in the air was terribly off, and the inherently racist convulsions of paid transactions poisoned what was once seen as a rather benign – if inconvenient – relationship between locals and expats.

The *Art et Liberté* movement may have been rather short-lived but, in hindsight, their way of viewing the rapidly changing cultural landscape has undoubtedly influenced the interpretation of pharaonic and feminine imagery that would be portrayed in the auteur cinema of the late 1960s and early 1970s. And while they were rather critical of Gamal Abdel Nasser and his policies – most of them even forced into exile or imprisoned during his presidency – their work also foreshadowed the inevitability of the 1952 revolution.

Before leaving the Egypt of WWII behind, it would behoove one to take a brief detour with Tahiya Carioca, one of the truly great performers in Egyptian cinema. Multi-talented Carioca's career began as a dancer, one of the best proponents of *raks sharki* (classical Egyptian belly dancing) in the 1930s and 1940s. She soon moved onto acting, and her charismatic presence on-screen won her considerable acclaim. At the height of WWII, she met an American soldier posted in Cairo, whom she married, eventually moving with him to Los Angeles. The details of the union remain rather vague (Carioca possessed an indomitable spirit, and was married at least eight times, so most biographers gloss over this part), but what we do know is how utterly bored she was by Hollywood and the Beverly Hills elite. She had no intention of being a veteran's wife and was sure that she could continue her career in America. But there was a very specific role to play for the foreign muse, which Greta Garbo and Marlene Dietrich had mastered. Carioca balked at the

Tahiya Carioca at the height of her fame.

idea of being boxed in, chained to her glittery dancing costume for all
eternity. But as an Egyptian-Arab woman, she was granted even less leeway
in presenting herself, and the vulgarity of the proposition appalled her. She
had no patience for it, especially when she saw how quickly Egypt was
changing, and by contrast her life in America felt completely stagnant. She
divorced and returned to Cairo, where she knew she could make her own
path, beyond the grim gaze of studio executives in their Bel Air mansions.

1952: The Pharaoh Comes to Life

In the documentary *In Search of Oil and Sand* (2012), Mahmoud Sabit
explores his family's archives, particularly an amateur film they were
shooting for sport shortly before the revolution, titled *Oil and Sand*. The
family in question is the Egyptian royal family; King Farouk and his
brethren, and their shenanigans are captured in an Orientalist epic that
may have been produced by the same Hollywood studio that gave life to
Rudolph Valentino's *The Sheikh* in 1921. The acting is, of course, over-the-
top campy, and the plot is incongruous at best. But it wasn't meant to be
seen by outsiders. It was just a way for the royal family to while away the
time. However, what makes the surviving footage so remarkable are the
scenes they shot on the eve of the 1952 revolution (or, as some would refer
to it, a wildly popular military coup led by Mohamed Naguib and Gamal
Abdel Nasser, stars of the Free Officers Movement). Much of the royal
family seemed to be completely out of step with the political climate
engulfing the country, and their filmic escapades reveal a critical
obliviousness that, in its own way, harkens to the inevitability of massive
societal change. The dated Bedouin imagery in *Oil and Sand* did not bode
well for them, and 1952 was certainly nothing like 1921.

The onset of Nasserite politics in the 1950s and 1960s led to a
tremendous shift in how the country would view itself, and the methods
employed by the state and other interested parties to shape the national
consciousness present a breathtaking awareness in the supremacy of visual
representation. Nasser was by nature a cinephile and remains perhaps
Egypt's most image conscious president. While some thinkers and artists
of the time saw him as a tyrant in disguise – surrealist Georges Henein

being one of them – they still admired his ability to unite not just Egyptians but the Arab populace at large in a war against imperialist forces.

Popular culture experienced another groundswell of innovation and heightened production, even as the Ministry of Culture's Censorship Board was granted more power than the past. The Egyptian state funded newsreel production at an impressive rate – a format whose influence on documentary and avant-garde cinema has in some ways been taken for granted. It would also prove vital in shaping the collective imagination, and the rich symbolism entailed within each news magazine shot and distributed to the public via movie theatres soothed the soul with a heady mix of ultra-nationalism and a distinct sense of agency. Egyptian destiny made international headlines and the audience loved watching the drama unfold.

Deliberate image-making was even more important in mainstream cinemas, and it is during Nasser's reign that the figure of the peasant – usually an innocent farm girl – became the most relatable on-screen icon. Faten Hamama's 1959 film *The Nightingale's Prayer* was a turning point in the actress' dramatic career, a tale of love and revenge against the injustice perpetuated by a bourgeoisie engineer. The twin dichotomies of the countryside versus the city, the rich versus the poor, were never more magnified. Indeed, the feminine figure of a peasant (meant to symbolise Egypt) continues to be a popular trope in the country's cinema, representing strength, beauty, and unwavering moral certainty.

Egypt's pharaonic heritage was resurrected yet again during Nasser's reign, but largely in the ways feared by the surrealists years before. The erstwhile president encouraged an awkward embrace of the country's heritage, celebrating the pharaohs' militaristic might to conjure the supremacy of the present-day army. In fact, at an earlier moment in Nasser's presidency when warmer relations with America seemed possible, his administration was instrumental in bringing Howard Hawks' 1955 epic *Land of the Pharaohs* to life on-screen. One of the largest productions in filmic history at the time, it was shot on location in Egypt, and Nasser provided over a thousand military men as extras. The film is a fictional account of the building of The Great Pyramids, and explicitly endorsed Hollywood's view of Egypt's sumptuous past. This is almost impossible to imagine happening in the current climate, where obtaining a filming permit requires infinite patience, and the government's tight grip on how the state's operations are presented on-screen means that seemingly inconsequential frames of information are censored.

Meanwhile, ancient Egyptian heritage felt farther away than ever in the populace's mind, as it embraced Arab Nationalism with open arms, and looked to the future with youthful optimism. The pharaohs would appear from time to time in cinema, but usually in harmless comedies tinged with only the faintest strains of satire. One notable example is the fantasy film, *Bride of the Nile* (1963), starring Egypt's version of Elizabeth Taylor, Lobna Abdel Aziz. The lovely blue-eyed actress was a remarkable presence in many Egyptian films during this period, and her skill was admired as much as her beauty. Her striking features are interesting to note, if only to help underscore the very subtle role colourism played in cinema during this period, and its eventual bubbling up in later decades.

While *Bride of the Nile* was a fantastical romantic comedy centered on the ancient figure of a virginal Nile Maiden rising from the dead, other films celebrated ancient Egyptian heritage, but more as a beautiful backdrop to musical comedies, such as 1965's *Love in Karnak*. Entire dream-like folkdance sequences took place in Luxor led by the Reda Troupe, under the bemused watch of silly, guileless pharaonic rulers who relished the performances with child-like glee.

The cinema's true reckoning with the past did not emerge as part of the cultural firmament till after the 1967 defeat of the Arab-Israeli War. The stunning loss presents a profound rupture in the Egyptian psyche, as all of the Nasserite bravado and hope quickly fell to pieces. Nasser – after briefly submitting his resignation, a decision that Egyptians defiantly protested in the streets – subsequently appeared in public speeches and filmed newsreels possessing a far humbler aura. He wanted to be genuinely embraced by his people again but, at the same time, his administration understood the need to project strength in order to boost morale. One incredible newsreel, dating to 1969, is a ten-minute recap of the destruction wrought by the war, followed by images of innovation and development in the fields of agriculture and medicine, ending with an astounding sequence jump cutting Nasser's profile with that of the Sphinx, and a final title card that reads 'Victory is Ours'.

While mainstream images found new ways to conflate the state with pharaonic imagery, the newly auteur-driven cinema of the late 1960s and

Film stills: a series of snapshots from the newsreel, ending with 'Victory is Ours.'

1970s provided another angle altogether. Shadi Abdel Salam, who previously worked as an art director and costume designer in countless films – both Egyptian and international productions – sought to bring to life the central dilemma of modern Egyptian identity, and the collective amnesia felt when it came to the country's ancient heritage. It is one thing to evoke pharaohs in song and dance, but quite another to question their haunting presence in the country's psyche. Alienation with the past and its meaning was explored in *The Mummy,* or *The Night of Counting the Years* (1969). The film is set in Egypt, 1881 – shortly before British colonial rule ensured its footprint on the nation. For decades, a familial tribe robs pharaonic graves in the nearby necropolis of a temple, living off the sales of the treasures. When the tribe's leader dies, his sons learn about the graves' mysteries and are compelled to continue their father's business. But the youngest, Wanis, refuses to partake, for reasons not fully understood by him. Torn between loyalty to his family and moral duty towards his country's cultural heritage, he is plagued by doubts and the tragedy of the uncertain. The film took numerous artistic risks, such as its use of classic Arabic as a form of speech rather than the colloquial Egyptian dialect audiences were used to, a move that adds more historic weight to the action unfolding on-screen. And Abdel Salam, possessing his own unique aesthetic style, directs a *mise-en-scène* flowing with strongly featured actors (all square jaws, kohl-rimmed eyes, lightly tanned skin), against the backdrop of the tomb's inscrutable hieroglyphics. The characters are in a strange pantomime with the past, their bodies intuiting a language they have lost for centuries.

The question of Egyptian identity continued to haunt Shadi Abdel Salam's career, but *The Night of Counting the Years* is perhaps his clearest thesis statement on the matter – the present enforces a disconnect with the past. And, in this film, the bourgeois and colonialists attempted to rob Egyptians of their heritage – by robbing them of their memory first, antiquities second.

Underground / Overground

A brief return to the influence of the surrealist movement helps to explain some of the cinematic imagery of post-1967 Egypt. One of the pioneers,

Étienne Sved, a French-born national forced into exile for a short period in Egypt due to his Jewish heritage, was a powerful force within the group. His sketches and photography provide deeply evocative snapshots of the country in the 1940s, where it was slowly becoming clear that irrevocable change would soon occur. One photographic series in particular comes to mind, featuring pharaonic statues shot in a disturbingly disembodied manner – he would focus on the tips of their feet, the stone bodies seemingly floating elsewhere. The enigmatic pictorials are summoned in later films, which also used pharaonic imagery to poke fun at the country's elite, invoking governmental figures without risking the ire of the censorship board. One example of this is the 1971 movie *Adrift on the Nile*, which has a penultimate sequence with one of the film's major stars, Mervat Amin, drunkenly leaving a trail of kisses on an ancient statue.

Film still: *Adrift on the Nile* (1971)

Ghostly slabs of stone and random body parts made another appearance in Youssef Chahine's deeply personal *Alexandria Again and Forever* (1990), whose highlight is a satirical dream sequence featuring former blue-eyed matinee idol Hussein Fahmy as a pompous (and rather well-fed) pharaoh, who asks Chahine (playing himself) to oversee an audition of the most beautiful legs in a line-up featuring faceless, entangled limbs. The conflation of the pharaonic with both decadence and a darker Sphinx-like force is meant to be a sly stick-in-the-eye of the corrupt men and women running the country. Thus, the underground work of Sved and his peers found its way into mainstream iconography, decades later.

The Egyptian moving image's uncomfortable depiction of racial elements has been one of the industry's unspoken secrets for decades. While it would be unfair to impose the West's racial constructs on another country's past, robbing it of its specific context, it can be rightfully ascertained that Egypt's racial attitudes were influenced as much by its own unique and diverse history as the spectre of colonialism. There are moments in classic Egyptian films that seem out of place today, such as child star Fairouz's dance donning black-face in one of her most beloved movies. Most Egyptians would note that the sequence bore no malicious intent – that they were largely innocent of the West's (especially America's) sins and were simply copying funny scenes they viewed in Hollywood movies.

The truth, as always, lies in the grey area of things. While Egyptians perhaps did not share the deeply racist attitudes of other countries, the local Nubian population, for instance, have historically suffered a great deal of superstition and even mass displacement during Nasser's attempts to build the Aswan High Dam in the 1960s. In popular cinema, the few dark-skinned heroes were comedians, such as Ali El Kassar. Otherwise, black or Nubian actors were relegated to the roles of porters or extras. They were rarely marketed as performers capable of carrying their own star-studded vehicles. And, in the controversial case of noted filmmaker Youssef Chahine, they were sometimes reduced to the confines of their bodies; the physicality of dark-skinned actors linger in some of his later works as a peculiar homoerotic fascination that one can deem to be just as dehumanising.

A few dramatic actors exhibited just the right amount of tanned skin and ruggedly Semitic features to turn them into working class heroes; namely, Farid Shawky, whose entire career with filmmaker Salah Abu Seif remains the most successful pairing in star-making history. However, this is not exactly seen as breaking the colour mold within the industry, and such a move would not come till much later with the rise of Ahmed Zaki, arguably one of the most talented actors of his generation.

Zaki's rise to stardom and the difficulties he faced due to his darker skin tone is well documented. The crucial difference between him and someone like Farid Shawky was that the latter more often than not played a very specific role: the tough-guy prototype, sticking it to the elites. Zaki did not play to type – he melded a Brando-esque understanding of technique with mass popular appeal that proved to be undeniable, especially at the pinnacle of his career in the 1980s and 1990s.

But his path to celebrity was notably problematic. He took on smaller parts throughout the 1970s both in theater and film and was repeatedly passed over for roles for which producers felt it would be best to market a light-skinned actor. One infamous story surrounding the making of the political thriller, *Al Karnak* (1975), centers on a distributor's insistence to cast another actor in the lead role, since he felt that marketing the film with the dark-skinned Zaki would be impossible in Gulf countries and their neighbours throughout the region.

Of course, he who laughs last laughs longest, as the adage goes, and Zaki's talent would become impossible to ignore. His eventual prominence rivaled that of his immediate predecessor, Farid Shawky, and the public flocked to every new film he made. Curiously, he took on the role of both presidents Nasser and Al Sadat in historical pieces, but he was never asked to play a pharaoh.

Melancholy of the Present

Artists such as Shadi Abdel Salam would perhaps view the current reality in abject horror – the importance of Egyptian heritage on-screen has receded even farther in the collective memory. As cinematic production became severely depleted in the mid-to-late 1990s, so did the desire to make sense of the country's past. A sense of stasis took over, and any reckoning with historical identity was relegated to the trivial romantic melodramas of television. The pharaoh became the most potent symbol of alienation, synonymous with a tyrannical government and an authoritative military establishment. During Hosni Mubarak's presidential reign, his face was hastily superimposed on hospitals, schools, and highways, some of the architecture consistently invoking ancient Egyptian antiquities, but only in the most superficial terms. In the fight against rising Islamism, the image of the pharaoh was the only one deemed powerful enough to combat the austere long beards and black veils of political Islam. This prominent discourse shifted for a brief moment in the aftermath of the 2011 Revolution, but demonstrative interrogation has been driven underground yet again. As the broader culture slowly became more insular, materialistic, and craven, the government's chauvinistic embrace of the pharaoh, the peasant, and other iconoclastic figures lost their sincerity and instead came to represent the height of artificiality. History stopped making sense.

WOMEN WRESTLERS

Ricci Shryock

At the Festival of the King of Oussouye, girls and young women participate in traditional wrestling alongside the men. The area, in Senegal's southern Casamance region, is home to most of the country's female wrestlers. Almost every year, coaches from the Senegal Women's National Wrestling Team – who compete in the African Championships and Olympics when they qualify – come to the festival to scout new talent. The festival features traditional Senegalese wrestling known as *laamb*, which differs in style and rules from freestyle, Greco-Roman wrestling that is practised at the international level. However, according to Senegal Men's Wrestling Head Coach, Lansana Coly, the strength and skills of the two are similar enough. Coly is from the Casamance region, and he launched the women's team 20 years ago with three wrestlers, whom he recruited at the 1996 Festival of the King of Oussouye.

Today, according to many of the girls in the Oussouye area, female wrestling has lost its popularity due to some young women in the area no longer viewing it as feminine. For centuries the sport has been used as a way for women from the Jola group to display their womanhood among one another. Black and indigo blue are the traditional colours to wear if you are going to wrestle, though people also wear other colours these days. Girls and young women often wear beads to dance and support the male wrestlers, before removing the decorations to then wrestle themselves.

In September 2017, the men and boys at the festival wrestled for two days before they cleared away the giant circle in an open green field. That was the signal it was time for the women to join in the fun.

FIVE POEMS

Mustafa Abu Sneineh

Maqdisi the Geographer

You say the 'Dead Sea' is a fabrication of the Greeks
That you called it the 'Upturned Lake'
The sun's a crown of thorns
around the forenoon, you say
And on your body, the clay
Cleopatra's last words

Is it the Dead Sea or the Upturned Lake?
—It makes little difference, as long
as the eyes of the earth
are generous with their water
As your eyes
are generous
with their salt.

[Abu 'Abd Allah Muhammad ibn Ahmad al-Maqdisi, also known as
al-Bashshari, (947-991) was a geographer and traveller, and author of *The
Finest Divisions for Knowledge of the Regions*, considered one of the most
important medieval works of geography.]

Bisan Checkpoint

We could have walked on the Sea of Galilee
If we hadn't been crucified at Bisan checkpoint.
Hours of sacred passion,
Hours waiting to be saved by some mighty hand.

Our last supper was cooked by the sun
And the soldiers got drunk from our chalices.

A long, slow crucifixion between Jerusalem and Tiberias,
without wood or nails
No-one will believe the screams of the crucified,
without wood or nails
No books or hymns will repeat them
and the sun will grill our bodies for the barbarian soldiers.

Bombs in Baghdad always explode in Jerusalem

They said an Iraqi peasant had shot down an Apache with his Brno rifle
during the 'Final Battle'
An Iraqi peasant from Karbala by the name of Ali Ubayd Mingash.
Jerusalem was turned upside down at the news.
Apparently the Apache was dropping instructions to surrender
along with 25,000-dinar bills
and it was noted that the Brno was Czech,
first manufactured in 1924.
Love Saddam Hussein or hate him, everyone believed the Iraqi TV report.
Even I believed it, as I listened to the wretched rain hammer down
without watering a single tree.
My whole family believed it, and from March 2003 onwards
they reserved a seat for death at dinner.

This poem's one of the lies of that war
Lies, these letters and words,
and a liar, that Iraqi peasant

because
martyrs belong to God alone
and because
bombs in Baghdad always explode in Jerusalem.

Syria

They repeat your name in the British parliament
On the Underground, on Twitter, in fleeting reports
They repeat it in Herodotus's Histories
Syria, Syria—
These neo-Hellenes won't admit
that the Athens we built with our words
was Black Athena.

Syria
There are many seas I could drown in
Many clouds I could offer bitter cups of rain to
Only your name now signifies me—
The name I hear between pirates and mercenaries' teeth
Between the teeth of Herodotus.

Poison

Instant coffee from Osem, labneh from Tnuva
Two hundred and fifty grams of Emek cheese
and Soglowek olive mortadella.
A loaf of happy bread from Angel Bakeries
A glass of Tapuzina mango juice
And halva with Aleppine pistachio from Strauss.
I say the name of the Lord
And tuck in to my poison.

[These are the names of popular Israeli food manufacturers.]

Translated from Arabic by Katherine Hall

POEMS

Brandino Machiavelli

On the front seat

On the front seat,
Your favourite,
At the top of number 19 bus
Your arm
Was gently stroking
Against mine
But not willingly,
Like mine.

Your arm
Was careful
Not to send
Any signals
That might signal
A signal
Of being pleased
By the gentle
Intentional
Stroking of my arm
Against yours.

The beauty of the world

The beauty of the world
Lies in its infinite, forgiving, healing sadness

Which covers with its tender mantle
The unbearable inhumanity of life.

I am like a large, rough horned

I am like a large, rough horned
Ocean marine shell
Created over the decades, spire over
spire
By its marine creator, and then
Abandoned by its keeper, and polished
clean
By the resounding ocean waves.
It can now
Be picked up, and blown into,
And hum a poignant,
Melancholy note, echoing
Past delusions. But no one knows,
Or cares, or can remember,
And no one ever will.

I want to write

I want to write a short, famous
Poem, full of corrections to be admired later,
About the feeling of the sound of voices
Wafting up from downstairs
That keeps my mind from wandering
Over the soft green grass,
Thick with daisies, and clumps
Of prickly thistles, way up the Alps;
The sharp air, the crisp and blinding
Light into the blue blue sky, shimmering
Over a cold Alpine lake.
Rocks litter my path. An immense silence
Fills the air. Beauty continues to flow,

Peak after peak way far beyond
To crowded noisy polluted humanity
Somewhere a thousand miles away.

I am at the end

I am at the end
Of a long corridor of rooms.

Stretching for centuries along a wall of
jasmine,
Unknowing, silent and eternal;

Each room filled with memories
Of brightly-coloured unfinished lives.

Cold ocean waves

Cold ocean waves
Roll away slowly, patiently, ahead
Under my heaving hull,
Over the deep blue brooding sea
Endlessly
Promising nothing.

The flowing, healing wind

The flowing, healing wind above the sand
Is truer than the deaf, still tears
That hide down deep
Beneath the shifting dunes.

Now, behind the scenes,

Now, behind the scenes,
Hollow laughter and suppressed rage
Beneath a soft surrender.
The rare oriental carpet
Looks thin upon the wall. Once, underfoot, alive,
Its flight was thick with perfume,
colours and understanding.
Its dangers only increased the yearning.

The entire Universe has come together

The entire Universe has come together to create me.
It has taken all the eons of time
For the infinite coincidences to pass
And coalesce
So I could Be.
The Universe could not survive without me, or you, that flower, or that
fly,
Every single tiny event is irreplaceable,
For the survival of the whole.

Today, tomorrow, now,
My emptiness complete
My role almost concluded,
I'm but a new, future coincidence.

And chance, and freedom and happiness and sadness, all predetermined,
All fitted into the infinitely small point containing all the Universes,
All as close as our jugular vein and distant as the farthest star
And all
As beautiful and pointless as an ocean wave
smashing against the long defenceless shore.

Baron's Court Tube Station

Baron's Court Tube Station is never judgemental
Like Earl's Court Tube,
Which scowls if you are not in a hurry.
Baron's Court smiles if you are going,
It consoles if you are returning
If you are nearing your end it will remind you of the good times,
Of the rusty metal flowers in the awnings at Crevalcore train station
Lost in the plains of Italy,
The hot smell of the freshly harvested wheat-fields in July,
The silence on the straight flat hot white roads without mysteries,
Just pebbles twisting the bicycle wheel as it rolls on the fine dust.
Baron's Court will always give you some extra time
It will whisper that it's all part of life
And that time heals.
Earl's Court doesn't give you a chance.

To Be

To Be alive
is the essence
of the Universe.

To Love
is the essence of Being alive.

REVIEWS

UNWANTED BONES *by Sahil KWarsi*
THE PRICE OF A RAINFOREST *by Giles Goddard*
DRESSED TO BE BLESSED *by Misha Monaghan*

UNWANTED BONES

Sahil K Warsi

Historians can only be admired for the alchemy required in blending together fragments, ellipses, and lacunae into a narrative that expresses a reality of the past in the context of the present. This balancing act reveals them more immediately, I believe, as artists, than just chroniclers and interpreters. Indeed, Kim Wagner's *The Skull of Alum Bheg* is a work of art. Yet, lest you think this review will be a litany of the book's wonders, let me forewarn you: one need not like a work to recognise it as art, for art goes beyond demonstrated mastery and skill to provoke and unsettle.

I really did want to like *The Skull of Alum Bheg*. Having read Wagner's first book on the 1857 uprising, I expected his signature style of gripping, fast-paced narrative. On this count he did not disappoint. As in his other popular historical writing, Wagner delves deftly into vast primary source material to illustrate the intricate and multifaceted social histories of events (and non-events even) connected to the 1857 Sepoy Rebellion and its legacy. In this book, he attends specifically to the unfurling and aftermath of the uprising in Sialkot. Through clipped prose, Wagner contours the broad social dynamics, cross-hatching with statistics and figures and contrasting with passages from first-hand accounts. One pleasantly feels less that one is reading an historical account than a heady whodunnit, albeit a heavily researched and annotated one.

Kim A Wagner, *The Skull of Alum Bheg: The Life and Death of a Rebel of 1857*, Hurst & Company, London, 2017.

Style and flourish alone do not, unfortunately, constitute good history. Finishing the book, I was left perplexed and frustrated. How was it, I wondered, that despite having enjoyed the ride I had arrived with a feeling of having been blindfolded and thrown in the back of a pickup? Thinking I had perhaps fallen victim to my own expectations, I resolved to re-read the book, attending to it as an object rather than an experience. This second reading proved insightful. I had indeed expected too much of the book, but whereas I initially wanted to fault Wagner – 'How dare you not deliver me my consumerist due!' – I felt I could only grieve at the project's misconstrued objectivity.

These are maybe harsh words, so I must be clear on one thing: writing history is hard and writing good history even harder. I do not pretend to do it; I am not a historian. However, as an anthropologist, I have an acute appreciation of the challenge in researching and writing about those who do not, cannot, or will not speak. Undertaking a 'subaltern prosopography', as Wagner describes his work, is no mean task. One must contend with a near complete absence of primary sources on the sepoys' own experience of the uprising while attempting to contextualise and communicate their relationships, their ambitions, and – in the case of Alum Bheg – their grisly fate. This Wagner executes skilfully and communicates accessibly, and he must be lauded for doing so. But there is perhaps a fine line between artistic and artful, and my misgivings about *The Skull of Alum Bheg* are ultimately not because of the exquisiteness of the tableau, but the distortion in perspective and unfortunate choice of frame.

The premise of the book promises a *dastan*-like experience, a form of story-telling where audiences are carried through nested tales of mystery, trickery, and perhaps even moral insight. An email to Wagner from new owners of a pub in Southeast England alerts him to the existence of a skull with a biographical note tucked away inside. This note becomes the vehicle carrying readers into the past, affording a birds-eye view of the uprising in Sialkot, an outpost on the margins of the wild west of mid-1800s British India that is now in Pakistani Punjab near the border with Indian Kashmir. Through the introductory tale of the mystery of the skull, Wagner sets the tone and presents his framework for thinking through and about the uprising and writing history more broadly. This is followed by three chapters that outline the tensions brewing across India in the prelude to the uprising, and the specific context of the sepoys, the British military, and European and American missionaries in Sialkot. The subsequent three chapters present a blow-by-blow description of the happenings and movements of people in Sialkot from the day before the uprising through the outbreak of revolt. These chapters aim to illustrate how the uprising was not an organised mass rebellion against the British in India and are followed by another four chapters on the military defeat of the Sialkot *sepoys*, their fate in the context of British retribution, the longer-term pursuit of survivors of the rebellion, and the practice of public executions in the wake of British victory. The book ends with a chapter on the European colonial practice of head hunting – let us at least not call it 'collection' – and a short epilogue tying up the stories of the characters introduced in the story of the Sialkot uprising.

The straightforward structure and engaging style of the book make it an undeniably pleasant read. I was, however, also expecting a critical engagement with the history of the uprising and, as promised to readers in the introductory chapter, a critical and nuanced understanding of the 'enduring legacies' of imperialism. My own orientation to British imperial history in India is varied. I grew up on a steady stream of Indian popular media generally steeped in disdain for colonialism. These sentiments fermented through academic study in the humanities and hardened during a decade of living in the United Kingdom in which raj-mania has become *en vogue* (was it ever not?). Still, somewhere in the recesses of my mind, behind the fantastical Bollywood representations of overthrowing the British yoke, angry Urdu novels, and dazzling postcolonial critiques, there is a parallel tune. Stemming from the same region as Alum Bheg, though a couple of generations later, my grandparents' nostalgia for the failing imperial machine they served in has always been a reminder that history – or indeed reality – is rarely ever unitary.

I could thus only agree with Wagner's assertion that 'the biggest stumbling-block to constructive debates about the history and legacies of the Empire today is the overwhelming reliance on the notion of the so-called "balance sheet of Empire".' I hoped that in the maelstrom of contemporary public discussion on engaging with the past and present of colonialism, *The Skull of Alum Bheg* would offer a considered inquiry into realities and lessons of the British colonial enterprise in India. There are two reasons why it fails to do so. First, the simplistic theoretical box set up for the work to fit into does not suit the complexity of the intervention it seeks to make. Second, by not attending to this complexity it attempts an objectivity that only further replicates certain colonialist narratives and misses an opportunity to effectively consider any 'enduring legacies' of colonialism.

The basis for Wagner's approach is sound. Of course, one cannot always judge people of the past by moral metrics of the present, let alone caricaturise colonisers and colonised in ways that deny their human predicaments and agency. However, in placing his work to respond to extremes of 'mindless empire-bashing' or 'jingoistic empire-nostalgia', which he emblematises through Shashi Tharoor and Niall Ferguson, I felt the bar was being set unnecessarily low for readers. Similarly, while I agree reducing the past into binaries of good or bad is crude, I cannot help but feel that a lack of judgement or consideration of the morality and ethics of past events and actions is, at best, careless history. The misplaced objectivity in presenting all sides as similarly complex, in the end, ignores the very real power relationships under which people lived and acted.

Ultimately, and contra Wagner's own aims, the attempted detached observation serves to replicate colonial attitudes and knowledge in the book. Despite stating that one must see the sources and forces of the uprising as diffuse and diverse, readers are consistently presented with easy stereotypes such as Muslims being less invested in the imperial enterprise, Hindus being more likely to be loyal to the British, local Punjabis being more amenable to British rule than the immigrant *purbiya* population (referring to people of the eastern Gangetic planes area), and so on. There is some consideration on issues such as caste difference and social class, but the absence of any explicit discussion to complicate such categories casts these reflections into the shadows of the vivid colonial accounts that move the narrative along. It was not until the second, close reading that I identified the problematisation of these categories at all.

Nonetheless, Wagner is not uncritical in engaging with his sources. Readers become intimately acquainted with the lives and sentiments of the missionaries and officers in Sialkot through their diary entries and reports that comprise the bulk of the narrative. Naturally, it is the nature of the colonial archive that 'subaltern' voices are virtually non-existent. Wagner does consider what such voices might have said based on the little information available, and indicates the European and American protagonists' classism, indirectly acknowledging the racism and prejudice expressed in their views. The constant presentation of colonial views followed by that of the silent subalterns', however, has the effect of erasing the political context within which relationships were being made and broken. By the time I got to the final chapter on head hunting, this alternating system of presentation seemed to lead to the conclusion that just as one cannot see resistance to colonisation as unified, one must appreciate how colonial attitudes and actions were not met with united zeal in Britain. This unsettling false equivalence is discomforting, to say the least, and comes across as an argument for #notallcolonisers that misses the point.

In contrast to *The Skull of Alum Bheg*, Wagner's first book on the uprising, *The Great Fear of 1857*, successfully draws readers' attention to the complexities of actors, motives, and outcomes in the context of the rebellion. It considers the uprising as it played out across various cities of British India, highlighting the disunity within the sepoy uprising and revealing the East India Company's fractured monopoly of power. Most of *The Skull of Alum Bheg* could easily have been a chapter in this first book if the aim was merely to highlight the historical multiplicity of the event of the uprising. Indeed, much of the contextual material presented in the second book appears to have been repurposed from *The Great Fear of 1857*. Transposing the argument and framing of *The Great Fear of 1857* onto the second book is neither germane nor effective when the uprising, British imperialism, and its legacy today are being explored through the question of how Alum Bheg's skull came to rest in an English pub. The framework set up for *The Skull of Alum Bheg* draws attention to colonial orientations to and engagement with the colonised, and their place in the present context. To argue here for a need to recognise that not all Britons supported colonialism seems a non sequitur and insensitive to the very real and continuing legacy of imperialism.

It is not until the final chapter on European colonial head hunting that the morality and ethics of imperial practice are really touched upon, and only in the final three paragraphs of the book are attempts made to follow the introduction's claim to consider 'enduring legacies of imperialism that are still with us today'. These final paragraphs were, for me, the most jarring. A paltry half paragraph explains how the presence of Alum Bheg's skull in an English pub remains a mystery. Breaking from the tone of the rest of the book, Wagner makes a bold assertion that 'it is high time for Alum Bheg to return home,' while recognising the bureaucratic hurdles to repatriating the skull. His observation that there are no South Asian groups pressing for return of human remains as there are in South Africa or Oceania is tone-deaf and ignorant of the difference between Alum Bheg's skull and those remains that are of continuing sacred value and political import to present communities elsewhere. Finally, lurking behind the concluding observation that Alum Bheg's execution intentionally deprived him of a proper burial, the spectre of the question as to how this skull is part of and representative of current orientations toward British history looms large and unexplored.

Despite my misgivings, *The Skull of Alum Bheg* is well-written and it undoubtedly moved me, as good art does. While I found it disappointing in many ways, the book led me to what I can only express as surprise at my own capacity for indifference. Particularly during my second reading, I found myself without any sense of empathy for the deaths of the British men, women, and children in Sialkot and other British Indian cities. The horrific description of their deaths somehow only deepened my frustration with the inadvertent whitewashing of the book. Naturally, this realisation was itself horrifying. Perhaps for a moment I could understand how someone would be driven to the extremes of 'mindless empire-bashing' or 'jingoistic empire-nostalgia'. It is for this reason that Wagner's stance that he does not intend to offer a view on the merits or faults of colonialism through the book make me uncomfortable.

To refrain from taking a position assumes that history is something that only exists in the past and is thus beyond our critique. With regard to colonialism, it ignores the context of the present in which Oxford academics are undertaking research as part of a multidisciplinary five-year *Ethics and Empire* project to 'test the critiques against the historical facts of empire' and thereby 'develop a nuanced and historically intelligent Christian ethic of empire'. Or similarly, where a leading peer-reviewed journal like the *Third World Quarterly* can publish articles such as 'The Case for Colonialism', that unironically argues for a return to colonialist governance and expansion. In this context, how we read and present the archive does matter. Wagner is no apologist for colonialism and makes this clear both in and outside the book. He warns readers that those seeking a simplistic moralising view of history, regardless of their political orientations, will be disappointed with *The Skull of Alum Bheg*. However, in treating experiences of colonisers and colonised as commensurable from the perspective of the present, he misses a real opportunity to consider why thinking about colonialism is important today. Why is it that Alum Bheg's skull makes Britons uncomfortable today in a way it didn't before? What does it mean that people don't feel it belongs here anymore? Many such questions that actually attempt to consider the continuing legacy of Britain's imperial past remain woefully unasked and unthought in the book.

For what it is worth, I disagree with Wagner. I think ultimately the place of Alum Bheg's skull is in Britain. It represents the honest and uncomfortable discussions that remain to be had around the practice of empire and its reverberations through to the present. As Bahadur Shah Zafar, the last Mughal Emperor who was exiled from India following the uprising, writes in the introductory *ghazal* to his *diwan*:

کانٹوں کو مت نکال چمن سے او باغباں
یہ بھی گلوں کے ساتھ پلے ہیں بہار میں

'O gardener, do not remove the thorns;
they too were cultivated alongside the blooms of spring!'

THE PRICE OF A RAINFOREST

Giles Goddard

How much is a rainforest worth? Not much, apparently. In late 2017, I spent a couple of months of my sabbatical in Malaysian Borneo. The journey there involved flying over thousands of square kilometres of clear-cut land, abundant and mysterious forest burnt and replaced by an endless monoculture of palm oil plantations. This, despite decades of fervent advocacy to preserve the rainforest, and scientific consensus that the tropical ecosystem is a vital carbon sink. Why? Because the economics, apparently, don't stack up. There's no money in preserving the forest; only in destroying it and using the land for short term cash-crop exploitation. Which, in turn, provides an immediate and measurable increase in Malaysia's Gross Domestic Product (GDP) and an increase in governmental tax take. The wellbeing of the indigenous tribes deep in the forest is sacrificed for the sake of fulfilling the rich world's insatiable demand for shower gel.

To lay all of this destruction at the door of one economists' measure of national financial weight would be to lay too heavy a burden on the notion of Gross Domestic Product. But, argues Ehsan Masood, in *The Great Invention,* the crudeness and bluntness of GDP as a measure of national financial health has had profound and baleful consequences for global wellbeing and environmental health. I have a clear memory of *il sorpasso* – the moment in 1987 when Italy's GDP overtook the UK's. There were disquieted articles in the broadsheets about the spiralling decline of Britain's economic strengths, followed ten years later by relieved comment marking the moment when Britain overtook Italy again.

Everyone enjoys a league table. The Premier League, the tennis rankings, TV reality shows with their precisely calibrated competitiveness – each is carefully followed both by those with vested interests and by those who simply enjoy the show. The leaders of countries are no different. They watch, carefully, the relative sizes of the economies of nations. Is their

CRITICAL MUSLIM 27, JULY–SEPTEMBER 2018

country large enough to be part of the G20 group of global economies? Or even the G7, which became the G8 when Russia joined in the late 1990s (and then got suspended in 2014).

GDP, the tool most commonly used to measure the size of national economies, has, for economists and politicians, an important function. It is one of the fundamental terms of the grammar of capital. It shows clearly how much value a nation's economy is producing. It can be expressed in a simple mathematical formula: $Y = C + I + G + (X - M)$. C is what consumers spend in shops; I is what businesses spend; G is spending by governments; X is what companies sell to customers abroad; and M is what we buy from sellers overseas. In other words, Y, or GDP, is a measure of what we sell, what we make, what we spend as a government, and what we export, minus what we import. It seems, at first glance, to be a reliable and robust measure of the relative strength of global economies. The bigger the better – a large GDP is apparently indicative of the strength of an economy, and one could be forgiven for assuming that GDP growth is invariably a good thing.

Ehsan Masood, *The Great Invention: The Story of GDP and the Making (and Unmaking) of the Modern World*, Pegasus Books, New York, 2016.

This is where Masood's fascinating account of the development of GDP is so valuable – it is also an investigation of why GDP is in fact a blunt instrument which can lead to a distorted approach to the health of an economy and the wealth of a nation's citizens. The government of Pakistan, for example, pursued a National Plan after independence which enthusiastically embraced industrial investment at the cost of provision of hospitals and schools. The growth rate in GDP was around six per cent between 1960 and 1965, with industrial output increasing at 14 per cent per year. But it became apparent as the Plan entered its first decade that much of this growth was unsustainable, being mainly funded by loans and precarious development grants – and that the benefits of GDP growth had accrued mainly to a very small number of elite, super-rich families. Mahbub-al-Haq, the first chief economist of Pakistan's Planning Commission, made a famous speech in 1968 in Karachi in which he said:

Society has every right, in fact it has a duty, to resist the emergence of a privileged class of entrepreneurs which is pampered by fiscal concessions, which is sheltered by prohibitive tariffs, which is nurtured by artificial incentives and which makes its living on the bases of imperfect and inefficient competition.

Al-Haq had discovered, first hand, the damage that could be done by managing an economy solely on the basis of increasing GDP. Yet how did this particular measure of economic strength become so authoritative? Its genesis is surprisingly recent. Policy makers and financiers in the North Atlantic economies were hampered, during the depression years of the 1930s, by a lack of statistical information on national income and expenditure. Masood quotes an exchange from a Congressional inquiry in 1931:

'We are woefully lacking in payroll statistics, are we not?'

'Yes.'

'Now let us consider statistics on consumer purchases.'

'In the first place, we do not have very good coverage... We have lost the identity of commodities completely by the time they get to the consumer...'

'You cannot answer the question.'

'I would hate to guess it within 100 percent.'

A roll-call of senior economists, headed by John Maynard Keynes, were involved in the development of GDP as a standard measure of national economic strength. It reached more or less its current form shortly after the second World War in order to assist the US in its implementation of the Marshall Plan to rebuild Europe, and has, with some tweaks, retained its dominant place in economic discourse ever since.

The trouble is, money can't buy you love. As Robert F Kennedy pointed out on the presidential campaign trail in 1968:

Our gross national product...counts air pollution and cigarette advertising and ambulances to clear our highways of carnage. It counts special locks for our doors and the jails for the people who break them. It counts the destruction of the redwood and the loss of our natural wonder in chaotic sprawl....Yet the gross national product does not allow for the health of our children, the quality of their education, or the joy of their play.

Although Kennedy referred to GNP – gross *national* product – his criticism could also apply to GDP. The difference between the two is that GNP takes into account the economic activity of a country's corporations and individuals *beyond* its borders. GDP only includes activity *within* national borders. The USA's GNP is thus significantly higher than its GDP as it has a high level of external activity.

The difference between GNP and GDP therefore does not invalidate Kennedy's criticism. GDP values only what is bought or sold. It does not include intangibles and unsold goods such as volunteering, housework, informal caring, community engagement, or social capital. GDP assumes that saleable economic activity is the fundamental way that nation states express value, and it is, at best, a crude way to express that activity.

This is not news. In 1989, the Nobel prizewinning economist Amartya Sen said to Mahbub al-Haq, 'Look, you are a sophisticated enough guy to know that to capture complex reality in one number is just vulgar, like GDP.' Masood goes further in *The Great Invention* and argues that the effect of GDP is more insidious and more destructive than this. The exclusion of items which are hard to measure because they are rarely, if ever, bought or sold, means that the most significant measure of economic strength is *unable* to take into account issues such as environmental degradation, climate change, or individuals' health and wellbeing. Indeed, ill health can result in a larger GDP, for example through higher levels of medical treatment for higher levels of heart disease in the population. Conversely, areas of recreation such as national parks and factors indicating the health of the natural world such as biodiversity are not costed and therefore ignored. The effect of that has been to privilege economic growth at the cost of the common good and societal wellbeing. Pollution, air quality, loss of biodiversity and increasing occasions of extreme weather are only included in GDP insofar as they affect income and expenditure. They are marginal to GDP and yet crucial to the wellbeing of society. Furthermore, the immediate effect of the emphasis on GDP is a focus on economic growth at the cost of everything else. Growth depends on consumption. The world's resources are finite, and the higher the growth, the quicker they are consumed. Pope Francis has spoken about this in his encyclical *Laudato Si*, published in 2016:

Economic powers continue to justify the current global system where priority tends to be given to speculation and the pursuit of financial gain, which fail to take the context into account, let alone the effects on human dignity and the natural environment. Here we see how environmental deterioration and human and ethical degradation are closely linked. Many people will deny doing anything wrong because distractions constantly dull our consciousness of just how limited and finite our world really is. As a result, whatever is fragile, like the environment, is defenceless before the interests of a deified market, which become the only rule.

Unsurprisingly, since very early in the history of GDP, attempts have been made to counteract the potentially destructive effect of the measure. In 1971, the newly crowned King Wangchuck of Bhutan, aged 16, attempted to synthesise growth and greenery, and to quantify his citizens' wellbeing. The young monarch announced, 'our country's policy is to consolidate our sovereignty, to achieve economic self-reliance, prosperity and happiness for our people.... Gross National Happiness is more important than Gross National Product.' Bhutan has become a poster nation for an alternative approach to finance and the economy. Bhutan's forests are preserved by tight planning policies and its economy has remained largely agricultural. It is small and inaccessible enough for it to be able to pursue an independent approach. But it also now has a functioning and vibrant parliamentary democracy, and has successfully steered away from options, recommended by US-based consultants McKinsey, which could have derailed the emphasis on Gross National Happiness.

The concept of measuring happiness has now been picked up across the world, not least by the UK's former Prime Minister David Cameron who, during his term of office, enthusiastically endorsed government-sponsored happiness surveys. The happiness industry has even taken hold of the World Economic Forum, the club for the super-rich and powerful which meets annually in Davos, Switzerland. Measuring individual happiness, however, is one thing – measuring environmental damage and collective wellbeing is another. A leading light in the attempt to counteract the orthodoxy of GDP, Robert Costanza, encountered significant opposition to his attempts to put a value on the global environment, developing a methodology which initially valued 'natural capital' at US$33 trillion. And Mahbub al-Haq was instrumental in producing the Human Development Index as an alternative to GDP. But his work was holed below the waterline at first publication, as it ranked the US at number 19. According to Masood, 'the US probably never forgave for the humiliation of a lowly position in the first HDI tables.'

To the frustration of Masood and many others, GDP still remains enthroned as the primary measure of economic strength, at the same time as measures of unhappiness (over 25 per cent of teenage girls in the UK now display symptoms of depression) and environmental threat (there was unprecedented hurricane activity in the Atlantic in the summer of 2017) are increasing.

The Great Invention does not end with an upbeat flourish, confidently looking forward to a time when countries will collectively adopt an economic measure which genuinely encourages global wellbeing. On the contrary, it ends with a challenge to those who seek to change GDP so that it can measure the things that matter to us all. Masood concludes from his research and investigations that the failure to influence the measure is less about data quality than it is about political might and the ability of campaigners to engage with authority in the debate – and ensure that the interests of the major economies are also respected.

But there may be a more fundamental reason why GDP has retained its primacy and its influence. The league table of relative economic national strengths, exemplified in *il sorpasso,* is a manifestation of the human tendency to measure, to quantify, to codify, to determine. The years of the Enlightenment in Western Europe – 1750-1820 – saw a dramatic upsurge in the activities of measurement in the natural and economic world. Carl Linnaeus's *Systema Natura* was the first attempt to codify the entirety of the known natural world, and Adam Smith's *The Wealth of Nations*, published in 1776, effectively heralded the birth of economics as a separate academic discipline.

It may be that this focus on economics as a science has meant that notions of happiness or wellbeing, or the general good of society, have become by definition excluded from economic theory. The Pope's *Laudato Si* addresses this explicitly. Section IV – 'Politics and Economy in Dialogue for Human Fulfilment' is a hard-hitting and comprehensive challenge to the way in which the market, underpinned by the focus on GDP, has diminished the ability of nation-states to ensure the wellbeing of their citizens. Parts of it are worth quoting at length:

The financial crisis of 2007-08 provided an opportunity to develop a new economy, more attentive to ethical principles, and new ways of regulating speculative financial practices and virtual wealth. But the response to the crisis did not include rethinking the outdated criteria which continue to rule the world. Production is not always rational, and is usually tied to economic variables which assign to products a value that does not necessarily correspond to their real worth.

The encyclical is very much worth reading in full. It connects spiritual and physical wellbeing with the care of creation and the need to develop a new economic theory. And it ends with a challenge that applies to individuals, communities and wider society:

We must regain the conviction that we need one another, that we have a shared responsibility for others and the world, and that being good and decent are worth it. We have ethics, goodness, faith and honesty. It is time to acknowledge that light-hearted superficiality has done us no good.

In a way, the Pope also challenges woolly solutions, such as the World Economic Forum's 'add happiness and stir' prescription at its recent Davos meetings. The large-scale structural damage caused by an obsession with GDP cannot be undone by feel-good solutions for individual happiness.

This is partly why, in my day job as a priest in a parish in Waterloo, London, I have had many conversations about the connection, or lack thereof, between mindfulness and prayer. It is my slightly provocative contention that mindfulness focuses on the individual at the cost of the community. The practice of mindfulness, when it is embedded within a capitalist, consumer-driven system, seems to offer short-term individual solutions to problems which would be better solved communally – loneliness, alienation, anger. Whereas prayer is, at its best and most radical, an activity which both acknowledges and strengthens community. Mindfulness, as it is branded and packaged now, is a manifestation of a compartmentalised and individual approach to the world. It is a philosophy for a world which measures success in terms of economic growth, whereas the ancient spiritualities offer a vision of wholeness which relies on the health of the whole of community.

'The avarice of plenitude keeps you occupied till you reach the grave,' warns the Qur'an (102:1-2). Despite this divine admonition, around

31,000 square miles of rainforest are cut down each year – 416 million trees each month. After measurable improvements in the early years of the twenty-first century, the rate of destruction is increasing again. The disconnect between consumption and wellbeing is a manifestation of wider disconnect between the spiritual and the economic. The damage wrought by our obsession with GDP is a symptom – albeit a serious one – of this. If we are to enable humanity and creation to continue to flourish, says Masood, we must do better.

DRESS TO BE BLESSED

Misha Monaghan

Like many Muslim women across the world I have had a complicated relationship with the way I dress. Although I have never covered my hair, the importance of my body and the clothes I could wear was impressed upon me from a young age. Well into my early twenties, my Pakistani grandmother had a habit of assessing my apparel before I left the house to discern the level of 'piousness'. This sexualisation of me, my sisters, and many of my other female relatives, was not deemed unusual or problematic in any way. Women were told to protect themselves from the advances of men but men were not taught to view women in any way other than as sexual beings.

I did not grow up with role models like Dina Torkia, a mixed race British Muslim woman like me who has managed to retain her 'pious' identity while also being seen as someone who can dress any other fashionista under the table. My mixed heritage confused me further; I had Scottish cousins who were allowed to wear frilly dresses and strappy tops in their teens but my Muslim background and Pakistani grandmother vehemently forbade the showing of more skin than necessary for fear of whipping any passing man into a sexual frenzy.

Throughout my formative years I toyed with what it meant to be a mixed race Muslim woman in Britain. I considered wearing a hijab to more easily fit in with my Indian and Pakistani relatives, but then eschewed the idea for fear that it would alienate my Scottish ones. I never really understood how I could consolidate all of my identities.

There were also some completely intangible rules that I still cannot make sense of. My maternal grandfather was from Hyderabad Deccan, India, where the wearing of a sari is a rite of passage for a woman after her marriage. It is a sign of graduation to a higher plane of being. I looked at the women around me and could not understand how it was deemed acceptable for them to have at least five inches of their back and stomach showing but I was nearly disowned for not wearing a baggy top over my apparently extremely tight jeans. I was even more flummoxed by the rules that my mother and grandmother imparted to me regarding the 'pious fashion' around us. It was perfectly permissible for me to wear a short sleeve *shalwar kameez* but anything that revealed a shoulder would be frowned upon. The same rules did not apply to women who chose to cover their hair — they were to be held to a higher standard. I vividly remember the strong critique of a second cousin of mine that my mother, grandmother and sisters launched into when they had seen that she decided to wear a headscarf but then also wore short sleeves. Did she not realise that the rules had now changed for her? Elbows were a big no-no.

Elizabeth Bucar, *Pious Fashion: How Muslim Women Dress*, Harvard University Press, Cambridge, 2017.

I was also bewildered as to why my style of dressing was permitted to become less 'pious' when I would eventually and apparently inevitably get married. My grandmother's favourite phrase to us when she was critiquing the piousness of our dress was to announce that once we got married we could 'run around all day in bikinis' for all she cared.

As a Muslim woman with lived experience of navigating the rules of dressing myself, I approached *Pious Fashion* with some anticipation. Perhaps Elizabeth Bucar could explain all those intangible rules that I could not comprehend. Bucar's research shows us how important the topic of clothing is for women in Muslim communities around the world. Just as it is for non-Muslim women, the female body has and always will be a hot topic. From debates regarding the taxation on women's sanitary products to the #MeToo movement, there has been a significant and long-awaited upsurge in the prevalence of discussion about wrongs done to women.

One of the most common arguments made against Islam is that women are deemed to be oppressed and the physical expression of this oppression is the necessity for women to veil themselves in all sorts of ways. Bucar attempts to unravel the assumption that the Islamic veil is a sign of oppression. Instead, she proposes that 'pious fashion', as she defines it, has different connotations based on its context. Her chapters cover three locations. She intentionally decided that she would veer away from more traditional Arab regions of the world when focusing her research and as a result landed in Iran, Turkey and Indonesia.

Each of these countries has its own rich history of and relationship with women and the way they present themselves. Iran has had quite a reputation for using apparel for both women and men as a political instrument. The Turkish state has also had a controversial relationship with the headscarf. It was banned from public institutions under 'public clothing regulation'; women who chose to wear headscarves were denied entry into universities and barred from civil serve and government jobs. The ban was eventually lifted in October 2013 by the AKP government. Nor surprisingly, recent years have seen an upsurge in the number of women choosing to wear the headscarf. Indonesia's Muslims make up 87.2 per cent of its population, making it the largest Muslim country in the world by population, and the interpretations of appropriate Islamic dress for women are as diverse as its population.

Bucar shows us that fashion is not frivolous. It is an expression of something we need to take note of. Art is a mirror to our times. Fashion is art and like all other forms of art it gives us a unique insight into the world around us. Bucar discusses this early on in the book, citing one of my favourite scenes from the film *The Devil Wears Prada*. Meryl Streep's character, Miranda, the powerful fashion magazine editor, verbally obliterates Anne Hathaway's Andy when she dares to scoff at the pains her team are taking to decide between two items that, in Andy's eyes, are the exact same shade. In her tirade Miranda explains to Andy exactly how obtuse she is in thinking that her choice of frumpy clothing somehow separates her intellectually from the others at the magazine, when in fact every choice she has made in her clothing has been meticulously orchestrated by the fashion powers-that-be.

Bucar also shows that Muslim women are not a monolith. They do not all dress the same and their fashion choices are not entirely dictated by the men in their lives. It is a book that will make many Muslim women feel vindicated. I felt a sense of camaraderie with many of the women she mentions. They, like me, know that there were some intangible rules about their fashion choices but were not necessarily able to explain the their root causes. Unfortunately, Bucar too is unable to tease out the causes in her study either.

My issue with this book is that it contains relatively little in the way of anecdotes or explanations from the women being interviewed. There were short extracts from interviews but the majority of the work is based on the analysis of these women from Bucar's perspective. Although this is somewhat helpful, there are two inherent issues. Bucar presents many of these women as blindly fumbling through the world of fashion without having the elevated and academic understanding that she has of their environment. Secondly, her work and conclusions are based on observations she made over relatively short periods of time. How much can her three to four months' worth of fieldwork across three different highly diverse nations really tell us about women and their fashion choices? This of course does not mean that people outside of communities cannot provide us with a useful analysis of particular situations, but Bucar's book does not do this. We are given a fleeting understanding of the political background of each city she is in and how that could have potentially affected women's dress in these nations. This is then followed with Bucar's 'fashion snapshots', which were minimal and – for fear of sounding like a child transitioning to non-illustrated books – had very few illustrations. She then rounds every chapter off with identifying and assessing the fashion authorities in each region. In theory this works well as an academic paper but not as a book hoping to give the reader rounded and empathetic insights.

The lack of quoted dialogue from the interviewees and true appreciation of the motivations behind their choices, in their own words, left me disassociating from the book. It had the overall effect of taking the life out of the prose. This is part of the issue with reading books written by people who do not have a lived experience of the phenomenon they are writing about. Bucar would have benefitted from passing the microphone more often. She did not succeed in capturing me in her journey and the book felt inorganic and dry as a result. I struggle with believing that her study helps us truly understand why and how women in the locations she focused on choose their dress and what influences them on a deeper level.

There is obviously great merit in viewing Muslim women not as an oppressed mass but as individuals with agency. My frustration stems – in reality – from the very necessity, and ultimate futility, of such ethnographic studies. The core message of *Pious Fashion* is that Muslim women dress differently throughout the world. Their choices are based on possibly hundreds of years of decisions that have been made through a variety of different actors and sectors, which eventually lead to the clothes on their backs today. This is not and should not be a revelation. It is common sense and something that can self-evidently be said of all women everywhere. Why must there be a perpetual separation of Muslim women from the norm?

There is nowhere in the world that is devoid of the trends that Bucar is unveiling in her book. Politics, history, media and a host of other devices have been influencing women and their fashion for millennia across the world. Yes, many Muslim nations are inherently patriarchal, but this does not differentiate them from any other nation in the world. Yes, Muslim women sometimes dress in a particular way. So what? Muslim women do not need trivial and irrelevant explanations for the choices they make. They need space to express themselves however they see fit.

ET CETERA

LAST WORD ON MALE BEAUTY *by Avaes Mohammed*
THE LIST: TEN MIGHTY MAKEOVERS
CITATIONS
CONTRIBUTORS

ON MALE BEAUTY

Avaes Mohammad

He was a man already in his nineties when I first met him, too old to walk very much unaccompanied. Whenever we were granted audience with him he'd be sat almost motionless atop a heavily padded sofa. Flawlessly smooth skin, piercingly sharp eyes, and lips pursed intentfully. My master was iridescent.

I'd heard as an adolescent of how the companions of the Prophet Muhammad, peace be upon him, would sit so motionless before him that a bird could have landed upon their shoulders and not been disturbed. If I'm perfectly honest, the way I related to this and other depictions of the time of the Prophet wasn't entirely unlike the way I related to folk tales: a time where men and women of valour and chivalry vehemently fought injustice, striving always to do the right thing and where even the laws of nature conspired towards their aid.

Being part of that audience however, I now understand what that scene over 1,400 years ago could have felt like. We too, this disparate band of seekers from around the world who had collected in a Moroccan outback to sit before a man we'd each taken as our spiritual master, were, just as that scene would have been, sat as statues before him, transfixed and filled with awe. Our master hardly spoke and when he did it was through hushed, croaky Moroccan Arabic, the meaning of which reached us via echoed translation. It wasn't that we'd come to see our master do anything in particular. He just sat there.

Yet the impact he had upon us all was palpable. Floods of tears coursed down the cheeks of some of us whilst others were so overcome with humility they dared only to snatch glimpses of him from lowered heads. As though feasting upon his presence, it was usually the walks back to our accommodation where we'd attempt to digest what had just happened. Backdropped by the blue-black silhouettes of mountains and illuminated under a cacophony of night stars spilt over our heads, we'd try and understand what exactly it was that just happened to us. Our meagre attempts echoed one another in nothing but their voids most of the time, hardly able to articulate a drop from the ocean of feeling within us all.

Nevertheless, what was graspable for us was that we'd each been subjected to a beauty unlike anything we'd known before. This beauty defied definitions which I, at least, had tacitly grown to accept, one where beauty was synonymous with seduction, used in order to arouse base, carnal human qualities. Hanging over me from vast billboards in order to generate feelings of either inadequacy, lust, or both, just so I might buy something. Such beauty screamed to the world, demanding that it stand apart, distinct and separate. Yet the beauty I'd seen in my master harmonised with everything around it whilst also projecting itself onto its environment, illuminating all with its own light and so making everything brighter.

Our attempts to capture our master's beauty and all it meant took us deep into the night. *He's radiant*, one would say. *Piercing*, would reply another. Stunning, in the literal sense of the word, capturing its perceiver like prey before captivating them in order to facilitate an effortless absorption. By simply looking upon him, it was as though we were developing a new literacy around this term, beauty. It was no doubt his physical form our eyes locked themselves upon, but our gaze travelled much farther. Like a light, his beauty shone outwards from within through his body and into the outside world, resulting in him appearing more luminous than anything around him. This was a beauty that didn't scream for focus and attention, rather, it commanded it.

Throughout all of our discussions and discourses, never once had anyone mentioned that there may be something strange in the fact that the subject of our absorption was in fact an elderly man. Whilst its true we'd all taken him as our spiritual guide and master and as such were naturally predisposed towards his adulation, we were still young heterosexual men born and raised in the West who most likely had never let ourselves become so affected by the beauty of another man before. Yet our passions for our master have never once seemed strange or deviant from any professed norm for us.

We were all well aware that every interaction with our master was a spiritual lesson for us, a means of accessing Allah and His exemplar and paragon, the beloved Prophet Muhammad. Such is the role of these guides, men and women who themselves have undertaken the spiritual rigour necessary to have reached the status of *insaan-i-kamil*, the perfected human, so they may exist as echoes of the Prophetic Way in contemporary times. To see such men and women is akin to seeing the Prophet. The way my master turned his body so as to give full attention to whomsoever he spoke, it's exactly as I'd heard the Prophet had done. The way he walked, with humility and so as not to burden the earth, was exactly as I'd read the Prophet had done. The pleasure he took in feeding people, in giving whatever came to him to those around him, that he remained calm and grateful despite what happened to him. My master and people like him make real what seem like folk tales, proof that a man even greater than them lived amongst us over 1,400 years ago.

One Ramadan night I saw my master outside under the night sky, finding myself again transfixed. As others thronged around him I absorbed him from a distance. I can't recollect when, but at some point, I found myself looking between the moon that suspended itself just behind him and his own face. As soon as I'd realised what I was doing, I recalled reading somewhere an account of one of the Prophet's companions who stood before him, perhaps similarly to the way I had just been, gazing between his blessed countenance and the sight of the moon. The companion explains how that night he was so stunned by the beauty of the Prophet that he caught himself comparing him to the moon in order to decide which was the more beautiful. He concluded in favour of the Prophet.

That a man in the deepest deserts of Arabia over 1,400 years ago would stand before another man in a scene as poetic as this only strengthened my association of that period with folk tales. Until of course I found myself in the exact same scene.

In fact, the appreciation of the beauty of the Prophet by his male companions appears to be a feature of their relationship with him. His favoured poet Hassan ibn Thabit writes:

When I saw his light shining forth,
In fear I covered my eyes with my palms,
Afraid for my sight because of the beauty of his form.
So I was scarcely able to look at him at all.

Later in the same poem he goes further than simply evoking this heightened beauty; he describes it as proof itself of The Prophet's appointed stature:

Even if he had not brought any clear signs with him,
The sight of him would dispense with the need for them.

Among the many other companions who spoke of his beauty are Abu Hurairah, stating that he 'did not see anyone more handsome as the messenger of Allah (peace and blessings of Allah be upon him). It was as if the brightness of the sun had shone from his auspicious face'. A sentiment echoed by the Prophet's wife, Aisha, according to whom, 'The Holy Prophet was the most handsome of all people, regarding his countenance and complexion he was the most illustrious and brilliant person.' His cousin and son-in-law Ali mentions as part of a detailed description of his form that those who would have glanced upon him by chance would no doubt have been left impressed by him but as soon they drew closer becoming more familiar, they'd have fallen in love.

Countless commentators have since sought to decipher a more meaningful significance from the Prophet's unique beauty, claiming it a reflection of divine light itself. However, what had been especially notable to me is the very consideration of his beauty by other men. That the beauty of any other man can be ruminated over with such passion and heartfelt intent, without any erotic implications, has previously been to me, quite frankly, a matter of surprise.

The surprise here is largely because I'd become so used to beauty being used to induce lust and denote sex. The great icons of beauty in our age are often unpossessable symbols of sexual allure that reflect back at us our comparative lackings. Lackings that are readily mined and exploited by the wheels of consumerism. The prescriptive and limiting designations by which beauty is offered dictate that beauty precedes desire and as such a heterosexual man or woman may only engage in appreciation of beauty in the other gender.

Perhaps it's this obscuration between beauty and eroticism that has prevented some from computing the relationship between Rumi, the thirteenth century scholar and mystic, and his master Shams without framing it in sexual terms. No doubt the praise poetry between this particular disciple and his master is passionate and the allusions graphic, yet reducing all love and beauty to the sexual sphere alone surely prevents us from understanding all it has to offer.

Highlighting and expanding upon the beauty of the master as perceived by the disciple is a key feature of Sufi poetry, as is beautifully illustrated by the writings of the thirteenth century poet of Delhi, Amir Khusrow, in praise of his spiritual master Nizamuddin Auliya. An incomparable poet whose work has left indelible imprints upon the very language of the subcontinent, the rapture induced in him by the beauty of his master can be found across his work. *Aaj Rang Hai (Today There is Colour)* is among his more popular verses sung into the very fabric of the region, everywhere from Bollywood to village weddings, celebrating this rapture with the lines:

I've never seen such colour O Beloved of God,
I've searched the whole world.
It's your colour that I love Nizamuddin

An already established court poet, having taken Hazrat Nizamuddin as his master, he immersed himself and his art fully into the presence of his Sheikh and master. Everything he wrote from this point rings as an evocation of this love as though nothing else existed for Khusrow anymore.

Man too shudam too man shudee
Man tan shudam too jaan shudee

I have become one with you and you have become one with me
I, the body. You, its life.

Adopting the motif of a burning lover, he often takes for himself the female role, the bride within this wedded relationship, burning deep within the pangs of her lover's flames. In his Persian ghazal *Nami Danam Che Manzil Bood,* Khusrow elaborates on the very form of his male master with imagery that could sit just as well amongst the English Romantic Poets:

An image of a fairy's body, cypress slim with tulip cheeks
Heart's affliction from head to toe, the place I was last night

Being playful with the gender roles across this male-male relationship, he's also found feminising his master as the beautiful fair maiden, or *gori*. This in fact becomes the term of his final literary address to Hazrat Nizamuddin as he gives breath to the following verses whilst gazing upon his corpse:

Gori sove sej per much per dare kes
Chal Khusro ghar apne, saanjh bhaee chahu des.

The fair maiden rests on a bed of roses,
Her face covered with a lock of hair;
Let us oh Khusrow return home now,
Dark dusk has settled across all corners of this world.

Khusrow himself died only months after his master of what was literally a broken heart.

This historic appreciation of the male form through the eyes of other males can therefore be traced back within the Islamic heritage to the time of the Prophet and has been kept alive by Sufis predisposed to seeking absorption within the being of their master. This begs the question however of why it should be restricted to Sufis alone. The hadith 'Allah is beautiful and loves beauty', speaks generally and to all audiences; and the Qur'an declares, 'Indeed, we created the human with the fairest stature.' (95: 4). Thus our attention is pointed to the beauty of the human form more generally. It is useful to understand how the Qur'an itself defines beauty. One recent study by Hasan Bolkhari Ghehi, an Iranian philosopher of art, uses the following verse to expound upon Qur'anic beauty: 'He Who has made everything which He has created most good (beautiful: *al-husn*): He began the creation of man with [nothing more than] clay' (32:7). According to Ghehi, the word 'most good' (in Arabic: *al- husn*) in this verse is the most comprehensive word in the Arabic language for expressing beauty. The fact that Allah has created a thing means that the thing is most good and beautiful, or in other words, everything created by Allah is most good and beautiful by the very fact that Allah has created it.

Beauty is therefore universal and so too should be its appreciation. This definition of beauty, a divinely sourced goodness, is inherent to all beings regardless of gender or race, or any other precursor of identity. The beauty that I'm so absorbed by in my own spiritual master is no doubt the goodness that emanates from within him. As is the beauty I allow myself to see in any other male or female. This understanding doesn't distance admirers from their subject of beauty but rather invokes it for themselves because to recognise this goodness is to invite it in and make room for it. While it may not invoke the same arresting exhilaration I felt under the starry nights of Morocco, such everyday appreciation of one another enables beauty to grow within the perceiver, rather than them shrivelling before impossible comparisons.

TEN MIGHTY MAKEOVERS

There are makeovers, and then there are makeovers. The word itself indicates a radical change in appearance. But some changes are more radical than others, or more sustainable than others, or both. In 1988, for example, media powerhouse Oprah Winfrey shocked her viewers when she lost 67 pounds (or more than 30 kilograms) and pulled a wagon of fat – representing the amount she had shed – onstage. As dramatic as it was, Winfrey's weight loss was not sustainable – in the ensuing decades, she has made public her struggles with her fluctuating size and weight. Whatever one's opinion of her, at least Winfrey has dared to confront the darker side of how we are pressured to conform to societal expectations about physical appearance. This has not stopped the proliferation of the makeover industry, with titles such as *Extreme Makeover*, *Ambush Makeover*, *How to Look Good Naked*, and *What Not to Wear* gracing our television screens.

It's easy to purse our lips in disapproval at the lengths that people will go through for that perfect personal makeover. Or to indulge in a bit of schadenfreude at botched cosmetic procedures or unconvincing hair implants. But perhaps makeovers are neither merely personal nor merely physical. For example, could radical, self-consciously adopted changes in ideological beliefs be a kind of makeover as well? The journey of Maajid Nawaz, founder of the Quilliam Foundation, comes to mind – a decision to ditch Islamist fanaticism to become a poster-boy for right-wing-lite counter-jihadists surely counts as a theological and political makeover. Or does it?

Ultimately, a makeover is a conscious decision to transform an old self, perhaps an undesirable one, into a new self that is at peace internally and with its surroundings. And sometimes that's legitimate and can result in a transformed, more positive state of being. But then again, individuals – or communities – that have gone through this meaningful process of change might not like the trivialising connotations of 'makeover'. Also, who gets to evaluate or monitor the goals of the makeover? What differentiates a makeover from a conversion, or repentance, or even genuine maturity? With these questions in mind, we present, in no particular order, our list of ten mighty makeovers – the good, the bad, and the ones the jury's still out on.

1. Mecca

The holiest city in Islam has undergone quite the revamp in recent years. The Saudis must have been watching 1990s re-runs of home improvement shows because the new look is more *60 Minute Makeover* than *Grand Designs*. Home to the Kaaba, Islam's most sacred site, this venerated city is the pinnacle towards which the world's 1.8 billion Muslims pray five times a day. Described by fourteenth-century traveller and scholar Ibn Battuta as a city of elegance, pilgrims from around the world would undertake year-long epic journeys on foot to perform the Hajj (pilgrimage). The serene desert landscape is now unrecognisable, turned into an arcade of shopping plazas and hotels for those used to the finer things in life. Package-holiday tourists can sign up for a VIP Hajj/Umrah experience with all luxury trimmings, and the vulgar face of capitalism is no better symbolised than by the five-star Clock Tower Hotel that looms over the city. In the words of Ziauddin Sardar, 'Mecca has been turned into Disneyland'.

2. Bradford Literature Festival

The grand Victorian architecture of the former mill town has stood witness to a number of seismic events over the past sixty or so years. Post-war immigration, particularly from the Mirpur region of Pakistan, has transformed the city into a thriving hub of cultural diversity. Not, however, without a few hiccups along the way. The Curry Capital of Europe, as it has been dubbed, was the scene of major low points in race relations in the UK, namely the demonstrations against author Salman Rushdie and the notorious burning of his book, *The Satanic Verses*. Since then, racial tensions and social problems have flared intermittently, making Bradford a bellwether for the health of the multicultural project. In recent years, the city has seemingly shrugged off its infamy thanks to a couple of inspirational local women. Syima Aslam and Irna Qureshi subverted the book-burning symbolism long-associated with Bradford to found the critically-acclaimed and hugely successful Bradford Literature Festival (BLF). Now in its third year, BLF has plugged into its Yorkshire literary heritage as well as celebrating the rich art traditions of recent settled communities to show the world that this much-maligned city can set the literary world on fire, in more ways than you think.

3. Madonna

The Material Girl burst onto the pop scene in the early 1980s and has reinvented her image and sound to remain effortlessly ahead of the curve ever since. It is no coincidence that her 2004 concert tour was named the Re-Invention World Tour. Her iconic transformations have seen her ditch the frizz of her 'Like a Virgin' era to embrace the peroxide bob and bold red lipstick for 'Papa Don't Preach' and rave electronica embodied in her acclaimed 1998 album *Ray of Light*. Throwing shade on all who came after her (Lady Gaga you such a wannabe), the Queen of Pop has proved the omnipresent culture vulture, flirting with Hinduism, Buddhism, embracing Kabbalah (a form of Jewish mysticism), getting us all excited by temporarily acquiring a hot Muslim boyfriend and, of course, scandalising the Roman Catholic Church. She played the quintessential English lady about town during her marriage to the English film-maker of impeccable pedigree, Guy Ritchie. And how can we forget her role as Earth Mother – adopting the obligatory African orphan-child and raising her rainbow family-nation? Bitchy sniping aside, Madge, we salute your influence as a feminist trailblazer and champion of queer communities. Oh, and we would like to see your 50-year-old self rock a leotard like she does in the video for 'Hung Up'. Time goes by... so slowly, so slowly.

4. The Muslim Institute

Readers of *Critical Muslim* will no doubt be aware that the esteemed quarterly is a joint project between the Muslim Institute and Hurst & Co. Those who have not read up on the Institute's history may be oblivious to the fact that the Institute itself has undergone its fair share of reincarnations. 'The Muslim Institute for Research and Planning' was founded in 1974 to promote the revival of Muslim scholarship and was soon publishing ground-breaking research on science, economics and the future of Muslim civilisations. The year 1979 proved to be a watershed when the then director, Kalim Siddiqui, became enamoured with the Iranian Revolution and aligned himself closely with the Islamic Republic's new regime. This created a split within the Institute, with many founding members resigning in protest at the path Kalim Siddiqui was pursuing. During the ensuing years he set up the Muslim Parliament and the Halal Food Authority, but these initiatives were overshadowed by his continuing ties to Iran. After his death in 1996, Dr Ghayasuddin Siddiqui, who had been involved in the Muslim Institute's early years, became the director and severed all links with the theocratic state. In 2009, Ghayasuddin Siddiqui invited founding member of the original Institute, Ziauddin Sardar, to re-invent the organisation. At a gathering of friends and associates of the Institute at Sarum College, Salisbury, 4–6 December 2009, it was decided that the old Institute would cease to exist and a new Muslim Institute would be formed, consisting of a network and community of Fellows dedicated to pluralistic thought and critical thinking.

5. Planes that unveil

Flying while Muslim has become one of the pitfalls of the age in which we live. But who has heard of transformative air miles? We are talking about your post-Ramadan escapees fleeing the scorch of the Gulf Arab sun to re-locate their households from Jeddah and Doha, to their vacant luxury apartments in Knightsbridge for a summer of driving supercars up and down London's Edgware Road. The transformative phenomenon occurs at departure, when pristine *ghutras* and accompanying *keffiyehs*, black *abayas* and *niqabs* are discerningly donned. As the plane approaches the English Channel a discreet disrobing of passengers seems to occur. Blonde-highlighted tresses and Jimmy Choo footwear become the order of the day, while the immaculate *thawb* is removed in favour of Diesel jackets and Gucci jeans. It gives a whole new meaning to the concept of cross-cultural travel.

6. Alec Baldwin as Donald Trump

The election of Donald Trump as US President in 2016 might have provoked horror within the country and beyond, but it was also a goldmine for political satirists. The most iconic of these has been the eerily convincing transformation of Alec Baldwin into the Orange Menace on *Saturday Night Live* (SNL). Debuting in October 2016, at the height of the presidential campaign debates, Baldwin's multiple award-winning turn as the Donald was not without controversy either. Former SNL cast member Darrell Hammond – the show's resident Trump impressionist up till then – admitted he was crushed by the decision to replace him with Baldwin. But Baldwin's casting has been undeniably fortuitous. It's not that he doesn't do a fantastic job – he does. The rest of the SNL team, however, are no slouches either – think of Tina Fey's screamingly funny impersonation of former governor of Alaska and failed vice-presidential candidate Sarah Palin, or Melissa McCarthy's *tour de force* as Trump's former press secretary Sean Spicer. Neither, however, have had the privilege that Baldwin has enjoyed of an ongoing Twitter feud with the subject of their portrayals. To Baldwin's claim that parodying Trump was turning into 'agony', Trump tweeted: 'Alec, it was agony for those who were forced to watch. Bring back Darrell Hammond, funnier and a far greater talent!' Baldwin fired back in response: 'Agony though it may be, I'd like to hang in there for the impeachment hearings, the resignation speech, the farewell helicopter ride to Mara-A-Lago. You know. The Good Stuff. That we've all been waiting for.' As the kids would say, 'Boom!'

7. Mahathir Mohamad

On 9 May 2018, Malaysian voters witnessed a miracle. A whopping 82 per cent of them turned up at the polls to boot out an increasingly draconian, corrupt, nationalist, and Islamist coalition government – led by the United Malays National Organisation (UMNO) – which had held the country in its grip for an uninterrupted 61 years since independence from the British. One major factor for this David-and-Goliath moment was the role played by former Prime Minister Mahathir Mohamad.

Mahathir has a track record of mighty makeovers. His 22-year UMNO-led administration, from 1981 to 2003, is credited with transforming Malaysia from a largely agricultural economy to an industrial and technological powerhouse. But his administration had sinister elements, too – he silenced his critics mercilessly and was embroiled in his share of financial scandals. Mahathir was, of course, also responsible for persecuting his protégé, Anwar Ibrahim, who was framed on charges of sodomy and imprisoned for several years. Mahathir and Anwar put their differences aside to join forces against the UMNO government of Nujib Razak, who used the same tactics as Mahathir to send Anwar to prison for the second time on charges of sodomy.

The turning point might have come during a 'public' forum – which Mahathir was not invited to – discussing whether he was too old to return as leader. In the middle of a presentation that asserted he was senile, the former premier turned up unannounced, sat in the front row, and tweeted a picture of himself with the caption: 'I'm here guys. Say it to my face.' Several jaws dropped – some in horror, most in admiration.

A few weeks afterwards, a shell-shocked Najib had to announce his resignation. Shortly afterwards, as leader of the incoming governing coalition, literally called the Alliance of Hope, the 93-year-old Mahathir was sworn in as the country's new (old) premier. Or should that be old (new) premier? Either way, he says he's a good guy now and has promised to clean everything up. But can a leopard change its spots? We shall see.

8. Meghan Markle, Duchess of Sussex

An impassioned sermon, tinged with liberation theology, delivered by the first African-American bishop of the Episcopal Church in the US. A soulful rendition of the classic, 'Stand by Me', by an all-black gospel choir. Prayers of intercession by the Reverend Rose Hudson-Wilkin, who looked like she could have stepped out of the film *Black Panther* (yes, we have black people in Britain, too, and some of them are Anglican priests). A stirring cello solo by the 19-year-old prodigy Sheku Kanneh-Mason. A star-studded audience that included Oprah Winfrey, Serena Williams, and Idris Elba. When biracial Meghan Markle met ginger Prince Harry, did she foresee that she would be responsible for this 'rousing celebration of blackness' (in the

words of *Guardian* columnist Afua Hirsch) at Windsor Castle, one of the
bastions of the British monarchy? But not everyone has been that impressed
by the unprecedented diversity on display at the latest royal wedding. As
much as she had a bit of 'Meghan Sparkle Mania' herself, the *Washington
Post*'s Karen Attiah was doubtful that Princess Meghan would be able to
continue being as outspoken about racial or other forms of justice after
marriage. And one royal wedding cannot centuries of imperial racism
undo. What tangible benefit, for example, could Harry and Meghan's
nuptials possibly have for the many Britons of Afro-Caribbean descent who
have had to suffer the indignity and anguish of the Conservative
government's 'hostile environment' immigration policy? Only time will
tell if Markle's makeover – from mixed heritage American actress to
Duchess of Sussex – has truly inspired the makeover of the monarchy.

9.*Yusuf Islam* / *Cat Sevens*

You can be forgiven for thinking that the great makeover for the British
singer-songwriter Cat Stevens was his conversion to Islam in 1977. And
what a metamorphosis it was, too – Stevens was barely thirty, a hitmaker,
and a heart throb who decided to ditch his musical career and stardom
completely in compliance with his new-found faith. His was a particularly
austere and severe interpretation of Islam – in 1989, he courted
controversy for seemingly supporting the *fatwa* calling for Rushdie's death.
But the terrorist attacks of 9/11 seemed to provoke another, subtler phase
of soul-searching. In 2006, he returned to music, recording his first all-
new pop album since 1978, *An Other Cup*, complete with musical
instruments (which he had earlier considered *haram*, or forbidden). And
this was not a one-off – he started touring again, now simply as Yusuf. His
journey this time around is less dramatic but no less remarkable. His 2017
album, *The Laughing Apple*, is credited to 'Cat Stevens/Yusuf' and earned
him a Grammy nomination for Best Folk Album. Yusuf's second makeover
is not without its difficulties, though. As he puts it, 'Criticisms came from
some small sections of the Muslim Community who quite incredibly
assumed that because I was making music I had left Islam – God forbid!'
Perhaps Yusuf's return to music is not so much a second makeover as a
harmonising of his seemingly conflicting but deeply held identities as a

Muslim and as a musician. In his own words, 'I once went through a stage where I turned my back on everything that I'd done before, but of course that was a radical and overzealous reaction to the spiritual happiness that I'd felt in Islam.

10. Children of bus drivers

What do Sajid Javid (Britain's first home secretary to come from a Muslim background), Sadiq Khan (London's first Muslim mayor), and Sayeeda Warsi (the first Muslim to sit in the British cabinet) have in common? Besides their first names all starting with 'S', that is? They're all children of bus drivers, of course! Specifically, they're children of post-war Pakistani immigrants who came to Britain in the 1960s in pursuit of a better life. Who says there is no social mobility in Britain? And political differences aside, there's a bit of a children-of-bus-drivers bonding thing going on between the three. When Labour's Khan won the London mayoral election in 2016, Javid, from the Conservatives, was quick to tweet his good wishes, saying, 'From one son of a Pakistani bus driver to another, congratulations.' Javid's message was retweeted by Warsi, also a Tory, who added, 'From this daughter of a Pakistani bus driver to a son of a Pakistani bus driver, congratulations.' Observing this burst of cross-party, intra-class and intra-cultural mirth on Twitter, the Conservative activist Tim Montgomerie quipped, 'Bus drivers are clearly the new Etonians.' If only.

CITATIONS

Introduction: Making Muslims Beautiful by Shanon Shah

The London Modest Fashion Week was held on 17-18 February, 2018, at Victoria House. More details can be found at: https://www.lmfw.co.uk/ To date, one of the most comprehensive studies on Muslim fashion is Lewis, Reina. *Muslim Fashion: Contemporary Style Cultures*. London: Duke University Press, 2015.

On Muslim women enduring online abuse in Malaysia, see: Biswas, Soutik. 'The Online Abuse Hurled at Malaysia's Muslim Women'. *BBC News*, 21 August 2017, http://www.bbc.co.uk/news/world-asia-40337326.

And on Muslim women enduring secularist heavy-handedness in France, see: Cockburn, Harry. 'Armed Police Force Woman to Remove Burkini on French Beach'. *The Independent*, 24 August 2016. http://www.independent.co.uk/news/world/europe/burkini-swimwear-ban-france-nice-armed-police-hijab-muslim-a7206776.html; Lichfield, John. 'Muslim Girl Sent Home by School in France over Long Skirt'. *The Independent*, 9 May 2016. http://www.independent.co.uk/news/world/europe/muslim-girl-sent-home-by-school-in-france-over-long-skirt-a7019706.html.

Selfies and Other Gazes by Samia Rahman

The opening poem from Rupi Kaur is from her 2015 collection, *Milk and Honey*, published by Andrews McMeel Publishing. Longer works referred to or cited in this article are: Susan Sontag, *On Photography*, (Penguin, London, 1979) and Roland Barthes, *Camera Lucida*, (Hill and Wang, New York, 1981).

The news articles referred to can be accessed at https://www.hellomagazine.com/healthandbeauty/2015031624027/top-5-best-apps-for-selfies/;

https://www.lennyletter.com/story/alicia-keys-time-to-uncover; https://www.cosmopolitan.com/uk/beauty-hair/makeup/news/a43804/alicia-keys-stopped-wearing-makeup/; https://www.thetimes.co.uk/magazine/the-sunday-times-magazine/the-interview-kit-harington-game-of-thrones-actor-5m2fkj57f;https://www.theguardian.com/lifeandstyle/2018/may/14/i-never-thought-i-was-beautiful-neelam-gill-and-the-fight-against-the-pressure-to-be-pale.

Giovanna Borradori is professor of philosophy at Vassar College, US, and her lecture, 'From Selfie to Selfie: Glimpsed, Revisited and Quickly Forgotten' was delivered at Goldsmiths, University of London on 20 March 2018/

Beauty in Islam by Doris Behrens-Abouseif

The main secondary sources for this article, based on Arabic sources, are: Doris Behrens-Abouseif, *Beauty in Arabic Culture*, (Princeton 1999) and José Miguel Puerta Vílchez, *Historia del Pensamiento Estético Árabe*, (Madrid 1997); English translation: C. Lopez-Morillas, *Aesthetics in Arabic Thought: from pre-Islamic Arabia through al-Andalus*, (Leiden 2017). Citations of the latter refer to the Spanish text. 'Abbās, I. *Tārīkh al-naqd al-adabī ʿinda al-ʿarab*. 2nd ed.,(Amman 1993); Abu Deeb, K. *Al-Jurjānī's Theory of Poetic Imagery*, (London 1979); idem, Literary criticism, in: *The Cambridge History of Arabic Literature. Abbasid Belles-Lettres,* eds. J.Ashtiany & T.M. Johnstone, (Cambridge 1990), 339-387; Allen, T., *Imagining Paradise in Islamic Art*, (Sebastopol/ Calif. 1993); Idem, and *Five Essays on Islamic Art*, (Solipsist Press 1988); Allen, R. and D. S. Richards (eds.), *Arabic Literature in the Post-Classical Period, (*Cambridge 2006); Arnold, T. W., *Painting in Islam*, (New York 1965); Basset R., 'Burda', *EI2*; Behrens-Abouseif, D. 'Beyond the secular and the sacred: Koranic inscriptions in medieval Islamic art and material culture', in: *Word of God, Art of Man: The Koran and its Creative Expressions; Selected Proceedings from the International Colloquium, London, 18-21 October 2003*, ed. F. Suleman, (Oxford 2007), 41-9; Bencheikh, J.E., *Poétique Arabe. Essai sur les voies d'une création*, (Paris 1975); Dahiyat, I. M., *Avicenna's commentary on the poetics of Aristotle*, Leiden 1974; Ettinghausen, R., Al-Ghazzālī on beauty, in: *Art and Thought, Issued in Honor of Dr. Ananda*

K. Coomaraswamy on the Occasion of His 70ᵗʰ Birthday. (ed. K. Bharatna Iyer), (London/Luzac 1947), 160-65., (repr. in: *Islamic Art and Archaeology. Collected Papers*, ed. M. Rosen-Ayalon, (Berlin 1976), 16-21); Ettinghausen, R., Early realism in Islamic art, in: *Studi Orientalistici in Onore di Giorgio Levi Della Vida,* (Rome 1956), 1:250-73 (repr. in: *Islamic Art and Archaeology. Collected Papers*, ed. M. Rosen-Ayalon, (Berlin 1976), 158-181); Farmer, H. G., The Influence of music: from Arabic Sources, in: *Proceedings of the Musical Association* 52 (1925-26):89-124 (repr. in *Studies in Oriental Music,* 1:291-328); idem, *Studies in oriental music* (reprint of publications from the years 1925-66), ed. E. Neubauer, 2 vols., (Frankfurt 1986); idem, al-Kindī on ethos of rhythm, colour, and perfume, in:*Transactions of the Glagow University Oriental Society.* 17(1955-56):29-38; Gardet, L., 'Djanna', *EI2;* Gaudefroy-Demombynes, *Ibn Qotaiba. Introduction au livre de la poésie et des poètes,* (Paris 1947); Geries, I., *Un Genre littéraire Arabe: al-maḥāsin wa-l-masāwi',* Paris 1977; Goichon, A.-M. (trans.), *Ibn Sīnā. Le Livre des directives et remarques. (kitāb al-ishārāt wa-l-tanbīhāt),* (Paris 1951); Goodman, L.E., *Avicenna,* London/NewYork 1992; Goodmann, Lenn E., *Islamic Humanism,* (Oxford 2003); Grabar, O., *The Mediation of ornament,*(Princeton 1992); idem,The Iconography of Islamic architecture, in: *Content and Context ofVisual Arts in the IslamicWorld,* ed. P. Soucek, (London 1988), 51-60; von Grünebaum, G., *Kritik und Dichtkunst. Studien zur arabischen Literaturgeschichte,* (Wiesbaden 1955); Hamori, A., *On the Art of medieval Arabic literature,* Princeton 1974; idem, 'Did medieval readers make sense of form? Notes on a passage from al-Iskāfī', in: *In Quest of an Islamic Humanism*, ed. A.H. Green, (Cairo 1984), 39-47; Hillenbrand, C., Some aspects of al-Ghazālī's views on beauty, in: Giese, A. and Ch. Bürgel (eds.), *Gott ist schön und Er liebt die Schönheit. Festschrift für Annemarie Schimmel,* (Bern 1992), 249-265; Kahwaji, S., 'Ilm al-Djamāl, *EI2;* Kuehnel, E., *Die Arabeske,* (Wiesbaden 1949); Kirmani, N., *Gott ist Schön,* (Munich 1999); Marçais, G., Remarques sur l'esthétique musulmane, *Annales del'Institut d'Etudes Orientales.* 4(1938):55-7; idem, Nouvelles remarques sur l'esthétique musulmane, *Annales de l'Institut d'Etudes Orientales.* 5(1942-47):31-71; Mahdi, M., Islamic Philosophy and the Fine Arts, in: *Architecture and Community*, eds. Renata H. and D. Rastorfer, (NewYork 1983); Necipoğlu, G., *The Topkapi Scroll. Geometry and Ornament in Islamic Architecture,* (Santa Monica 1995); idem, 'L'idée du décor dans les régimes de visualité islamiques' in: *Purs décors?* *Arts de l'Islam, regards du XIXe siècle*, ed. Rémi Larousse, (Paris 2008); Neubauer, E., *Musiker am Hofe der frühen Abbasiden*, (Frankfurt a.M. 1965); Pellat, Ch., *Arabische Geisteswelt dargestellt von Charles Pellat auf Grund der Schriften von al-Ǧāḥiẓ 777-869,(* Zürich/Stuttgart 1967); Rosenthal, F., *Four Essays on art and literature in Islam*, Leiden 1971; idem, *Das Fortleben der Antike im Islam*, (Zürich/Stuttgart 1965) ; Sabra, A.I. (trans. & comment.), *The Optics of Ibn al-Haytham. Books I-III On Direct Vision*, 2 vols., (London, 1989); Sawa, G. D., *Music performance practice in the early ʿAbbāsid era*, (Toronto 1989); Schimmel, A., *Calligraphy and Islamic culture*, (New York 1984); Shehadi, F., *Philosophies of music in medieval Islam*, (Leiden/New York/Köln 1995); Shiloah, A. (trans. & ed.), al-Kātib, al-Ḥasan Ibn Aḥmad Ibn ʿAlī, *La Perfection des connaissances musicales (Kitāb kamāl adab al-ginā')*, (Paris 1972); Sperl, S., *Mannerism in Arabic poetry - A structural analysis of selected texts (3rd century AH/9th century AD- 5th century AH/11th century AD)*, (Cambridge/New York 1989); Trabulsi, A., *La Critique poétique des Arabes*, (Damascus 1995); Ward, G.R., Beauty, in: *Encyclopaedia of the Koran*, (Leiden/Boston/Köln 2001); ʿUṣfūr, J. *Qirā'at al-turāth al-naqdī*, (Kuwait 1992); idem, *al-Ṣūra 'l-fanniya fī l-turāth al-naqdī wa-l-balāghī*, (Cairo 1992); Van Gelder, G.J., *The Bad and the Ugly. Attitudes towards invective poetry (hijā') in classical Arabic literature*, (Leiden/New York 1988).

The selected primary sources referred to in this article are:

al-Farābī, Iḥṣā' al-ʿulūm, ed. ʿU. Amīn (Cairo 1949); al-Ghazālī, *Iḥyā' ʿulūm al-dīn*, 16 vols.,(Cairo 1357/1938-39); al-Ḥarīrī, *Sharḥ maqāmāt al-Ḥarīrī*, commented by Ibn al-Khashshāb and Ibn Barbarī, (n.p. 1326/1908-9); Ḥāzim al-Qartajannī, *Minhāj al-bulaghā' wa sarāj al-udabā'*, (Tunis 1966); Ibn Ḥazm, *Ṭawq al-ḥamāma*, (Beirut 1992); Ibn Khaldūn, *al-Muqaddima*, (Beirut n.d.); Ibn Qayyim al-Jawziyya, *Rawdat al-muhibbīn*, Cairo n.d; al-Iṣbahānī, *Kitāb al-aghānī*, 24 vols.,(Cairo 1963); al-Farābī, *Kitāb al-musīqī al-kabīr*, ed. Gh. ʿA. Khashaba (Cairo 1967); al-Jāḥiẓ, *al-Ḥayawān*. eds. ʿA. Hārūn & M.B. Ḥalabī (Cairo 1948); al-Jāḥiẓ, (attributed to), *al-Kitāb al-musammā bi-l-maḥāsin wa-l-aḍḍād. (Le Livre des Beautés et des Antithèses)*, ed. Gerlov Van Vloten (Leiden 1898); (repr. Amsterdam 1974); al-Jurjānī, ʿAbd al-Qāhir, *Asrār al-balāgha fī ʿlm al-bayān*, (Beirut 1995); al-Kātib, al-Ḥasan Ibn Aḥmad. *Kitāb kamāl adab al-ghinā'*, ed. Gh.ʿA. Khashaba, (Cairo, 1975); al-Masʿūdī,

Murūj al-dhahab, Beirut 1982; al-Nawājī, *Ḥulbat al-kumayt fī l-adab wa-l-nawādir al-muta'alliqa bi-l-khamriyyāt,* (Cairo 1299/1881-82); al-Washshā, 'Abū Ṭayyib Muḥammad Ibn Isḥāq, *Kitāb al-muwashshā,* ed. R. Brünnow (Leiden 1886); Hämeen-Anttila, Jaakko, 'Al-Suyūṭī and Erotic Literature', in: (ed.) Antonella Ghersetti, *Al-Suyuti, a Polymath of the Mamluk Period.* Proceedings of the themed day of the First Conference of the School of Mamluk Studies (Ca' Foscari University, Venice, June 23, 2014), Leiden 2016

Beauty Pageants by Nadia Rasidi

The following online sources informed the writing of this article: 'Ann Fiona Ratu Cantik 1Malaysia 2010.' *Utusan Online,* www.utusan.com.my/utusan/info.asp?y=2010&dt=0524&pub=Utusan_Malaysia&sec=Dalam_Negeri&pg=dn_20.htm; Astro Awani. 'Gadis Somalia Pakai Hijab Burkini Di Pertandingan Ratu Cantik AS.' *Astro Awani,* www.astroawani.com/gaya-hidup/gadis-somalia-pakai-hijab-burkini-di-pertandingan-ratu-cantik-124105; 'High Heels and Hijabs.' *Al Jazeera America,* projects.aljazeera.com/2014/miss-muslimah/; King, Elizabeth. 'A Look Back at the Sexist, Racist History of Beauty Pageants.' *Racked,* 7 Mar. 2016, www.racked.com/2016/3/7/11157032/beauty-pageant-history; Middleton, Rachel. 'Malaysian Religious Officers Detain Transgender for Organising "Haram" Beauty Pageant.' *International Business Times UK,* 4 Apr. 2016, www.ibtimes.co.uk/malaysian-religious-officers-detain-transgender-organising-haram-beauty-pageant-1553129; The Star Online. 'Beauty Pageant Contestants Who Dispute Ban Can Be Charged in Syariah Court.' *The Star Online,* 25 July 2013, www.thestar.com.my/news/nation/2013/07/25/beauty-pageant-contestants-who-dispute-ban-can-be-charged-in-syariah-court/

A Beautiful Death by Hasina Zaman

For further background on the notion of a good death, refer to the BBC Two programme 'How to Have a Good Death'. BBC, 15 May 2007. https://www.bbc.co.uk/programmes/b00790y5.

The quote from Elisabeth Kübler-Ross is from her book *On Grief and Grieving* (2005) – the quote in this essay can also be found here: https://www.goodreads.com/work/quotes/243726-dem-leben-neu-vertrauen.

The quote from Lemony Snicket is from *Horseradish: Bitter Truths You Can't Avoid* (2007) and can also be found here: https://www.goodreads.com/quotes/13155-it-is-a-curious-thing-the-death-of-a-loved.

Statistics and other information on death, suicide and mental illness can be found at the following websites: 'Dealing with Sudden or Violent Death'. Dying Matters, https://www.dyingmatters.org/page/dealing-sudden-or-violent-death; 'Gender Differences in Suicide', *Wikipedia*, https://en.wikipedia.org/w/index.php?title=Gender_differences_in_suicide&oldid=841429934; 'Statistics and Facts about Mental Health', Mind, the mental health charity - help for mental health problems, https://www.mind.org.uk/information-support/types-of-mental-health-problems/statistics-and-facts-about-mental-health/#.WwAX_kgvy00; 'Suicide: Facts and Figures', Samaritans, https://www.samaritans.org/about-us/our-research/facts-and-figures-about-suicide.

On the relationship between terror management theory and death, see: Burke, Brian L., Spee Kosloff, and Mark J. Landau. 'Death Goes to the Polls: A Meta-Analysis of Mortality Salience Effects on Political Attitudes: Terror Management and Politics'. *Political Psychology* 34, no. 2 (April 2013): 183–200. https://doi.org/10.1111/pops.12005.

Shaykh Yasir Qadhi's khutbah at the East London Mosque can be accessed at: *Legacy of Muhammad (Pbuh) & The Tafsir of Surat Al-Kawthar*, 2015. https://www.youtube.com/watch?v=otODwdORGZs&feature=youtu.be.

Beautiful (Pop) Sounds by Jonas Otterbeck

This article is based primarily on the author's interviews and first-hand observations, but also relied upon the following sources: Berkowitz M. (2002). 'Religious to Ethnic-National Identities: Political Mobilization Through Jewish Images in the United States and Britain, 1881–1939' in S.

M. Hoover & L. Schofield Clark (eds), *Practicing Religion in the Age of the Media: Explorations in Media, Religion, and Culture*. New York: Colombia University Press. Najmabadi, A. (1991). 'The Hazards of Modernity and Morality: Women, State and Ideology in Contemporary Iran' in D. Kandiyoti (ed.) *Women, Islam and the State*. London: MacMillan.

Wellness by Irum Shehreen Ali

Works cited include: Harvard Health Publishing 'Yoga Benefits Beyond the Mat'. *Harvard Medical School*, February 22, 2015; Hendricks T, de Jong J, Cramer H 'The Effects of Yoga on Positive Mental Health Among Healthy Adults: A systematic Review and Meta Analysis'. *Journal of Alterative Complementary Medicine*, July 2017; NHS Choices 'How Mindfulness Helps Mental Wellbeing'. *NHS.com*, April 22, 2017; Bee Wilson 'Why we fell for clean eating'. *The Guardian*, 11 August, 2016; Ruby Tandoh 'The Unhealthy Truth Behind "Wellness" and "Clean Eating"'. *Vice.com*, 13 May, 2016; Annaliese Griffin 'Women are flocking to wellness because modern medicine still doesn't take them seriously'. *Quartz.com*, 15 June, 2017; Meeyong Cha, Simon Rice, Jesse Gritton, et al 'Social Networking Sites, Depression and Anxiety: A Systematic Review'. *JMIR Mental Health*, 23 November, 2016; Shelby Lorman 'What 65 Studies Can Tell Us About Facebook and Mental Health'. *thriveglobal.com*, 14 September, 2017; Women's Marketing 'Health and Wellness is the Next Trillion Dollar Industry'. *Womensmarketing.com*, 19 December, 2016; Kathleen Chaykowski, 'Meet Headspace, the App That Made Meditation a $250 Million Business'. *Forbes.com*; 8 January, 2017; International Coach Federation (ICF) & PWC '2016 ICF Global Coaching Study'. *ICF*, December 2017; Maya Kacharoo-Levine 'How Do YouTubers Make Money? A Pro YouTuber Explains Just How The Whole System Works.' *Bustle.com*, 10 August, 2015. Renee McGregor *Orthorexia: When Healthy Eating Goes Bad*, (London, Watkins, 2017); Fardouly J, Wilburger B, Vartanian L 'Instagram use and young women's body image concerns and self-objectification: Testing meditational pathways.' *New Media and Society*, 1 February 2017; Salma Haidrani 'How The Wellness Movement Ostracizes Women of Color.' *TheEstablishment.com*, 14 July, 2016; Jessamyn Stanley *Everybody Yoga*. (New York, Workman Publishing, 2017); Amanda Hess '"I

Feel Pretty" and the Rise of Beauty-Standard Denialism'. *The New York Times*, 23 April, 2018; Michael Pollan *In Defense of Food: An Eater's Manifesto*. (New York, Penguin, 2009).

The author's conversations with Nazia Du Bois, Mehrangez Rahman and Jeremy Mooney-Somers greatly helped shape this piece.

Taming the Barbarians by Henry Brefo

Works referred to and cited in this piece are: Ahmed, Leila (2012) *A Quiet Revolution: The Veil's Resurgence, From the Middle East to America*. New Haven: Yale University Press; Al-Khalili, Jim (2011) The *House of Wisdom: How Arabic Science Saved Ancient Knowledge and Gave Us the Renaissance*. London: Penguin; Alibhai-Brown, Yasmin (2014) Refusing the Veil: (Provocations), London: Biteback Publishing; Baines, Barbara, (1981) *Fashion Revivals from the Elizabethan age to the Present Day*, London: Drama Book Specialists; Bianca London (2018) 'Four Muslim women reveal why they choose to wear - or not wear - the hijab in today's society', Available at http://www.glamourmagazine.co.uk/article/women-reveal-why-they-choose-to-wear-a-hijabd; Boucher, Francois and Yvonne Deslandres (editors) (1987) *20,000 Years of Fashion*, New York: Henry N Abrams; Davenport, Millia (1965) *The Book of Costume*, New York: Crown; Faroqhi, Suraiya and Christoph K Neumann (editors) (2004) *Ottoman Costumes: From Textile to Identity*, Istanbul: Eren Yayinlari; Herwees, Tasbeeh (2018) 'Stop Using Muslim Women to Sell Soda.' Available at: https://www.good.is/articles/pepsi-ad-muslim-woman-kendall-jenner; Said, Edward (1978) *Orientalism*, New York: Pantheon; Samuel Pepys, *Diary*, edited by Robert Latham and William Matthews (London, 1970), Vol 7: 373; John Evelyn, *Diary*, edited by E. S. Beer (Oxford, 1959), Vol 3: 460; and YouTube (2018) 'Is Britain STILL a Racist Country?' Available at: https://www.youtube.com/watch?v=OTi1SCVI6Xo.

Skin Shades by Yovanka Paquete Perdigao

Books referred to and cited in this article are: Durba Ghosh (2006) *Sex and the Family in Colonial India: The Making of Empire*. Cambridge Studies in

Indian History and Society; Meeta Jha (2015) *The Global Beauty Industry: Colorism, Racism, and the National Body (Framing 21st Century Social Issues)*, Oxon: Routledge; Kimberly Jade Norwood (2014) *Color Matters, Skin Tone Bias and the Myth of a Postracial America*, Oxon: Routledge; Carina Ray (2015) *Crossing the Color Line: Race, Sex, and the Contested Politics of Colonialism in Ghana*. Ohio University Press.

Articles cited include: CNN. 'People for sale', available at: https://edition.cnn.com/specials/africa/libya-slave-auctions; Neha Mishra, Ronald Hall, 'Bleached girls: India and its love for light skin, available at: https://theconversation.com/bleached-girls-india-and-its-love-for-light-skin-80655; Hanna-Johara Dokal, 'We need to discuss colourism in the Middle East', available at: http://www.gal-dem.com/need-discuss-colourism-middle-east/; Mira Jacob (01/05/17) Priyanka Chopra on Getting Comfortable in Her Skin and Why She Won't Settle for the 'Exotic' Indian Character, available at: https://www.glamour.com/story/priyanka-chopra-june-cover-interview; Sana Uqba, 'Dubai's Modest Fashion Week "excludes" Black Muslim bloggers', available at: https://www.alaraby.co.uk/english/society/2017/12/13/Dubais-Modest-Fashion-Week-excludes-Black-Muslim-bloggers

Aranya Johar's video, 'A Brown Girl's Guide to Beauty' can be found at https://www.youtube.com/watch?v=ZX5soNoPiII

On slavery in Mauritania, see the report, 'Global Slavery Index 2013. Mauritania' by the Walk Free Foundation, available at https://www.globalslaveryindex.org/

Nose jobs, Iranian style by Nima Nasseri

This piece was mostly based on reportage and interviews in Iran, supplemented by the following academic works: Asef Bayat. 2010. *Life as Politics: How Ordinary People Change the Middle East*. Stanford University Press, Stanford; Marzieh Kaivanara, 09 October 2017, 'Beauty in Iran: Paradoxical and Comic' (https://www.researchgate.net/publication/320908671_Beauty_in_Iran_Paradoxical_and_Comic) and her forthcoming book, *Normative Space and Space of Normativity: Normal(s) ized Bodies and Boundaries in Tehran*; Sara Lenehan. 2008. *Reasons for Rhinoplasty: Understanding Tehran's Nose Job Boom*. MPhil Thesis. Oxford University.

News articles cited include: 'By a nose: Iran leads the world in rhinoplasty surgery', 5 March, 2013 (https://www.washingtontimes.com/news/2013/mar/5/iran-leads-world-female-nose-jobs/); 'The beauty obsession feeding Iran's voracious cosmetic surgery industry', 1 March, 2013 (https://www.theguardian.com/world/iran-blog/2013/mar/01/beauty-obsession-iran-cosmetic-surgery); 'Iran va Brazil; record dar-e jarahiy-e zibayi-e jahan (Iran and Brazil; The world record holders for cosmetic surgery)', 24 September 2011 (http://hamshahrionline.ir/details/146492); 'The porn star who went to Iran for a nose job', 3 August 2016 (http://www.bbc.com/news/blogs-trending-36954386?utm_content=bufferb974c&utm_medium=social&utm_source=pinterest.com&utm_campaign=buffer); 'Iran bans teachers with acne, unsightly moles and dental problems', 24 August 2017 (http://www.euronews.com/2017/08/24/iran-bans-teachers-with-acne-unsightly-moles-and-dental-problems); '"Infertile, hairy and cancer-stricken" Iranian women banned from becoming teachers', 29 August 2017 (http://en.royanews.tv/news/11335/2017-08-29).

Egyptomania by Yasmin Desouki

Academic and other written texts that were referred to include: Antonia, Lant. 'The Curse of the Pharaoh, or How Cinema Contracted Egyptomania.' *The MIT Press*, Vol. 59 (Winter, 1992), pp. 86-112.
Bardaouil, Sam. *Surrealism in Egypt: Modernism and the Art and Liberty Group*. I.B. Tauris, 2017. Colla, Elliot. 'Counting the Years: Shadi Abd al-Salam's Words.' *Discourse*, Vol. 21, No. 1, Middle Eastern Films Before thy Gaze Returns to Thee (Winter, 1999), pp. 127-139. Wayne State University Press. El Dessouki, Ibrahim. Eds. El Qayloubi, Mohamed, Samy, Helmy. *Silent Egyptian Documentary Cinema (1897-1930). el cinema el masreya el samta el wathiqaya* (1897-1930). Ministry of Culture, 2010. Elnaccash, Ataa. 'Egyptian Cinema: A Historical Outline.' *African Arts*, published by UCLA

James S. Coleman African Studies Center. Vol. 2, No. 1 (Autumn, 1968), pp. 52-55. Marei, Diaa. 'The History of Newsreels in Egypt.' (*Tareeekh el gareeda fi misr*). Master's thesis, High Institute of Cinema. 1979.

The films cited in this article are, in chronological order:

Cléôbatra (Cleopatra). Dir. Lama, Ibrahim. 1943. Egypt
Land of the Pharaohs. Dir, Hawks, Howard. 1955. USA. Warner Bros. Pictures.
A'roos El Nil (Bride of the Nile). Dir. Abdel Wahab, Fatin. 1963. Egypt
Gharam fi al-Karnak (Love in Karnak). Dir. Reda, Ali. 1967. Egypt.
'Two Years of Firm Determination.' *Arab Newsreel,* No. 1150, 1970. Dir. Murad, Hassan.
Thartharah fawq al-Nil (Adrift on the Nile). Dir. Kamal, Hussein, 1971. Egypt.
Al Karnak (The Karnak). Dir. Badrakhan, Ali. 1975. Egypt.
In Search of Oil and Sand. Dir. Omar, Wael and Philippe Dib. 2012. Egypt.

The Last Word on Male Beauty by Avaes Mohammad

This article relies upon insights from the following sources: Najib-ur-Rehman, M. (2016). *The Mohammadan Reality*. Lahore: Sultan ul Faqr, pp. 122-125; Das, R.K. (2004). *Ameer Khusro The Great Indian,* New Delhi: BPI (India), pp 79-92; Aga Khan Trust for Culture. (2011), *Jashn-e-Khusrau, A Collection*, New Delhi: Roll Books, pp 157, 184; Ghehi, H B; 'Aesthetic and Concept of Beauty in Quran,' *International Journal of Arts* 2017, 7(1): 1-5
Wikipedia has a biography of the Prophet's favourite poet, Hassan ibn Thabit, available at: https://en.wikipedia.org/wiki/Hassan_ibn_Thabit

CONTRIBUTORS

Alev Adil is an Anglophone Cypriot poet, performance artist and scholar ● **Irum Shehreen Ali** is a London-based sociologist, writer and project manager ● **Doris Behrens-Abouseif** is Emeritus Professor in the History of Art and Archaeology, SOAS ● **Henry Brefo** is a PhD candidate at the University of Birmingham, and co-founder of *Afrikult*, an online forum on African literature and culture ● **Yasmin Desouki** is a Cairo-based film archivist and independent researcher ● **Canon Giles Goddard** is the vicar of St John's Church in Waterloo, London ● **Brandino Machiavelli** is a retired filmmaker ● **Avaes Mohammad** is a poet, playwright, chemist and teacher ● **Nadia Mohd Rasidi** studied racism in sitcoms for her doctorate in American Studies from King's College London ● **Misha Monaghan** is Executive Assistant at the Muslim Institute ● **Mahmoud Mostafa**, a Sufi, is a translator based in London ● **Nima Nasseri** is a Middle Eastern analyst, a teacher and an engineer ● **Jonas Otterbeck** is Professor at the Institute for the Study of Muslim Civilisations, Aga Khan University, London, and Professor of Islamic Studies at Lund University in Sweden ● **Yovanka Paquete Perdigao** is a Bissau-Guinean writer and one-third of the acclaimed podcast, 'Not Another Book Podcast' ● **Samia Rahman** is Director of the Muslim Institute ● **Shanon Shah** is Deputy Editor of *Critical Muslim* ●**Ricci Shryock** is a photographer and video journalist based in Dakar, Senegal ● **Mustafa Abu Sneineh** is a Palestinian poet and writer from Jerusalem ● **Sahil Warsi** is an anthropologist who brings a bit of Texan Indian flair to the North of England ● **Hasina Zaman** is the CEO of Compassionate Funeral Directors, based in East London.